中国当代律师系列丛书

Chinese Lawyers for Foreign-Related Matters

# 中国涉外律师

赵 伟 主编

## 中国改革开放40周年纪念特刊！

当代法学泰斗江平教授，耄耋之年，赤子之心，题写总序言！

知识产权出版社
全国百佳图书出版单位

**图书在版编目（CIP）数据**

中国涉外律师：汉文、英文、日文 / 赵伟主编. —北京：知识产权出版社，2019.5

ISBN 978-7-5130-6082-0

Ⅰ. ①中… Ⅱ. ①赵… Ⅲ. ①涉外案件 – 律师业务 – 中国 – 汉、英、日 Ⅳ. ①D922.13

中国版本图书馆CIP数据核字（2019）第027018号

**内容提要**

1978年12月18日，党的十一届三中全会隆重召开。中国共产党用改革开放的伟大宣示把中国带入一个崭新的时代。2018年，我国迎来改革开放40周年。40年来，中国实施改革开放，可谓春风化雨，改变了中国，更影响了世界。近年来，涉外法律人才辈出，各地重点培养涉外人才，也为中国律师队伍增加了新鲜血液。在广大律师及企业强烈要求下，我们决定在2018年，中国改革开放40周年之际编辑《中国涉外律师》，力求在整理律师信息方面更准确、更及时、更完备。

责任编辑：龚 卫 李 叶　　　　　　　　　　责任印制：孙婷婷

封面设计：段维东

## 中国涉外律师
ZHONGGUO SHEWAI LÜSHI

赵 伟 主 编

| | |
|---|---|
| 出版发行：知识产权出版社 有限责任公司 | 网　　址：http:// www. ipph. cn |
| 电　　话：010 – 82004826 | http://www. laichushu. com |
| 社　　址：北京市海淀区气象路50号院 | 邮　　编：100081 |
| 责编电话：010 – 82000860转8120 | 责编邮箱：gongwei@cnipr.com |
| 发行电话：010 – 82000860转8101 | 发行传真：010 – 82000893 |
| 印　　刷：北京建宏印刷有限公司 | 经　　销：各大网上书店、新华书店及相关专业书店 |
| 开　　本：889mm×1194mm　1/16 | 印　　张：8.75 |
| 版　　次：2019年5月第1版 | 印　　次：2019年5月第1次印刷 |
| 字　　数：260千字 | 定　　价：80.00元 |

ISBN 978 – 7 – 5130 – 6082 – 0

# 总序

在有关律师的问题上，我发表过的文章不少，尤其是中国律师制度初创时期，几乎涉及律师制度的方方面面，我都作过专题报告。

西方国家对律师是非常重视的，他们对人权的重视、对法治的重视，在很大程度上都表现在对律师作用的重视上。当个人被捕的时候，警察马上要说，你有请律师为自己辩护的权利。辩护的权利可以自己行使，也可以请别人行使。律师的权限也很大，无论是审判还是侦查期间，律师都可以参与其中。而且，律师在社会上，也得到了很高的尊重。

西方国家法律制度中，律师的地位和作用在审判中表现得尤为明显。律师和检察方是平等的，控辩双方是站在同样的位置上，而法官则代表法院，高高在上并且绝对中立。在审理过程中，控方从法律的角度提出了控诉被告人的理由，然后律师则要通过自己的工作，向法官和陪审团证明控方的控诉是站不住脚的，使法官相信被告人的无辜或者轻罪。从法律地位上来说，控辩双方的地位是完全一样的。相较而言就这个司法状况来说，中国还远没有达到这么文明的高度。

律师制度的建立是为了维护国家法治，不仅是实质，而且也是形象。如果一个国家的律师都是在政府的管理下，没有任何自己的独立思考，那就说明国家法治有缺陷了，不能够限制政府的权力了。一个国家的法治健全不健全，首先在于公权力是不是得到限制。而公权力对于律师的限制，影响律师对公权力的监督能不能自由进行。"律师兴则国家兴"，只有律师制度发达了，国家的民主、法制才能够更加完善。中国的律师制度已经恢复有30多年了，30多年来律师经历的甜酸苦辣，大家心里都有一本账。在司法改革进程中，律师的作用是不能埋没的，他们为中国法治进程、人权保护的艰苦奋斗应该留在史册中！

尤为欣喜地看到"中国当代律师"系列丛书收录了各领域的优秀律师、专业律师的事迹和经典的案件，透过一个个标志性的案件让我也看到了中国律师的希望！

耄耋之年，赤子之心，欣然提笔，是为序！

## 目录　Contents

## 目录　Contents

## 目录 Contents

# 一、中国涉外品牌律师事务所

中国涉外律师

# 金杜律师事务所
## KING&WOOD MALLESONS

## 金杜律师事务所（简称"金杜"）

### 金杜介绍

金杜律师事务所被广泛认为是全球最具创新力的律所之一，能够提供与众不同的商业化思维和客户体验。作为在中国内地、香港特别行政区、澳大利亚、英国、美国和欧洲重要法域拥有执业能力的国际化律师事务所，金杜在全球最具活力的经济区域都拥有相当的规模和法律资源优势。我们面向全球，为客户锁定机遇，助力其在亚洲和世界其他区域释放全部发展潜能。凭借卓越的法律执业能力和对中国文化的透彻理解，我们为中外客户就各类境内及跨境交易提供全方位的法律服务。

金杜在中国内地及香港特别行政区的办公室分布于北京、上海、深圳、广州、三亚、杭州、苏州、南京、青岛、济南、成都、香港等十多个重要商业中心城市。金杜拥有广阔的全球法律服务网络，我们在新加坡、日本、美国、澳大利亚、英国、德国、西班牙、意大利等欧洲主要城市和中东均设有办公室，是一家能同时提供中国法（大陆法和"香港法"）、英国法、美国法、澳大利亚法、德国法、意大利法服务的全球性律师事务所，我们拥有的巨大法律人才库使我们能充分了解本土情况和法律实践并能提供多种语言服务。

因此，金杜平台能够为客户提供在亚洲以及更大范围开展业务的独到视角及市场洞察力，确保我们的客户在他们开展业务的任何地域均能获得同样高品质且具商业化和创新性的法律服务。

### 业务领域

公司并购、证券与资本市场、私募股权及投资基金、银行与融资、竞争与贸易监管、国际贸易、劳动法、税务、海关、环境法、争议解决、知识产权。

## King & Wood Mallesons

### About KWM

Recognized as one of the world's most innovative law firms, King & Wood Mallesons offers a different perspective to commercial thinking and the client experience.As an international law firm in the world able to practice PRC (China Mainland), Hong Kong SAR, Australian, English, the US and a significant range of European laws, our presence and resources in the world's most dynamic economies are profound. We open doors to global clients and unlock opportunities for them as they look to unleash the fullest potential of the Asian Century. Leveraging our exceptional legal expertise and depth of knowledge in the China market, we advise Chinese and overseas clients on a full range of domestic and cross-border transactions, providing comprehensive legal services.

In China Mainland and Hong Kong SAR, King & Wood Mallesons has more than ten offices in Beijing, Shanghai, Shenzhen, Guangzhou, Sanya, Hangzhou, Suzhou, Nanjing, Qingdao, Jinan, Chengdu, Hong Kong and other major commercial centers. We are a global law firm which provides an one-stop legal services covering laws in PRC (mainland of China and Hong Kong SAR), the UK, the US, Australia, Germany, Italy, etc. With a large legal talent pool equipped with local in-depth and legal practice, we provide legal services in multiple languages.

The King & Wood Mallesons platform, therefore, is able to provide its unique perspectives and market insights in Asia and greater regions and ensures that wherever our clients are doing business, we deliver the same high quality, commercial and innovative legal services.

### Practice Areas

Corporate M&A, Securities & Capital Markets, Private Equity and Investment Funds, Banking & Finance, Competition &Trade Compliance International Trade, Labor& Employment, Tax, Customs, Environmental Law, Dispute Resolution, Intellectual Property.

网址：www. kwm. com
详情请登录中国律师年鉴网：www. yearbooklawyer. com

# 德恒律师事务所
## DeHeng Law Offices

## 德恒律师事务所（简称"德恒"）

### 德恒简介

德恒创建于 1993 年，原名中国律师事务中心，1995 年更名为德恒。拥有 37 个国内外分支机构和超过 2500 名法律服务专业人员，是中国规模最大的综合性律师事务所之一。

25 年来，德恒致力于为中外客户提供优质、高效的法律服务，为改革开放、经济建设、依法治国作出卓越贡献，承办了三峡工程、南水北调、京沪高铁、农行上市、中铁建上市等重大项目，创造了中国法律服务领域的多项第一，获得社会各界的肯定与好评。在"钱伯斯全球"（Chambers Global）、"钱伯斯亚太"（Chambers Asia-Pacific）、《亚洲法律杂志》（Asian Legal Business）等国内外知名法律媒体榜单与报道中，德恒的相关成就被认可。在资本市场、并购和融资等领域，德恒曾多次获得国内外"最佳 IPO 项目""最佳股权市场项目""最佳股权交易"等奖项。

### 专业人员

德恒律师大多拥有硕士、博士学位和中国律师执照，具有在国内外立法、司法、行政机关、大学、研究机构、跨国公司、大型国企及金融证券机构工作的经验。高效务实，以结果为导向是德恒律师一贯的作风。德恒律师熟稔中国的社会环境与挑战，熟谙中西方法律文化与实践，通过高超的沟通技巧与分析处理复杂法律问题的能力，能够智慧有效地帮助客户解决跨区域、跨文化的法律纠纷并保障权利。

德恒是首批获得从事证券法律业务、从事涉及境内权益的境外公司相关业务、基本建设项目招投标、破产管理人、境内外专利代理等法律服务资格的律所。此外，德恒律师还拥有国家一级注册建造师资格、建筑经济师资格、中国注册会计师、税务师、统计师资格，全国期货业从业人员资格、基金从业资格等。德恒律师能运用英文、法语、德语、日语、韩语、意大利语、俄语、西班牙、马来语等十多种语言提供专业的法律服务。

### 专业领域

作为处于领先地位的中国律师事务所，德恒的成功经验覆盖了公司证券、金融、争议解决、并购、跨境投融资、建筑工程与房地产、国际工程与项目融资、竞争法，知识产权、国际贸易、劳动与社会保障、企业拯救与破产、政府与公共服务、文旅体育与养老健康、生态环境与保护、海商海事、税法等众多业务领域。

DeHeng Law Offices is one of the leading law firms providing comprehensive legal services. It was founded in 1993 as China Law Office and was renamed in 1995 as DeHeng Law Offices, reflecting the firm's evolution from an institution of the Ministry of Justice to rapid emergence as an independent, private law firm with 37 domestic and foreign branches and over 2,500 legal service professionals.

For over 25 years, DeHeng has been committed to providing quality and efficient legal services for clients at home and abroad. The firm has made outstanding contributions to the economy's reform and opening-up, national development, and the prevalence of rule of law. The firm's accomplishments have been recognized by Chambers & Partners, Asian Legal Business, and China's legal media. DeHeng has received numerous deal awards recognizing its work in capital markets, M&A and financing (e.g. "Best IPO of the Year" "Equity Market Deal of the Year" and "Best Equity Transaction").

### Our Professionals

DeHeng has over 2 500 legal service professionals. Most hold domestic or foreign graduate degrees in law, and some of them have work experience in leading international law firms, in domestic and foreign legislatures, judicial organizations, government agencies, universities, and research institutes. DeHeng lawyers are solution oriented. They are familiar with both Eastern and Western legal cultures and practices. They know well the complexity of Chinese society, and untangle difficult cultural and legal issues through skillful communication and analysis.

DeHeng Law Offices was one of the earliest law firms in China to be qualified to render legal services in securities, cross-border investment, infrastructure, bankruptcy management, domestic and international patent prosecutions and other areas. Many DeHeng professionals are nationally certified specialists such as patent attorneys, construction engineers, tax advisers, etc. DeHeng serves clients around the world and can also work in French, German, Japanese, Korean, Italian, Russian, Spanish, Malay, etc.

### Practice Areas

DeHeng professionals have accumulated robust experiences in the areas of Capital Markets, Banking & Finance, Dispute Resolution, Mergers & Acquisitions, Crossborder Investment & Finance, Construction & Real Estate, International Construction & Projects, Antitrust & Competition, Intellectual Property, International Trade, Employment & Social Security, Bankruptcy & Restructuring, Government & Public Policy, Healthcare Industry, Environment, Maritime, Tax, etc.

网址：www.dhl.com.cn
详情请登录中国律师年鉴网：www.yearbooklawyer.com
— 003 —

# 北京市中伦律师事务所（简称"中伦"）

# Beijing Zhong Lun Law Firm(Zhong Lun)

## 简介

中伦创立于 1993 年，是中国司法部最早批准设立的合伙制律师事务所之一。中伦办公室分布在北京、上海、深圳、广州、武汉，成都、重庆、青岛、杭州、南京、东京、香港、伦敦、纽约、洛杉矶及旧金山 16 个城市，业务范围遍及全球 60 多个国家和地区。经过数年快速、稳健的发展壮大，中伦已成为中国规模最大的综合性律师事务所之一。

作为中国顶级律所之一，中伦深谙客户需求，对中国乃至全球市场有着独到理解和深刻洞见，具有丰富的法律服务经验。中伦人秉承进取精神，积极投身一线，总能在交易及争议中为客户提供全方位法律支持，始终保持市场领先地位。

## 律师队伍

目前，中伦律师事务所合伙人总数已近 300 人。每天，中伦全球 16 家办公室、1900 余名专业人员与世界各地的客户同频共振，为其提供独到的商业见解和与众不同的客户体验，在日益复杂的各地区环境中把握商机并降低风险。

## 荣誉

在最新的 2019 年钱伯斯亚太榜单中，中伦在推荐业务领域、律师上榜人数和上榜人次方面刷新了中国律所在该奖项的记录；在 2019 年法律 500 强亚太地区榜单中，中伦全面覆盖榜单设置的 18 个业务领域；同时，中伦 5 度荣膺《商法》"卓越综合实力律所"大奖并获得国际法律联盟（ILASA）中国最佳律师事务所金奖。

## Introduction

Founded in 1993, Zhong Lun is one of the first partnership law firms approved by the Ministry of Justice of China. The office is located in Beijing, Shanghai, Shenzhen, Guangzhou, Wuhan, Chengdu, Chongqing, Qingdao, Hangzhou, Nanjing, Hong Kong China, Tokyo, London, New York, Los Angeles and San Francisco. The business covers more than 60 countries and regions around the world. After several years of rapid and steady development, Zhong Lun has become one of the largest comprehensive law firms in China.

As one of the top law firms in China, Zhong Lun understands the needs of its customers and has a unique understanding and insight into China and the global market. It has rich experience in legal services. Zhong Lun are committed to the spirit of enterprising and actively participate in the front line. They can always provide customers with comprehensive legal support in transactions and disputes, and always maintain market leading position.

## Lawyer Team

At present, the total number of partners in Zhong Lun Law Firm is nearly 300. Everyday, Zhong Lun's 16 offices around the world and more than 1900 professionals resonate with customers around the world to provide unique business insights and differentiated customer experiences, capture business opportunities and reduce opportunities in increasingly complex regional environments risk.

## Honors

In the latest 2019 Chambers Asia-Pacific list, Zhong Lun has updated the record of the China Law Firm's award in the recommended business field, the number of lawyers on the list and the times of lawyers recommended on the list. In the 2019 list of the legal top 500 Asia Pacific region Zhong Lun comprehensively covered 18 business areas set by the list. At the same time, Zhong Lun won the " the Best Overall PRC Law Firms awards in the China Business Law Journals Firms of the Year" and won the Gold Award of the Best Law Firm of China in the International Legal Alliance Summit & Awards (ILASA). At the beginning of 2019, Zhong Lun won the award of "2019 China PRC Firms-Dispute Resolution" again.

# 天達共和律師事務所
# East & Concord Partners

## 天达共和律师事务所（简称"天达共和"）

### 关于我们

天达共和系由原天达律师事务所与原共和律师事务所于2014年合并而成立的一家大型综合合伙制律师事务所。原天达律师事务所与原共和律师事务所分别成立于1993年及1995年，均系国内最早成立的、颇具实力和影响力的知名律师事务所。合并后的天达共和，总部位于北京，并在上海、深圳、武汉、杭州设有办公室。天达共和现有专业人士近400名。我们的合伙人及顾问结构成熟稳定，由逾30年执业经验的业界元老、拥有国家部委、法院、检察院、国际仲裁机构、国际知名律所工作经验的法律专家和相当数量曾在欧美、澳洲、日本、新加坡等国家和中国香港、中国台湾地区接受法律教育或执业的中青年律师组成。中文、英语、日语、法语等多种语言是我们的日常工作语言。

### 业务领域

天达共和致力于为客户提供专业化法律服务，经过20多年的不断积累及锐意进取，已经在以下业务领域取得行业领先地位，赢得了客户的高度信任与赞誉，并连续多年被业界知名媒体如钱伯斯、亚太法律500强、国际金融法律评论等推荐或报道。

收购与兼并、资本市场与证券、争议解决、刑事诉讼、银行与金融、融资租赁与商业保理、反倾销反补贴、反垄断、知识产权、外商投资、海外投资、文化体育传媒、基础设施项目、房地产与建筑工程、能源与自然资源。

## East & Concord Partners

### Overview

The merger between the East Associates Law Firm and Concord & Partners in 2014 brought into being East & Concord Partners, one of the largest and the most comprehensive law firms in China. Briefly, East Associates Law Firm and Concord & Partners were established in 1993 and 1995 respectively, are among the earliest established law firms in China and both have nationwide influence and reputation. We are headquartered in Beijing and have branches in Shanghai, Shenzhen, Wuhan and Hangzhou. The firm has almost 400 professionals. And the structure of partners and consultants are mature and stable. In addition to experienced partners and consultants who have practiced law for more than 30 years, our firm is comprised of legal experts who have years of working experience in national ministries, courts, procuratorate, international arbitration institution and prestigious law firms and young and middle-aged attorneys who have gained qualifications and hands-on experience in law schools and firms throughout such as United States, Europe, Australia, Japan, Singapore as well as Hong Kong China and Taiwan China regions. Our working languages include Chinese, English, Japanese and French.

### Practice Areas

With 20 plus years of experience, East & Concord Partners is committed to providing professional legal assistance to our clients and has gained a leading position and earned clients' trust and recognition and has been frequently recommended and reported by well-known international legal media such as Chambers and Partners, The Legal 500, IFLR1000 and so forth in the following practice areas: Mergers and Acquisitions, Securities and Capital Markets, Dispute Resolution, Criminal Litigation, Banking and Finance, Financial Lease and Commercial Factoring, Anti-dumping and Countervailing, Antitrust, Intellectual Property, Foreign Direct Investment, Overseas Investment, Entertainment and Sports, Infrastructure and Project Financing, Real Estate and Construction, Energy and Natural Resources.

网址：www.east-concord.com
详情请登录中国律师年鉴网：www.yearbooklawyer.com

## 炜衡律师事务所（简称"炜衡"）

### 炜衡简介

炜衡是以司法部原"中国法律事务中心"部分骨干律师为核心于 1995 年初组建的合伙制律师事务所。经过 20 余年的发展壮大，炜衡在业界树立了良好的口碑，现已成长为中国知名的大型律师事务所。

### 炜衡理念与追求

炜衡秉承"洞察、沟通、解决、良知"的执业理念，致力于为中外客户提供全面、优质、高效的法律服务。

### 分支机构

炜衡总所设于北京，已在上海、广州、深圳、广西、西安、天津、厦门、宁波、南通、成都、石家庄、长沙、烟台、延安、沈阳、杭州、南京、苏州、澳大利亚悉尼、美国硅谷、日本东京等国内外地区设立了多家分所，中国台湾、中国香港地区以及加拿大和德国两国分所亦在筹建之中。立足中国、放眼全球的炜衡版图日趋完备。

### 业务领域

炜衡设有并购与投融资部、公司法律部、金融保险与信托业务部、矿产能源基建业务部、涉外业务部、诉讼仲裁部、证券与资本市场部、全球投资与移民业务部等业务部门。

具体业务涉及国际贸易、外商投资、境外投资、境外上市、企业收购与兼并、风险投资、资产重组、产权界定、股份制改造、股票债券发行与上市、知识产权、高新技术、电信、房地产、金融、信托、破产重整、清算、移民、反不正当竞争、反垄断、海事海商、反倾销等诸多方面。

### 炜衡涉外律师团队

炜衡律师绝大部分毕业于国内外知名法学院校，很多律师拥有政府部门及司法机关工作经历，理论功底扎实，实践经验丰富，积极参与相关司法解释、操作规程的起草和研讨，并出版了《证券法》《私募股权投资基金》《房地产工程建设》《企业商标全程谋略》《破产法论坛》《破产管理人工作规程》等几十部卓有影响的法学理论和法律实务著作。此外，多数炜衡涉外律师能以英语为工作语言，部分律师熟练掌握俄语，能够妥善处理欧洲、澳洲、美国、日本及俄罗斯等地区业务。

### 炜衡社会责任

炜衡律师始终关心国家和社会时事，先后向阿拉善治沙工作、母校捐资助学、母亲水窖、西部母亲爱心邮包、汶川地震、玉树地震、雅安芦山地震等捐款捐物。在北京市和上海市成立了炜衡法律援助工作站，为弱势贫困群体提供大量法律援助，维护和促进了社会的和谐稳定。

系统化的管理制度、行之有效的办案质量管理监控制度、优秀的律师团队、良好的知识结构、丰富的执业经验、高度的责任心，使炜衡有信心、有能力为国内外广大客户提供规模化、专业化、多元化、深层次的专业法律服务。

网址：www.whlaw.cn
详情请登录中国律师年鉴网：www.yearbooklawyer.com
中国涉外律师 —006—

炜者，盛大之火也　衡者，公平之器也

# W&H Law Firm

### About W&H

W&H Law Firm is a partnership firm established in early 1995 initiated by the key lawyers from the former "China Legal Affairs Center" under the Ministry of Justice. Through growth and development over more than two decades, W&H Law Firm has grown into a leading firm in China.

### W&H Philosophy

"Insight, Communication, Solution, Conscience" are the guidelines consistently adhered to by our lawyers in practicing law. "Comprehensive, Quality and Efficient Legal Services for domestic and international clients" are our paramount pursuit

### Offices

Headquartered in Beijing, W&H has established a number of branches in Shanghai, Guangzhou, Shenzhen, Guangxi, Xi'an, Tianjin, Xiamen, Ningbo, Nantong, Chengdu, Shijiazhuang, Changsha, Yantai, Yan'an, Shenyang, Hangzhou, Nanjing, Suzhou. W&H also has branches in Sydney, Australia, Silicon Valley, US and Tokyo, Japan, and are setting up branches in Taiwan China, Hongkong China regions as well as two countries, Canada and Germany. Based on China, the global dimension of W&H is becoming increasingly complete.

### Area of Practice

W&H has twenty two divisions, including M&A, Investment and Financing, Corporate Legal Services, Finance Insurance and Trust, Mining, Energies and Infrastructure, Foreign business, Litigation and Arbitration, Securities and Capital Market, International Investment and Immigration, etc.

The specific practices of W&H include: international commerce, foreign investment in China, outbound investment, overseas listing, corporate mergers and acquisitions, venture capital, asset restructuring, definition of property rights, joint-stock reform, stock and bond listing and issuance, intellectual properties, high-tech, telecommunications, real estate, finance, trust, bankruptcy and reorganization, liquidation, immigration, unfair competition, antitrust, maritime, anti-dumping and other aspects.

### Foreign Business Team

Most lawyers at W&H graduated from reputable law schools at home and abroad. Many lawyers have working experience in government departments and judicial organs. With strong theoretical knowledge, rich practical experience, many partners and lawyers at W&H actively participated in the drafting and discussion of relevant judicial interpretations and operating procedures, and published dozens of highly influential books regarding legal theory and practice, including Securities Law, Private Equity Investment Fund, Real Estate Construction, Comprehensive Strategies of Corporate Trademarks, Bankruptcy Law Forum, and Bankruptcy Administrator Operation Procedures.

In addition, most of W&H's foreign business lawyers can use English as their working language, some lawyers are proficient in Russian. W&H's foreign business team can properly handle business in Europe, Australia, United States, Japan, and Russia.

### Social Responsibility

W&H lawyers are always concerned about the state and social affairs, and make donations to Alashan sand work, Alma mater donation scholarship, Mother Reservoir, Western Mothers Love Parcels, Wenchuan Earthquake, Yushu Earthquake and Ya'an Lushan Earthquake. W&H has set up legal aid stations in Beijing and Shanghai to provide a lot of free legal aids for vulnerable and poor groups, and to maintain and promote social harmony and stability.

Systematic management system, effective case quality management monitoring system, excellent lawyer team, good knowledge structure, rich practice experience, and high sense of responsibility make W&H's lawyers to have the confidence and ability to provide domestic and international clients with comprehensive, specialized, diversified, in-depth and professional legal services.

## 中伦文德律师事务所（简称"中伦文德"）

中伦文德起源于 1992 年，是司法部最早批准设立的第一批合伙制律师事务所，也是中国第一家在英国伦敦和沙特利雅得设立分所的律师事务所。经过多年的发展，现已成为一家扎根于中国并面向国际化发展的大型综合性律师事务所，被《亚洲法律杂志》评为"中国前十大律师事务所"，并被多家专业机构授予荣誉。

中伦文德总部位于北京，并在国内设有 18 家分支机构，覆盖中国主要的中心城市；在巴黎、里昂、柏林、汉堡、悉尼和美国的各主要城市均设有机构，业务范围遍布海外。现有执业律师及专业人员 1000 余名。专业团队能用中文、英语、法语、韩语、日语和阿拉伯语等多种语言为客户提供法律服务，部分合伙人拥有境外的律师执业资格。中伦文德优秀的律师团队和国际化的地域分布能够为全球范围内的客户提供一流的法律解决方案。

中伦文德是中国大陆唯一一家加入国际律所联盟组织 INTERLAW 的律师事务所。并且是在中国政府促进"一带一路"的国际经济合作的大背景下，第一个由中国律所发起的新型国际律师组织——全球法律联盟（Global Legal Alliance，简称"GLA"）的联合创立者。GLA 是以项目信息、投资信息和法律服务信息交流为主的，由法律机构与法律人士组成的非盈利、非政府国际组织，旨在为全球范围内的法律服务机构和法律服务人士提供交流、学习与合作的公益平台。

2017 年中伦文德成立了中伦文德法律研究院、中伦文德雄安新区金融与投资发展研究中心，紧跟中国法律动态。

中伦文德多年以来的出色业绩不仅赢得了境内外客户的认可，同时也得到有关政府管理当局的高度肯定。中伦文德与中国各政府部门、各级司法部门和仲裁机构保持着良好的工作关系；与各会计师事务所、咨询机构有广泛的业务合作，能够最大程度上为境外客户提供专业的中国本土法律服务。

中伦文德作为大陆唯一律所
会员参加 INTERLAW 会议

中伦文德获得"一带一路"
杰出贡献奖

## Zhonglun W&D Law Firm

Founded in 1992, Zhonglun W&D Law Firm is one of the earliest-established Chinese law firms approved by the Ministry of Justice，and also the first Chinese law firm setting up offices in London (UK) and Riyadh (Saudi Arabia). After years of development, Zhonglun W&D grows to a large-scale, comprehensive, internationalized and first-class law firm now, nominated as top 10 law firms in China by Asian Law Business (ALB) and receiving awards of various aspects from different institutions.

Headquartered in Beijing, Zhonglun W&D have established 18 domestic branches covering almost every main cities in China. Our branches also reach Paris, Lyon, Berlin, Hamburg, Sydney and major cities in the US, etc. We have approximately 1000 lawyers and employees who are outstanding and experienced enabling us to provide first-class legal services to our clients. Our working languages include but not limited to Chinese, English, French, Korean, Japanese and Arabic. We have partners who are licensed to provide legal advice under Chinese, Anglo-American as well as Islamic law. Brilliant multi-lingual partners and widespread branch offices are our advantages to provide legal service for clients all over the world.

Zhonglun W&D is the only Chinese firm member of INTERLAW. At the same time, Zhonglun W&D initiated the establishment of Global Legal Alliance (GLA) under the "Belt and Road" initiative proposed by Chinese government under the international economic cooperation background. GLA is an non-profit non-government organization made up of legal institutions and legal professionals, founded for members to exchange project information, investment information and legal services information. GLA provides a public service platform for worldwide legal service agencies and legal service providers to communicate, to learn and to cooperate.

In 2017, Zhonglun W&D Law Firm has established the Zhonglun W&D Law Research Institute, Financial and Investment Development of Xiong'an new district Institute, focusing on the front of China's legal practice.

Our practice not only gains us reputations among our clients over the world, but also a high recognition from the Chinese government. Zhong Lun W&D maintains a good working relationship with government departments, judicial departments and arbitration agencies at all levels. We have established extensive business cooperation with plenty of accounting firms and consulting companies, enabling us to provide best Chinese law services for clients all over the world.

# 观韬中茂律师事务所（简称"观韬中茂"）

成立于 1994 年 2 月，是总部设于中国北京的专业化、综合性大型律师事务所。经过与创设于 20 世纪 50 年代的香港王泽长·周淑娴·周永健律师行，以及创建于 20 世纪 90 年代的上海市中茂律师事务所、上海市申达律师事务所的合并，观韬中茂现拥有 600 余名律师，150 余位合伙人，在法律服务、专业建设和律师团队等方面已成为中国领先的律师事务所之一。坚持追求卓越，诚信勤勉，高效优质是观韬中茂的理念，委托人合法权益高于一切是观韬中茂的价值观。

观韬中茂的法律执业领域涉及资本市场、公司业务与并购、银行与金融、房地产与建设、重组与破产、能源与自然资源、争议解决、国际贸易与 WTO、反垄断、私募与风险投资、工程与基础设施、知识产权、电信传媒与科技、金融创新与结构性产品、海商海事、行政法等业务领域。法律服务范围涵盖了银行、证券、保险、电信、科技、大型基本建设、房地产、机械制造、教育、生命科学与保健、交通、能源、矿产资源、环境保护、化工、医药、科研和其他服务业等各种行业。

观韬中茂除北京总部以外，在上海、深圳、大连、西安、成都、济南、厦门、香港、天津、广州、杭州、悉尼、苏州、纽约、武汉、多伦多、南京等地设有办公室。观韬中茂与亚司特（Ashurst）国际律师行建立了联盟关系，于 2018 年 2 月 8 日成立观韬中茂亚司特（上海自贸区）联营办公室，是

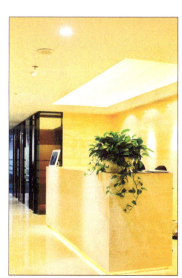

上海自贸区第四家获批试点的中外律所联营办公室。通过与亚司特律师行的紧密合作，使我们可以在全球的平台上，持之以恒地为我们的国内与国际客户提供有价值的、全方位的法律服务。

观韬中茂拥有一支理论深厚、经验丰富、勤勉尽责、服务诚信、业绩良好、追求卓越的律师工作团队，并拥有多名相关专业的法律专家，能够为不同行业、不同客户提供全过程的综合性法律服务。

# Guantao Law Firm

Guantao Law Firm, founded in February 1994 and based in Beijing, is one of the pioneer law firms in China. After merging with Peter C. Wong, Chow & Chow (a law firm established in the 1950s in Hong Kong China), Shanghai Zhongmao Law Firm and Shanghai Shenda Law Firm (both founded in the 1990s), Guantao has become a leading PRC law firm with a team of over 150 partners and 600 lawyers in total. We offer the insight of an integrated and professional law firm and uphold the principles of honesty and diligence, efficiency and quality. At Guantao, our top priority is to provide our clients with high quality service and help them achieve their business goals.

Guantao's practices include capital markets, general corporate, M&A, banking and finance, real estate and construction, assets restructuring, insolvency reorganisation, energy and natural resources, dispute resolution, international trade and WTO, antitrust, private equity and venture capital, projects and infrastructures, intellectual property, technology media and telecommunications (TMT), innovative financing and structured products, maritime and admiralty, administrative law and other relevant areas. Guantao advises clients from a wide range of industries, including banking, securities, insurance, telecommunications, technology, infrastructure, construction, real estate, mechanical engineering and manufacturing, education, life science and healthcare, transportation, energy, natural resources, environmental protection, chemical, bio-medicine, pharmaceuticals and scientific research.

Guantao has 15 offices in various major cities in China, being Beijing, Shanghai, Shenzhen, Dalian, Xi'an, Chengdu, Jinan, Xiamen, Hong Kong, Tianjin, Guangzhou, Hangzhou, Suzhou, Wuhan and Nanjing as well as three overseas offices in Sydney, New York and Toronto. Guantao has established strategic alliance with the UK-based international law firm Ashurst LLP. On 8 February 2018, Guantao and Ashurst launched a Joint Operation Office (JOO) in China (Shanghai) Pilot Free Trade Zone. The JOO is one of the only four approved by the PRC authorities to date. Through the strong relationship with Ashurst, Guantao aims to continue delivering service excellence and sharing resources and information for the benefit of its domestic and international clients.

Guantao lawyers are committed to excellence and integrity; they are experienced, hard-working, diligent and responsible, and have earned a reputation as experts in delivering comprehensive and innovative legal services.

网址：www.guantao.com
详情请登录中国律师年鉴网：www.yearbooklawyer.com
— 009 —

北京市华贸硅谷律师事务所
Huamao & Guigu Law Firm

## 华贸硅谷律师事务所（简称"华贸硅谷"）

成立于1994年，总部设在北京，目前在上海、天津、广州、太原、邯郸设有分所，是一家立足国内、面向海外的专业型律师事务所。曾连续获得北京市优秀律师事务所等荣誉。

华贸硅谷具有一流的专业律师。所内主要律师均具有法学硕士及以上学位，兼具深厚的法学功底和丰富的律师实践经验。拥有多名著名法学教授、会计学教授及法学博士生导师。华贸硅谷能够提供全方位的法律服务，能够用多种语言为客户提供法律服务。

华贸硅谷拥有一支在境内外从事商事争议解决的强有力骨干队伍，尤其在国内外仲裁方面，有4名国际仲裁员，在巴黎国际商会仲裁院（ICC）、伦敦谷物和饲料贸易协会（GAFTA）、香港国际仲裁中心、海峡两岸国际仲裁中心担任仲裁员；10余名中国国际经济贸易仲裁委员会仲裁员；20余名国内众多仲裁机构的仲裁员。在20余年的境内外仲裁、诉讼业务中，华贸硅谷积累了丰富的经验、广泛的社会联系、稳定的客户群，形成了专业、高效的独特的工作作风。

### 主要业务领域

境内外商事仲裁和诉讼、外商投资和对外投资、国际贸易、金融、信托、房地产、知识产权。

### 沈四宝教授

华贸硅谷创始合伙人、国际商会中国国家委员会（ICC China）仲裁委员会主席、深圳国际仲裁院理事长、Gafta中国贸易委员会主席。在近30年的仲裁实践中，处理过数百个涉外商事仲裁案，在境内外商事仲裁界具有较大影响。

# Huamao & Guigu Law Firm

Founded in 1994 and headquartered in Beijing, it sets up offices in Shanghai, Tianjin, Guangzhou, Taiyuan and Handan currently. It is a professional domestic-based and overseas-oriented law firm, and has won the award of Beijing Excellent Law Firm and other honors successively.

It has first-rate professional lawyers, many of them own a doctoral degree or a master's degree or above, and have profound legal knowledge foundation and abundant practical experience of lawyers. Besides, it also has many renowned law professors, accounting professors and doctoral tutors of law. It is capable of providing a full range of legal services for clients in multiple languages.

Moreover, it has a strong backbone team specialized in commercial dispute resolution both at home and abroad. In terms of domestic and foreign arbitration in particular, there are four international arbitrators who serve as arbitrators of the Paris Court of Arbitration of the International Chamber of Commerce (ICC), London Grain and Feed Trade Association (GAFTA), Hong Kong International Arbitration Center, and the Arbitration Center Across The Straits; more than 10 arbitrators of the China International Economic and Trade Arbitration Commission; and more than 20 arbitrators in many domestic arbitration institutions. In more than 20 years of practices in domestic and overseas arbitration and litigation, it has accumulated rich experience, extensive social contacts and stable customers, and fostered professional, efficient and unique work style.

Main business areas: domestic and foreign commercial arbitration and litigation, foreign investment and investment in foreign countries, international trade, finance, trust, real estate, intellectual property.

### 张丽霞博士

华贸硅谷主任、创始合伙人、全国优秀律师。任中国国际经济贸易仲裁委员会、香港国际仲裁中心、北京、广州、海南等等逾10家仲裁机构仲裁员；对外经贸大学、中国政法大学、澳门科技大学兼职教授；全国律协仲裁专业委员会副主任、第七届和第八届北京市律师协会仲裁专业委员会主任；北京市人大代表。

网址：www.ctsvlaw.com
详情请登录中国律师年鉴网：www.yearbooklawyer.com
—010—

# 天地和律師事務所
## T&D Associates

## 北京市天地和律师事务所（简称"天地和"）

　　天地和系经北京市司法局批准成立的合伙制律师事务所，是专注反垄断和反倾销法律服务的精品律所。天地和律师均毕业于国内外名牌法学院，在中国大陆执业多年，具有丰富的实践经验。其中，半数以上律师具有美国、欧盟和日本等国留学背景及国外法律执业经历。

　　天地和在反垄断领域成就突出。自2003年5月任勇律师创建中国第一个也是规模最大的反垄断团队以来，天地和为来自不同行业的跨国公司提供了大量的反垄断法律服务。至今，天地和已代表跨国公司在中国进行了320多项反垄断申报。同时，作为第一家参与中国反垄断执法机构发起的卡特尔和滥用市场支配地位调查案件的中国律所，天地和参与了大部分涉及跨国公司的卡特尔和滥用市场支配地位案件，成功地维护了客户的合法利益。在2010-2012年钱伯斯设立中国法律卓越奖期间，天地和先后三次荣获年度最佳中国律师事务所（竞争法/反垄断）。自2010年钱伯斯开始中国法律业务的评选以来，截至2018年，天地和团队已经连续9年被钱伯斯列为"竞争法/反垄断中国律师事务所——第一等"。

　　天地和在反倾销领域经验丰富。针对国际贸易救济中所涉及的反倾销、反补贴、保障措施和其他WTO项下的法律问题，天地和为中国、美国、加拿大、日本及欧洲等多个国家的客户提供了全方位的法律及咨询服务，涵盖钢铁、化工、家具、机械、纸张等多个产业领域，致力于为客户提供最准确和有效的法律意见。

### 主任合伙人——任勇

　　任勇律师是北京市天地和创始人兼主任合伙人，在反垄断和反倾销领域拥有丰富执业经验，是中国反垄断业务领军人物之一，也是中国反倾销业务开拓者之一。任勇律师不但在经营者集中申报、反垄断卡特尔调查和反垄断滥用市场支配地位调查领域拥有丰富实践经验，还全程参与了中国《反垄断法》的立法工作。同时，任勇律师在反倾销、反补贴及保障措施调查等方面也具有丰富应诉经验，并多次参与中国有关贸易救济立法的咨询工作。多年来，任勇律师为大量跨国企业提供了优质高效的法律服务，赢得了客户一致好评和业界赞誉。

　　任勇律师还担任中国国际经济贸易仲裁委员会和香港国际仲裁中心的仲裁员，同时也是北京律师协会反垄断专业委员会和反倾销专业委员会的委员。

　　此外，从2005年开始，任勇律师与对外经济贸易大学的竞争法中心共同主办反垄断法研讨会，参与者包括了来自中国反垄断法执法机构、美国司法部、美国联邦贸易委员会、欧委会竞争总署、日本公平贸易委员会的高级官员，反垄断法的顶级学者和专家，多家跨国公司等。此外，任勇律师还翻译了William Kovacic教授的《反垄断法和经济学》一书。

网址：www.tdlawyers.com
详情请登录中国律师年鉴网：www.yearbooklawyer.com
—011—

# T&D Associates (T&D)

T&D Associates, a boutique law firm in partnership approved by the Beijing Municipal Bureau of Justice, highly specializes in antitrust and antidumping law. All of T&D's partners and associates graduated from top Chinese and foreign law schools, have several years of legal practice experience in mainland China, and more than half of them have either studied or practiced law in other jurisdictions like the United States, the European Union and Japan.

T&D has made remarkable achievements in antitrust area. Since it was founded by John as the first and largest antitrust team in May 2003, T&D has been providing extensive antitrust legal services to multinationals in diverse industries. Up till now, T&D has represented multinationals in more than 320 merger notifications in China. Also, T&D is the first Chinese local firm to get involved in cartel and abusive cases initiated by Chinese antitrust authorities and most of the cartel and abusive cases involving multinationals were represented by T&D, in which T&D successfully safeguarded clients' legitimate interests. Between 2010 and 2012 when Chambers and Partners (Chambers) set up the Chambers China Awards, T&D has won three times the "Best Chinese Law Firm of the Year in Competition/Antitrust". As of 2018, T&D has been awarded nine times the "Band One Chinese Law Firm in Competition/ Antitrust" by Chambers since 2010 when the award started.

T&D has extensive experience in antidumping area. T&D has provided clients from several countries like China, the United States, Canada, Japan and the European Union with comprehensive legal and counseling services in international trade remedy cases, which involves issues such as antidumping, countervailing duty, safeguard measures and other legal issues under the WTO rules. These cases cover a broad range of industries including steel, chemical products, furniture, machinery and papers, etc. T&D is committed to provide clients with the most accurate and effective legal advice.

**Ren Yong, Managing Partner**

John Yong Ren is the founder and managing partner of T&D Associates with rich experiences in the fields of antitrust and antidumping, and he is regarded as one of the leading lawyers in antitrust area as well as one of the pioneers in antidumping area in China. John not only is experienced in handling merger filings, cartel investigations and abuse of market dominance investigations, but also fully participated in the legislative process of the Anti-monopoly Law of China. In addition, John has extensive experience in helping clients respond to antidumping, countervailing duty and safeguard measures investigations and he also actively participated in China's legislative process regarding trade remedies. Over the years, John has provided high-quality and effective legal services to a large number of multinationals and has earned acclaim both from the clients and within the legal profession.

John serves as an arbitrator in the China International Economic and Trade Arbitration Commission, an arbitrator of the Hong Kong International Arbitration Center, and as a panel member in both the Antitrust Committee and the Antidumping Committee of the Beijing Lawyers Association.

Since 2005, John has co-hosted multiple Anti-Monopoly Law Symposiums with the Competition Law Centre of University of International Business and Economics, with participants including senior officials from Chinese antitrust authorities, the US DOJ, the US FTC, the EU DG Comp, JFTC, Chinese top antitrust scholars and experts, various multinationals, etc. In addition, he translated the book of Antitrust Law and Economics written by Prof. William Kovacic into Chinese.

网址：www.tdlawyers.com
详情请登录中国律师年鉴网：www.yearbooklawyer.com
— 012 —

## 北京光汉律师事务所（简称"光汉"）

### 光汉介绍

光汉，作为经北京市司法局批准注册的专业法律服务机构，是一家专门从事国内和国际民商事法律业务的中国律师事务所。

### 业务领域

光汉律师团队均接受过国内外系统的法学教育并具有长期的执业经验，曾在国内外律师事务所、跨国公司、政府机构工作。光汉的主要业务范围包括公司、私募股权、兼并与收购、破产重组、外商投资、银行与资本市场、房地产与建筑工程、国际贸易等领域的争议解决。获益于光汉律师队伍的专业素养，光汉能够确保提供国际专业水准的法律文件并实现畅通的中西方文化、法律业务的交流。在处理涉外法律事务时，光汉与亚洲、欧洲和美洲多个著名的律师事务所建立了合作关系，使光汉不仅能够就客户提出的法律问题进行解答，并且能够切实保护客户在海内外的权益。此外，光汉律师团队在处置不良资产、清收债权方面经验非常丰富，已为多家银行、金融机构及央企持续提供近20年富有成效的法律服务。

# Guo & Partners

### About Guo & Partners

Guo & Partners is a Chinese law firm specialized in domestic and overseas business law. Its working languages are Chinese, English and German.

### Area of Practice

Guo & Partner's lawyers have received sophisticated legal education in P.R.C or overseas with extensive experience in practicing Chinese law in multinationals and government institutions. Some of Guo & Partners' lawyers worked for various State departments before devoting into private practice, and they had accumulated hands-on experience in dealing with governmental agencies. Guo & Partners' main business scope includes corporate, private equity, mergers and acquisitions, bankruptcy reorganization, foreign investment, banking and capital markets, real estate and construction engineering, international trade and dispute resolution.

Benefited from the outstanding qualifications, Guo & Partners provides legal advice that meets international professional standards while ensuring effective communications in legal concepts across Chinese and western cultures. Guo & Partners cooperates with a number of distinguished law firms in Asia, Europe and America. Guo & Partners has over 20 years of experience in the disposal of non-performing assets and debt collection for various banks, financial institutions and state-owned enterprises.

# 锦天城律师事务所（简称"锦天城"）

锦天城成立于 1999 年，总部设在中国上海，是一家提供全方位法律服务的、在业内享有盛誉和领先地位的中国律师事务所。锦天城已在中国大陆 18 个大城市（北京、深圳、杭州、苏州、南京、成都、重庆、太原、青岛、厦门、天津、济南、合肥、郑州、福州、南昌、西安、广州）及中国香港和英国伦敦开设分所，并在香港、深圳前海与史蒂文生黄律师事务所联营，年创收额达到人民币数十亿。

锦天城坚持优质、高效的服务理念和团队合作的方式，对客户的每一个项目和案件提供细致的法律分析和切实可行的法律建议，积极进取地解决法律问题。

## 锦天城的团队

锦天城有执业律师 2000 余名，其中合伙人（含高级国际法律顾问）500 余位。除以中文（普通话、上海话、粤语、闽南语）为日常工作语言之外，我们的许多律师还精通英语、日语、德语、法语等主要语种，并拥有美国多州、英国、法国及日本等地的执业资格。

锦天城的合伙人、高级国际法律顾问及律师专业精通、资历丰富。我们有许多商业律师曾在国际顶尖律师事务所和（或）领先跨国企业工作多年。我们的许多诉讼律师曾任职于最高人民法院、高级人民法院和各级人民检察院，也有多位合伙人目前担任着各地仲裁机构的仲裁员。另外，我们还有多位合伙人和律师曾就职于各级政府部门和立法机构。因此，我们对法律法规的适用、政府审批与监管要求以及各种复杂的法律程序有深刻理解，并能为客户提供行之有效的解决方案。

锦天城多位合伙人和律师曾应邀参与了多部重要法律法规的起草和制定工作，其中多数法律法规直至今日仍频繁应用于日常法律事务中。我们的合伙人和高级国际法律顾问也在多部国际投资、贸易和其他国际经济合作条约的起草工作中发挥了重要作用。

我们的专业团队通过紧密的合作，帮助大量企业客户完成诸多复杂、高端的商业交易，并成功代理了多个具有里程碑意义的案件。

## 我们的客户

锦天城的客户遍及全国和全球。我们的客户包括大中型国有企业、事业单位、跨国集团、外商投资企业、民营企业、新兴成长企业、投资银行、商业银行、非银行金融机构、私募基金、产业投资基金等等，行业分布广泛。许多客户已成为锦天城良好合作伙伴。

## 锦天城的愿景

锦天城的服务宗旨是：优质、高效、诚信、敬业。通过汇集法律行业的顶尖人才，提供良好的职业发展环境并有效地利用丰富的地方资源，我们致力于为每一个客户提供国际标准的法律服务，并在每一个法律服务项目中为客户创造最大商业价值。

# AllBright Law Office

## About Us

AllBright Law Office(AllBright) established in 1999 and headquartered in Shanghai, is a full-service Chinese law firm and enjoys an excellent reputation and status in the legal profession. AllBright has branch offices in eighteen cities in mainland China, in Beijing, Shenzhen, Hangzhou, Suzhou, Nanjing, Chengdu, Chongqing, Taiyuan, Qingdao, Xiamen, Tianjin, Ji'nan, Hefei, Zhengzhou, Fuzhou, Nanchang, Xi'an and Guangzhou, and other branch offices in Hong Kong China and London. It is also associated with Stevenson, Wong & Co. in Hong Kong China and Qianhai, Shenzhen, and the annual revenue of the law firm has reached billions of yuan. AllBright is committed to developing legal solutions and legal services for domestic and overseas clients in a rapidly changing business environment.

AllBright adheres to the quality, efficient service concept and team-work approaching to each customer's projects and cases to provide detailed legal analysis and practical legal advice to actively resolve legal issues.

## Our Professionals

AllBright has more than 2000 lawyers and over 500 partners (including senior international legal advisers). Except Chinese (Mandarin, Shanghainese, Cantonese, Minnan) as the daily work language, our lawyers are proficient in English, Japanese, German, French and other major languages, and have the practice of qualifications in United States, the United Kingdom, France and Japan.

AllBright's partners, senior international legal advisers and lawyers professional proficient are rich in qualifications. Our business lawyers have worked in international leading law firms and multinational companies for many years. Our litigation lawyers have served in the Supreme People's Court, the higher people's courts and all levels of the procrastinates, as well as many partners who currently serve as arbitrators for arbitration agencies around the world. In addition, we have many partners and lawyers working at various levels of government departments and legislative bodies. Therefore, we have a deep understanding of the application of laws and regulations, government approval and regulatory requirements, and various complex legal procedures, and provide effective solutions to customers.

Our partners and lawyers in AllBright have been invited to participate in the drafting and formulation of several important laws and regulations, most are still frequently applied to daily legal affairs. Our partners and senior international legal advisers have also played an important role in the drafting of several international investment, trade and other international economic cooperation treaties.

Through close cooperation, our professional team helps many enterprise customers to complete many complex and high-end business transactions. We have successfully represented several landmark cases.

## Our Clients

AllBright customers throughout the country and the world. Our clients include state-owned large and medium-sized state-owned enterprises, institutions, transnational groups, foreign-funded enterprises, private enterprises, emerging growth enterprises, investment banks, commercial banks, Non-bank financial institutions, private equity, industrial investment funds and so on, the industry widely distributed. Many customers have become good partners.

## Our Vision

AllBright's service aims at quality, efficiency, integrity and dedication. By bringing the top talent in the legal profession, providing a good career development environment and making effective use of the rich local resources, we are committed to providing every customer with the legal services of international standards and creating maximum business value for our clients in every legal service.

网址：www.allbrightlaw.com
详情请登录中国律师年鉴网：www.yearbooklawyer.com
— 015 —

## 华诚律师事务所（简称"华诚"）

华诚成立于1995年，总部位于上海，分支机构遍及北京、香港、哈尔滨、兰州、烟台、广州、芝加哥、东京等国内外城市（更多分支机构信息请参阅华诚官方网站）。20多年来，华诚秉承"诚信、思远、敬业、进取"的企业文化，已经发展成为由华诚律师事务所、华诚知识产权代理有限公司等多个实体组成的法律和知识产权服务综合体。

华诚目前的整体业务范围已经涵盖知识产权、公司商事、资本市场、金融与资产管理、破产与重组、文化娱乐体育、建筑房地产及基础设施、劳动人事、家事与财富管理、贸易海关及税务、诉讼与争端解决等众多领域。

多年来，华诚因其在商事战略布局、企业运营与管理、合规、知识产权代理和权利商业化、诉讼和争端解决等传统业务领域以及"互联网＋"等新兴法律业务领域的出色业绩而备受各行各业客户的认可与好评。作为最早获得ISO9001国际质量体系标准认证的法律服务机构之一，华诚始终严格控制其服务流程与品质管理，谨守一流涉外法律服务机构之风骨与水准。

华诚历年来被钱伯斯、法律500强、ALB等多家具有国际公信力的法律评价机构评为中国顶级法律和知识产权服务机构。此外，华诚还获得"全国优秀律师事务所""中国最值得信任的知识产权事务所"等荣誉称号，以及"上海市涉外咨询机构A类资质""上海市合同信用AAA等级企业""上海法院首批一级破产管理人"等资质。

### 华诚历程

2018年初，华诚烟台、广州办公室筹备中
2017年8月，成立华诚甘肃分公司
2016年8月，华诚迁至世纪商贸广场
2016年4月，成立华诚集团
2015年1月，华诚所入选上海高院一级破产管理人名册
2014年8月，华诚香港分所设立
2011年9月，华诚所被认定为上海市涉外咨询机构A类资质
2010年3月，华诚所通过ISO9001:2008国际质量体系标准认证
2008年3月，华诚北京办公室设立
2007年6月，入选上海高院破产管理人名册
2006年6月，华诚哈尔滨分所设立
2003年5月，华诚所被指定为涉外商标代理公司
2003年4月，华诚所迁址至上海文新报业大厦
2002年8月，成立华诚知识产权代理公司
2000年10月，华诚所迁址至上海新黄浦大厦
2000年4月，华诚所被指定为涉外知识产权代理机构
1998年9月，华诚所迁址至上海中华企业大厦
1998年9月，公信律师事务所正式更名为华诚律师事务所
1997年7月，公信律师事务所迁址至上海中岚大厦
1995年2月，华诚的前身：公信律师事务所成立

网址：www.watsonband.com
详情请登录中国律师年鉴网：www.yearbooklawyer.com
—016—

# Watson & Band

## About Watson & Band

Watson & Band was established in 1995 and is headquartered in Shanghai. It maintains domestic and international branch offices in Beijing, Hong Kong, Harbin, Lanzhou, Yantai, Guangzhou, Chicago and Tokyo (for more details on these offices, please refer to our official website). Over the last two decades, Watson & Band adhering to its philosophy of "Integrity, Strategy, Professionalism and Dedication", has developed into an integrated legal and IP services provider that is represented primarily by Watson & Band Law Offices and Watson & Band Intellectual Property Agent Ltd.

Watson & Band's current scope of practice includes various areas such as intellectual property; corporate and commercial law; capital market; financial and asset management; restructuring and insolvency; culture, entertainment and sports; construction, real estate and infrastructure; labor and employment; family law and wealth management; trade, customs and tax; litigation and dispute resolution; and investigation, etc.

Throughout the years, Watson & Band has been well-recognized and highly recommended by clients from various industries for its outstanding performance in traditional practice areas such as strategic business planning, corporate operations, management and compliance, IP agency and commercialization, litigation and dispute resolution and emerging practice areas such as "Internet +". As one of the first legal service agencies certified by the ISO9001 standard, Watson & Band strictly applies its service and quality management procedures and prudently adheres to the standards that are demanded of a top-tier international legal services firm.

For many years running, Watson & Band has been named a top-tier legal and IP services agency in China by various authoritative international legal rating services including Chambers and Partners, The Legal 500 and Asian Legal Business. Watson & Band also received great honors including the National Excellent Law Firm and China's Most Trustworthy IP Law Firm, as well as qualifications including Class A Qualification as a Shanghai Foreign Business Consultation Institution, Shanghai Contract Credit AAA Rated Enterprise and Top-Tier Bankruptcy Administrator in the Register of Shanghai Higher People's Court.

## Watson & Band History

·Early 2018, Watson & Band's new offices in Yantai and Guangzhou in progress

·August 2017, Watson & Band's new office in Gansu established

·August 2016, Watson & Band relocated to The Center

·April 2016, Watson & Band Group established

·January 2015, Watson & Band elected to the Shanghai Higher People's Court's Register of Top-Tier Bankruptcy Administrators

·August 2014, Watson & Band's new office established in Hong Kong China

·September 2011, Watson & Band recognized as Class A Shanghai Foreign Business Consultation Institution

·March 2010, Watson & Band passed ISO9001: 2008 International Quality Management System Standards Certification

·March 2008, Watson & Band's new office established in Beijing

·June 2007, Watson & Band elected to Shanghai Higher People's Court's Register of Bankruptcy Administrators

·June 2006, Watson & Band's new office established in Harbin

·May 2003, Watson & Band appointed as a Foreign-Related Trademark Agency

·April 2003, Watson & Band relocated to Shanghai Wen Xin United Press Tower (now known as "Shanghai United Press Tower")

·August 2002, Watson & Band Intellectual Property Agent Ltd. established

·October 2000, Watson & Band relocated to Shanghai New Huangpu Mansion

·April 2000, Watson & Band appointed as a Foreign-Related IP Agency

·September 1998, Watson & Band relocated to Shanghai China Enterprise Tower

·September 1998, Gong Xin Law Firm officially renamed Watson & Band Law Offices

·July 1997, Gong Xin Law Firm relocated to Shanghai Zhong Lan Mansion

·February 1995, Gong Xin Law Firm, predecessor of Watson & Band, is established

网址：www.watsonband.com
详情请登录中国律师年鉴网：www.yearbooklawyer.com
— 017 —

## 广东环宇京茂律师事务所

1993 年由原广东省对外经济贸易委员会组建成立，原名广东环宇商务律师事务所。2000 年，经司法部核准，正式更名为广东环宇京茂律师事务所。从 2001 年 3 月开始，本所实行合伙制。律所地处广州金融商业区的核心地带，总部位于广州标志性建筑中信广场。

本所是一家综合性的法律服务机构，是广东省知名的专业涉外律师事务所。经过多年的发展，本所目前拥有资深律师 40 余名，多毕业于国内外知名法律院校，拥有硕士或博士学位。依托于本所律师不同的专业背景和丰富的实践经验，本所有能力在各个领域为客户提供高质量的中国法律服务。同时，本所还聘请了中央和省一级政府部门的权威人士、专家及学者担任顾问。

本所提供的法律服务覆盖外商投资、国际贸易、海外投资、竞争法与反垄断、反倾销、海事海商、房地产与建设工程、公司融资和资本市场、公司收购、兼并及重组、私募股权与风险资本、银行与金融、结构性融资与资产证券化、项目融资、酒店和旅游开发与管理、城市基础设施、能源与自然资源、信息技术、电信、传媒与娱乐、知识产权、劳动法、破产重整与清算、争议解决、媒体和娱乐、税法等各行业领域，尤其在外商投资、国际贸易、资产重组并购和房地产等业务领域拥有强大的专业背景和多年的执业经验优势，在民事诉讼、刑事诉讼以及涉外仲裁方面也具有相当的优势，在业界及客户中享有广泛良好的声誉和口碑。

本所连续 3 年被权威法律杂志 —— 亚太法律 500 强评为亚太地区法律服务企业 500 强之一。2010 年，本所主任、首席合伙人何培华博士荣获"全国律政国际贸易精英律师"称号。本所代理过的影响较大的案例包括：香港昆利发展有限公司诉湛江海关行政纠纷案、美国公民诉中国政府及广东土产进出口集团公司烟花爆炸伤害索赔案、美国对湛江国联水产公司输美对虾反倾销调查案、广东省机械进出口集团公司与美国 HSQ 公司计算机工程合同争议仲裁案、德国皮特卡列公司对广州柴油机厂股权并购案、美国对广东生益科技股份有限公司 337 调查案等。

目前，本所与许多国家和地区的法律机构建立了良好的合作关系，其中包括美国 Varnum Riddering Schmidt & Hewlet 律师事务所，Sinkler Boyd, P.A 律师事务所，蔡擎柱律师事务所，康永华律师事务所，美国世强律师事务所（Steptoe & Johnson LLP）等。

本事务所全体同仁一如既往，推崇法律以人为本，秉承刚正不阿的精神，立足广东，面向全球，竭诚为社会各界提供一流的法律服务。

# Guangdong International Business Law Firm

Guangdong International Business Law Firm was founded in 1993 by and from then until 2001 under the supervision of the former Commission of Foreign Economic Relations and Trade of Guangdong Province. In March 2001 the firm has become a private law firm. Our headquarters is located on CITIC PLAZA, a landmark of Guangzhou.

The firm is a full service PRC legal service agency and a leading foreign-related law firm in Guangdong province. After years of development, we have formed an efficient team consisting of more than 40 senior lawyers, most of them have graduated from prestigious law schools in China and abroad and have professional backgrounds and extensive practical experience in different legal areas. Our team is competent to provide diversified legal service to our clients. We have also invited famous experts and scholars from all over the country to act as our counselors.

Our major practice disciplines include: Foreign Direct Investment, International Trade, Overseas Investment, Anti-Monopoly/Competition Law, Anti-dumping, Maritime and Admiralty, Real Estate, Banking and Finance, Bankruptcy & Restructuring, Capital Markets, Dispute Resolution, Energy and Natural Resources, FDI/Cross Border M&A, Hospitality, Intellectual Property, Labor and Employment, Media and Entertainment, Mergers & Acquisitions, Private Equity and Venture Capital, Project Finance and Infrastructure, Structured Finance & Securitization, Technology, Media and Telecommunications, Taxation and other areas. Noteworthily, we have great advantages and have built up reputation to provide legal services in areas of Foreign Investment, International Trade, Capital Reconstruction and Real Estate.

The firm is ranked as one of the top 500 law firms in Asia-pacific area by "The Asia Pacific Legal 500" for three consecutive years. The chief partner of our firm, Dr.He Peihua, was awarded the honorary title as "The National International Trade Elite Lawyer" in 2010. We have already dealt with a lot of cases successfully and some of them are of great social influence.

So far, friendly cooperative relations have been built up with legal institutions in different countries and regions, such as U.S. Varnum Riddering Schmidt and Hewlet, Sinkler Boyd, P.A., the Law Offices of Frederick W. Hong, NG and SHUN Solicitors and Notaries, Steptoe &Johnson LLP. With the powerful legal network covering both inside and outside Mainland China, surely we are able to gratify our clients' need for trans-regional even transnational service.

It has always been our law firm's goal to deliver customized services and practical solutions to our clients. What you need is what we care!

网址：www.univlaw.com
详情请登录中国律师年鉴网：www.yearbooklawyer.com
—018—

SINCERE PARTNERS & ATTORNEYS

## 星辰律师事务所（简称"星辰"）

星辰成立于 1993 年，是中国改革开放后成立的第一批律师事务所之一。星辰立足广东，为来自境外的和诸多走出国门的客户在珠三角、长三角乃至全国各地区的业务和发展提供服务，被评为"全国优秀律师事务所"。

### 办公机构

星辰总部位于广东深圳，在香港特别行政区、前海深港现代服务业合作区、贵州贵安新区等地设有分所，与香港简家骢律师行的联营进一步扩展了星辰的国际业务。星辰与北京、上海、南京、天津、重庆、沈阳、太原、长春、青岛、郑州等地 13 家享有盛誉的合伙制律师事务所结成"八方联盟"，被钱伯斯等国际机构评选为"中国最具影响的律师联盟"之一。

### 业务范围

星辰在中国境内的法律业务范围广泛，包含合作项目开发、银行业务、保险业务、公司法业务、商务服务连锁公司的设立和并购、知识产权保护策略、诉讼策略分析设计、涉外诉讼、涉外仲裁、境外仲裁在中国境内的执行、外商投资保护、中国企业到境外的投资保护、涉外婚姻家事诉讼、家族信托法律服务等，也为中国企业走出国门发展提供全方位的法律服务，包括项目尽职调查、与东道国律师联合服务、寻求东道国对投资的保护等。

### 星辰团队

星辰律师通晓多国语言及多地多种方言。人才优势不仅体现在法律专业性上，也体现在其多元化的个体优势上。星辰从业人员深入透彻的法律文化功底对于客户项目的成功具有不可替代的价值。所内有相当一部分律师曾经供职于政府机关、商事仲裁机构、劳动仲裁机构、社会服务组织、法律研究机构、跨国公司等，他们对法律的社会职能和实现法律的价值具有深刻的认知，并具有复合型的法律知识。作为一间大型综合性律师事务所，星辰在涉外法律服务上有着不可替代的价值，是粤港澳大湾区涉外法律服务的明智选择。

**兰才明**：星辰高级合伙人，香港分所首席合伙人，毕业于华东政法大学。从事法律工作 30 余年，擅长投资、并购、商业纠纷。于 2014 年在香港发起设立"一带一路"律师联盟及"一带一路"国际律师联盟有限公司，致力于涉外法律服务平台建设。

**王立**：星辰高级合伙人，复旦大学法学硕士。王立律师先后任职于深圳市人大常委会法工委和深圳市保税区管理局，具有立法和行政执法工作经验，擅长房地产法、公司法、涉外民商事诉讼和仲裁。

**母健荣**：星辰高级合伙人，芝加哥肯特法学院法学硕士、香港城市大学法学博士。母健荣律师曾参与大量外商投资及国际商事交易项目，擅长公司法、民商事诉讼与仲裁、国际商事争议解决。

**楼洪**：星辰高级合伙人，香港城市大学法学博士，深圳市"孔雀计划"海外高层次人才。楼洪律师擅长知识产权法、信息网络法、金融法、公司法及涉外民商事诉讼与仲裁。

**唐志峰**：星辰合伙人，香港分所执行合伙人，香港浸会大学社会学硕士，武汉大学经济法硕士。唐志锋律师曾为多家金融机构、证券公司、中外企业等提供法律服务。唐志锋律师擅长公司法、基金法及并购和重组、民商事诉讼等。

**刘缘**：星辰专职律师，中南财经政法大学国际私法专业硕士，拥有近 7 年的法律服务经验，主要执业领域为公司法及婚姻家事、民商事诉讼与仲裁。

**陈泳贤**：星辰专职律师，深圳大学国际法硕士。陈泳贤律师擅长国际私法、公司法、法律英语及涉外民商事诉讼和仲裁。

网址：www.sincerepartners.com

详情请登录中国律师年鉴网：www.yearbooklawyer.com

# SINCERE PARTNERS & ATTORNEYS

## Introduction

SINCERE PARTNERS & ATTORNEYS (SINCERE) which established in 1993, is China's first partnership law firms with good reputation, engages services in the wide range of banking, insurance, corporate mergers and acquisitions, foreign direct investment, overseas direct investment, human resources and employment, IP protection strategies, civil engineering and real estate, foreign-related litigation about marriage and family issues, trust, and dispute resolutions including foreign-related litigation and arbitration.

Based in Shenzhen, SINCERE offers commercial and legal services for foreign and domestic clients with regional, national and international interests with its dedicated team of professional lawyers. From 2015 to 2017, SINCERE was awarded "National Outstanding Law Firm" by the China Bar Association for providing comprehensive legal services to local and international clients who had legal demands both nationally and overseas.

## Global Connections

Headquartered in Shenzhen, Guangdong province, SINCERE has built an extensive network of branch offices both regionally and around the globe. Regional offices are located in Hong Kong Special Administrative Region, Qianhai Modern Service Cooperation Zone and Gui'an New District in Guizhou Province.

In 2004, SINCERE sponsored Bafang Lawyers Alliance with 7 well-known law firms across China and the alliance has 13 members up to now in such cities as Beijing, Shanghai, Nanjing, Tianjin, Chongqing, Shenyang, Taiyuan, Changchun, Qingdao and Zhengzhou. In 2018, SINCERE expanded its coverage when it formed a joint cooperation with Hong Kong law firm FRED KAN & CO. SINCERE has also cooperated with law firms in India, Southeast Asia, the United States, Japan and Canada as well as some districts, such as Macan China and Taiwan China. SINCERE has also played a vital role in China's "Belt and Road" strategy by forming a consortium and international lawyers for business ventures connected with this development policy.

## An Experienced Team

SINCERE's team can communicate in multiple languages and dialects and have served in government, commercial arbitration institutions, social service associations, legal research associations, and multinational companies, making it one of the most sought-after law firms in the Guangdong-Hong Kong-Macau Greater Bay Area and across the nation.

**Lan Caiming.** Senior partner of SINCERE, managing partner of the firm's office in Hong Kong. He graduated from East China University of Political Science and Law. Mr. Lan specializs in the field of Investment Law, M&A and commercial disputes resolution. He was the founder of the "Belt and Road" Lawyers Alliance and the "Belt and Road" International Lawyers Union Limited in Hong Kong in 2014 and was committed to the construction of a foreign-related legal service platform.

**Wang Li.** Senior partner of SINCERE, holds a Master's degree in Law from Fudan University. Mr. Wang has served for 5 years in the Legislative Affairs Commission, the Standing Committee of Shenzhen Municipal People's Congress and 3 years in Shenzhen Free Trade Zone Administration. Mr. Wang specializes in Real Estate Law, Corporate Law, PE Law, foreign related civil and commercial litigation and arbitration.

**Mu Jianrong.** Senior partner of SINCERE and holds a Doctor of Juridical Science. Dr. Mu has participated in a large number of foreign investment and international commercial transaction projects. She specializes in Company Law, civil and commercial litigation and arbitration and international commercial dispute resolutions.

**Dr. Lou Hong.** Senior Partner of SINCERE and holds a Doctor of Juridical Science from City University of Hong Kong and was qualified as the "Peacock Plan" Fellow of High-Level Oversea Talent by the Shenzhen Government. Dr. Lou specializes in Intellectual Property Law, Internet Law, Financial Law, Company Law and foreign related civil and commercial litigation and arbitration.

**Tang Zhifeng.** Partner of SINCERE and is vice managing partner of the firm's office in Hong Kong. He holds a Master's degree in Sociology from Hong Kong Baptist University and a Master's degree in Economic Law from Wuhan University. Mr. Tang has provided legal services for foreign and domestic financial institutions and securities companies. Mr. Tang specializes in Corporate Law, PE Law, mergers and reorganizations and civil and commercial litigation.

**Liu Yuan.** An attorney of SINCERE, has a master's degree in Private International Law. She has almost 7 years of legal practice experience. Her practice areas include Company Law, family dispute and civil and commercial litigation and arbitration.

**Chen Yongxian.** An attorney of SINCERE. She holds a Master's degree in law from Shenzhen University. Miss Chen specializes in Private International Law, Company Law, Legal English and foreign-related civil, commercial litigation and arbitration.

网址：www.sincerepartners.com
详情请登录中国律师年鉴网：www.yearbooklawyer.com
— 020 —

信任是一把钥匙，打开我和你的心门；信任是一座桥梁，缩短你与我的距离……当信任成为彼此的信念，信任的力量将生生不息……

*Trust is a key to the doors that lead to our hearts. Trust is a bridge that shortens the distance between us. Trust is the belief we share that makes us together. Trust is the power we hold that enables us stronger.*

# 广东广信君达律师事务所（简称"广信君达"）

广信君达成立于1993年1月，是广东最早成立的合伙制律师事务所之一；2012年11月，成为在广东率先采用特殊的普通合伙形式的律师事务所；2016年11月，成立了广东首家律师事务所党委；2017年6月，入驻广州第一高楼广州东塔，办公面积达7034㎡。

## 分支机构

广信君达总部设在广州，并在湖北武汉、深圳、中山、东莞、清远、佛山、广州南沙和白云、珠海、日本东京等地设有分所，在泰国曼谷、美国洛杉矶、马来西亚吉隆坡设有办公室。具有依托粤港澳大湾区、辐射全国、服务全球的地缘优势。

## 精英团队

广信君达以汉、英、日、德、法、韩等多种语言为国内外客户提供专业法律服务，具备提供一体化法律服务解决方案的能力。截至2018年9月1日，广信君达总部有合伙人114名，执业律师493名，其中20多位律师分别获得全国或广东省涉外法律领军人才、广东省刑事法律人才、广州涉外大律师、广州知识产权大律师等殊荣。

## 发展理念与目标

广信君达以"效率、信任、责任"为核心价值，不断探索、创新、进取，正努力打造成为华南地区首屈一指、全国行业排名前十的国际性专业化律师事务所。

## 涉外业务

广信君达立足中国和亚洲，为国内外客户提供证券与资本市场、金融与税务、知识产权、公司法、刑事辩护、跨境争议解决、国际仲裁等领域的涉外法律服务。

粤港澳大湾区是"一带一路"核心枢纽之一，其法律服务市场迸发出发展新活力。广信君达为涉及内地与港澳台联动的跨境业务企业提供法律服务，先后助力几十家企业在港交所主板上市，为近百家企业实现并购和发行债券提供法律服务。

与此同时，广信君达于华南地区在国际债券融资法律服务领域具有优势，为包括中国南方电网有限责任公司、中国奥园地产集团股份有限公司等在内的许多大型企业境外发行公司债券提供法律服务，协助客户成功进行了大量海外融资。

## 荣誉资质

广信君达自1993年以来，先后获得了中宣部、司法部"全国法律服务行业文明服务窗口"、司法部"部级文明律师事务所"、全国律协"全国优秀律师事务所"、《亚洲法律杂志》"中国南部最佳律师事务所"、《商法》"中国（广东）卓越律所""广州市十佳律师事务所"等多项荣誉，是第十六届广州亚运会组委会唯一常年法律顾问。

网址：www.etrlawfirm.com
详情请登录中国律师年鉴网：www.yearbooklawyer.com
— 021 —

# ETR Law Firm

## About ETR

Founded in January 1993, ETR was one of the first partnership law firms in Guangdong Province; in November 2012, became Guangdong's first law firm based on the form of special general partnership; in November 2016, the first law office CPC committee was founded at ETR in Guangdong Province; in June 2017, ETR moved to the Guangzhou East Tower, the highest building in Guangzhou, with an office area of 7 034 m$^2$.

## Branch Offices

ETR is headquartered in Guangzhou, and has branch offices in Wuhan, Shenzhen, Zhongshan, Dongguan, Qingyuan, Foshan, Nansha and Baiyun Districts in Guangzhou, Zhuhai, Tokyo in Japan, etc., and offices in Bangkok, Thailand and Los Angeles, U.S., Kuala Lumpur, Malaysia. It enjoys a geographic advantage in the Guangdong-Hong Kong-Macao Greater Bay Area to influence the country and serving the globe.

## Elite Team

ETR provides professional legal services to domestic and overseas customers in many languages, including Chinese, English, Japanese, German, French and Korean, and is capable of providing integrated legal service solutions. As of September 1, 2018, the ETR head office had 114 partners and 493 practicing lawyers, in which over 20 lawyers have won distinct honors like national or provincial leading foreign-related lawyer, provincial criminal legal talent, municipal foreign-related barrister and municipal intellectual property barrister.

## Development Philosophy and Goal

With "Efficiency, Trust and Responsibility" being its core value, ETR keeps exploring, innovating and progressing to become an international specialized law firm leading in southern China and ranking top 10 in the domestic industry.

## Foreign-related Affairs

ETR is based in China and Asia to provide legal services on securities and capital markets, finance and taxation, intellectual property rights, corporate law, criminal defense, cross-border dispute settlement, international arbitration, etc.

The Guangdong-Hong Kong-Macao Greater Bay Area is one of the core hubs of the "Belt and Road", and this regional legal service market is developing vigorously. ETR provides legal services to cross-border enterprises involving Mainland China interactions with Hong Kong China, Macao China and Taiwan China, and has helped tens of enterprises get listed on the HKEX Main Board, and nearly 100 enterprises realize M&As and issue bonds.

In the meantime, ETR has advantages in the field of legal services for international bond financing in southern China, and has provided legal services for the overseas issue of corporate bonds by many major enterprises, including China Southern Power Grid Company Co., Ltd. and China Aoyuan Property Group Limited, helping them with extensive overseas financing successfully.

## Honors and Qualifications

Since its foundation in 1993, ETR has won many honors, including "Civilized Service Window of the National Legal Services Industry" conferred by the Propaganda Department of the CPC Central Committee and the Ministry of Justice, "Ministerial Level Civilized Law Firm" by the Ministry of Justice, "National Outstanding Law Firm" by the All China Lawyers Association, "Best Law Firm of Southern China" by Asian Legal Business, "Excellent Law Firm of China (Guangdong)" by China Business Law Journal, and "Top 10 Law Firms of Guangzhou City", and was the only permanent legal counsel to the Organizing Committee of the 16th Guangzhou Asian Games.

网址：www.etrlawfirm.com
详情请登录中国律师年鉴网：www.yearbooklawyer.com
— 022 —

# 得伟君尚律师事务所（简称"得伟君尚"）

得伟君尚成立于1982年，是一家立足于湖北，以建设区域性领先律所为发展目标的合伙制、综合性律师事务所。曾先后被国家司法部、中华全国律师协会授予"部级文明律师事务所"和"全国优秀律师事务所"等荣誉称号。得伟君尚还是湖北地区唯一一家上榜国际知名律所评级机构钱伯斯律所名录的律所。

得伟君尚立志为社会提供高质量的专业法律服务，注重通过律师执业活动为客户创造和维护价值，促进公平正义，促进经济社会发展和国家法治建设进步。

### 服务机构与网络

得伟君尚总部位于湖北省省会武汉市。目前，已先后在北京、上海、湖北自贸区武汉片区、湖北自贸区宜昌片区等地设立分所。

2007年4月，作为中国华中地区唯一的一家创始成员，得伟君尚参与发起由国内多家地区性优秀律所与境外知名国际律所共同发起创设的全球性律所间合作组织——中世律所联盟（SGLA）。中世律所联盟先后被钱伯斯等多家知名国际律所评级机构定义为"中国最具影响力的律所间联盟组织"之一。目前，中世律所联盟成员在中国的执业机构，遍布北京、沈阳、大连、天津、济南、西安、兰州、重庆、武汉、上海、长沙、杭州、南京、南昌、昆明、广州、深圳、厦门、太原、贵阳、银川等大部分重要城市。与中世律所联盟各成员的良好合作，有效地提升了得伟君尚的服务范围和服务能力。

### 主要服务领域

得伟君尚是一家提供全方位法律服务的律所，为各类国际、外商投资机构、政府机构和国内企业提供专业化法律服务。在涉外、政府法律顾问、金融与资本市场、公司商事、财税、政府和社会资本合作等领域，我们一直致力于成为本地区法律服务市场的先行者，并努力通过统一的团队，从客户商业战略和实际操作角度为客户提供高质量的法律服务，帮助客户在中国商业和监管环境下实现其发展战略和经营目标。

得伟君尚涉外法律团队在外商直接投资，跨境并购、上市，跨境争议解决，境外投资和工程承包等领域，积累了丰富的专业经验，并在多起跨国并购、境外投资、国际工程承包等国际商业活动中，为中外客户提供了良好的法律服务。

2017年，得伟君尚被选定为第七届世界军人运动会法律服务商。

得伟君尚还设有湖北省内唯一一家经湖北省商务厅认定的国际贸易摩擦法律援助平台。

为支持、配合国家发展战略，得伟君尚先后在湖北自贸区武汉片区、湖北自贸区宜昌片区设立分所，积极探索为自由贸易试验区建设、发展，为长江经济带建设等提供法律服务的新领域、新思路和新方法，并取得了有益的成果。

### 得伟君尚律师团队

得伟君尚现有执业律师200余人，其中合伙人57名。得伟君尚律师绝大部分毕业于国内外知名的法学院校，大部分拥有硕士以上的学位。其中，近10名律师具有博士以上学位。得伟君尚不少律师还拥有政府部门和司法机关的工作经历，具备相当深厚的法律功底和丰富的实践经验。除以中文为日常工作语言外，得伟君尚有不少律师还精通英语、日语、法语等主要语种。

得伟君尚有多名律师兼具注册会计师、注册税务师、工程师等跨行业的专业资质资格。另有数名律师兼具美国纽约州等中国境外的律师执业资格。

得伟君尚现有一名律师担任第十三届全国人民代表大会代表，一名律师受聘担任湖北省人民政府参事，一名律师担任第十二届湖北省政协委员。得伟君尚有两名律师先后被授予全国优秀律师称号。

### 社会责任

得伟君尚重视拓展与法律职业共同体内其他组织、人员的合作与交流；注重通过提供实习、培训机会、捐资助学等方式培育行业发展新生力量；注重通过举办以及参与法律服务行业各类活动加强对律师职业价值的提炼和维护；关注法律服务均衡发展；积极参与对弱势群体的法律援助和对贫困人群的财务资助。

# Dewell & Partners Law Firm

### About Dewell & Partners

Dewell & Partners Law Firm (Dewell), established in 1982 and based in Hubei, is a partnership law firm with the development goal of building regional leading law firm in Hubei. Dewell is honored with "Law firm of Excellence at Ministerial Level" "National Outstanding Law Firm" and several other awards. Dewell is also the only law firm in Hubei Province that is named by international law rating agency, Chambers & Partners.

Dewell is determined to provide high-quality legal service, create and maintain values for clients through practicing of law, promoting justice and fairness, and facilitating in the economic and social development and ruling of law.

### Our Offices and Network

Dewell is headquartered in Wuhan of Hubei Province. Dewell has already set up its branch offices in Beijing, Shanghai, Hubei Free Trade Zone in Wuhan, and Hubei Free Trade Zone in Yichang.

In April 2007, as the only founding member of Central China, Dewell and other leading law firms at home and abroad founded Sino-Global Legal Alliance (SGLA), which is recognized by international law rating agencies as one of the most influential legal alliance in China. For now, members of SGLA spread all over China, including Beijing, Shenyang, Dalian, Tianjin, Jinan, Xi'an, Chongqing, Wuhan, Shanghai, Changsha, Hangzhou, Nanjing, Nanchang, Kunming, Guangzhou, Shenzhen, Xiamen, Taiyuan, Guiyang, Yinchuan and other important cities in China. Cooperating with SGLA has effectively raise Dewell's ability and range of our service.

### Our Main Service

Dewell provids legal service in comprehensive ways. We provide legal service for international institutions, foreign investment enterprises, governments and Chinese companies. In the field of international legal service, government legal consultant, finance and capital market, corporate and commerce, finance and tax, public private partnership and so on. We are devoting ourselves as the trailblazer of regional legal service market. We are making every effort, through the commercial strategy and practical operation, providing legal service of high quality and helping clients to achieve the strategic and managing goal in the commercial and supervisory environment of China. In 2017, Dewell is also selected as the legal service provider of the 7th Military World Games.

Dewell also has the only international commercial dispute resolution legal aid platform, which is recognized by Department of Commerce of Hubei Province. For the purpose of supporting and coordinating with the national development strategy, Dewell sets up its branch offices in Hubei Free Trade Zone in Wuhan and Yichang, exploring the new fields, new thoughts, new methods for legal service in construction and development in Free Trade Zone and Yangtze River Economic Belt.

### Our Team

Dewell has over 200 licensed lawyers, 57 of them are partners. Most lawyers in Dewell are graduated from reputable law schools at home and abroad. Over 10 lawyers have doctoral degree. Many lawyers have practiced in governments and judicial authorities, which entrusts them solid and reliable legal knowledge and plentiful practical experience. Apart from Chinese as working language, many lawyers are also proficient in English, Japanese, French and other main languages.

Dewell has several lawyers who are also qualified as certified public account, certified tax agent, engineer, and patent agent. Several lawyers qualify in practicing in New York State of United States and other countries.

In Dewell, one lawyer is the 13th deputy to the National People's Congress, one lawyer is the legal consultant of the government of Hubei Province, one lawyer is the 12th member of CPPCC of Hubei Province and two lawyers are honored with "National Outstanding Lawyer" prize.

### Our Social Responsibility

Dewell attaches much importance in expanding the cooperation and communication with other organization and people in legal professional community. We pay much attention to fostering new blood in legal community through providing internship and training opportunities and donating legal education. We concentrate in maintenance and refinement of the value of legal careers through holding and participating every kind of activities in legal service market. We focus on balanced development of legal service. We actively participate in the legal aid towards disadvantaged group and financial aid towards poverty group.

网址：www.dewellcn.com
详情请登录中国律师年鉴网：www.yearbooklawyer.com
— 024 —

# 山西艾伦律师事务所（简称"艾伦"）

艾伦成立于 2008 年，建所以来就致力于精英团队的建立，是一家立足国内、面向海外的合伙制律师事务所，目标是为政府部门、国内外高端客户提供精准、专业、高端、高效、持续的法律服务。本所多名骨干律师在保持传统诉讼业务的基础上锐意拓展新型法律服务领域。经过数年的稳健发展，艾伦吸引和培养了 40 多名律师，在涉外法律服务、政府法律服务、公司、企业、房地产、金融等专业法律服务领域业绩卓著、经验丰富，完全具备承接涉外法律服务、政府法律服务及大型法律专项服务的能力与条件。多年来我所获得"山西省优秀律师事务所""太原市优秀律所事务所""太原市三八红旗集体"、太原市司法局行政系统"创先争优"活动先进集体、支援新疆律师工作先进单位等荣誉称号。

艾伦创始人王志萍主任律师 3 次获全国优秀律师、山西省优秀律师、太原市劳动模范、太原市优秀律师等荣誉称号以及山西省妇联颁发的"三八红旗手"，同时入选全国律协涉外律师人才库。

团队精神、关注细节是 "艾伦文化" 的精髓。艾伦的律师队伍老、中、青比例配置适当。处理项目性法律事务均设立专业团队，集体分析讨论，分工合作。项目事务采用主承办律师负责制、团队成员分工合作配合的模式。项目团队律师及助理均经过资历、学历、专业、综合素质严格遴选程序确定入围。艾伦律师向客户提供项目性法律服务，依托经验丰富、专业突出、技能先进的律师团队。艾伦律师注重细节，专门设计适合客户自身业务特点的服务方案，真正体现了业务全面、专业突出、技能先进、经验丰富的合力优势。

事务所可提供多种语言的法律服务，能够为国内外客户提供英语、日语、韩语、德语等专业法律服务。目前已为美国、日本等国家以及中国香港、中国台湾等地区客户提供了有效的服务。同时，我所与美国明康律师事务所建立了长期的业务合作伙伴关系。

# Shanxi Ailun Law Firm

Shanxi Ailun Law Firm, founded in 2008, is a partnership law firm based in China and oriented to the globe. Our elite team provides precise, professional, premium, efficient and continuous legal services to government agencies, domestic and overseas premium customers, and actively explores new service areas in addition to traditional litigation. After several years of steady development, we have attracted and trained over 40 lawyers, who are exceptionally competent and highly experienced in foreign-related, governmental, corporate, business, real estate, financial and other legal services. Over these years, we have received a number of honorary titles, such as "Excellent Law Firm of Shanxi Province" "Excellent Law Firm of Taiyuan City" "March 8 Red-banner Holding Collective of Taiyuan City" "Advanced Collective in Excellence Building" of the administrative system of the Taiyuan Municipal Judicial Bureau, and "Advanced Organization in Assistance for Xinjiang Lawyers".

Our founder and director, lawyer Wang Zhiping, has received such honorary titles of "Outstanding Lawyer of China" (three times) "Outstanding Lawyer of Shanxi Province" "Labor Model of Taiyuan City" "Outstanding Lawyer of Taiyuan City" and "March 8 Red-banner Holder" (awarded by the Shanxi Provincial Women's Federation), and been admitted to the talent pool of foreign-related lawyers of the All-China Lawyers Association.

Teamwork and attention to detail are the essence of the Ailun culture. Our lawyer team has appropriate proportions of old, middle-aged and young members. A task force would be organized to provide legal services for a project through collective analysis and division of labor under the leadership of a chief lawyer. All lawyers and assistances of a task force have been strictly screened in terms of qualification, education, specialty and overall qualities. Our experienced, skilled and professional lawyers provide customized legal services for clients, showing our all-round competitive edges.

We can offer legal services in multiple languages, including English, Japanese, Korean and German. We have provided effective services to clients in the U.S., Japan and other countries as well as Hong Kong China, Taiwan China distrists of China. In addition, we have established a long-term partnership with Miller Canfield Law Firm.

网址：www.allan365.cn
详情请登录中国律师年鉴网：www.yearbooklawyer.com
— 025 —

## 山西恒驰律师事务所（简称"恒驰"）

恒驰拥有 600m² 的办公场所、精益求精的企业文化、专业的律师团队、大量的经典案例、丰富的科研成果以及众多的荣誉。

### 恒驰律师专注于高端诉讼与法律顾问

不论案件大小，恒驰律师都将依照事务所的专业流程为客户提供高端的律师代理服务。

恒驰律师以全面的事实分析、精准的证据安排、专业的法律论证为您提供最佳的诉讼方案。

恒驰律师以丰富的诉讼经验、精湛的庭辩技巧，在庭审过程中将诉讼方案发挥到最佳，让您体验到真正的高端诉讼法律服务！

恒驰律师事务所专业法律顾问团队在丰富的诉讼经验的基础上为您提供全面的法律风险防范体系，预防专业法律风险的发生，为企业保驾护航！

### 信息网络法律服务

恒驰拥有专业的信息网络法律服务团队，自 2000 年起始终关注信息网络法律发展，在信息网络法律领域取得了大量的理论科研成果。在电商平台法律框架、互联网金融、大数据产业、智慧城市、人工智能、"互联网＋"等领域有一定的实践经验，可为您的商业模式创新提供优质的法律服务！

## Shanxi Hengchi Law Firm

Shanxi Hengchi Law Firm has wide office space with area up to 600m², ever-improving corporate culture; professional lawyer team, a large number of classic cases, rich scientific research results and numerous honors.

**Hengchi lawyers specialize in high-end litigation and legal counsel**

Hengchi lawyers always provide clients with high-end lawyer agency services according to Hengchi professional procedures, regardless of large or small case.

Hengchi lawyers provide you with best litigation solution by virtue of comprehensive fact analysis, accurate evidence arrangement and professional legal argument.

With a wealth of litigation experience and excellent courtroom skills, Hengchi lawyers give full play to the litigation solutions during the trial to allow you to experience true high-end litigation legal services!

Hengchi professional legal consultant teams will provide you with comprehensive legal risk prevention system based on rich litigation experience so as to prevent professional legal risks and safeguard companies!

**Information Network Legal Services**

Hengchi Law Firm owns professional information network legal service teams. Since 2000, it has always paid attention to the development of information network law and made a large number of theoretical and scientific research achievements in information network law. Besides, it has certain practical experience in e-commerce platform legal framework, Internet finance, big data industry, smart city, artificial intelligence, "Internet +" and other fields, which enable itself to provide high-quality legal services for your business model innovation!

网址：www.hengchilawyer.com
详情请登录中国律师年鉴网：www.yearbooklawyer.com

# 二、向驻华商会、使馆、外向型机构推选的优秀涉外律师

北京 Beijing

## 陈波 律师

**执业经验**

陈波律师擅长公司证券、国际贸易、反垄断与反不正当竞争。

**代表性项目**

公司证券／金融：担任某国企并购基金参与中方投资联合体以35亿英镑收购英国Global Switch IDC公司项目法律顾问；担任亦庄国际投资发展有限公司以退市方式收购美国纳斯达克上市芯片半导体公司Mattson Technologies Inc.项目法律顾问；担任国家电网、英大传媒收购某出版社项目法律顾问；担任太平洋证券（601099）、东北证券（000686）的常年法律顾问；担任平安财产保险股份有限公司的保险代位求偿专项法律顾问；担任中能兴科（832618）全国中小企业股份转让系统挂牌和常年法律顾问；担任中电方大（430411）、金视和（831273）、蓝擎股份（833569）、鹰谷光电（838454）、能为科技（430282）、海润影业（836583）、常荣声学（832341）、嘉华美瑞（835251）等全国中小企业股份转让系统挂牌和常年法律顾问。

国际贸易：代表中国企业发起对美国汽车反倾销反补贴调查；代表中国企业应诉欧盟对华不锈钢案件反倾销调查；代表中国商务部和中国政府参加美国对华柠檬酸行政复审；代表中国企业发起对美国取向电工钢反倾销反补贴调查等。

**教育背景**

瑞士世界贸易研究院访问学者；对外经济贸易大学法学院法学硕士；对外经济贸易大学法学院经济学学士。

**职业资格**

中国律师执业资格。

**著作**

《南亚投资法律风险与典型案例》《西亚投资法律风险与典型案例》《中亚投资法律风险与典型案例》《新三板案例和解决之道》（法制出版社）。

**社会活动**

北京"一带一路"研究会常务理事

**工作语言**

中文、英语、日语

## Chen Bo(Judy)

**Professional Experience**

Ms Chen specializes in Financing & Insurance, International Trade, Anti-trust and competition.

**Representative matters**

Financing & Insurance: Acted as counsel participated in A well-known state-owned M&A fund participating in the Chinese investment consortium on acquiring UK Global Switch IDC with an amount of 3.5 billion GBP; E-Town International Investment & Development Co., Ltd. acquiring Mattson Technologies Inc., a Nasdaq-listed U.S. chip semi-conductor company by delisting; State GRID Corporation and Yingda media acquiring a publishing house project; Pacific Securities(601099) and Northeast Securities(000686): Ping'an Property Insurance Co., Ltd. Insurance Subrogation Special Project. Acted as National SME Share Transfer System Listing and Perennial Legal Adviser: ZNXK(832618), ZDFD(430411), JSH(831273), LQGF(833569), YGGD(838454), NWKJ(430282), HRYY(836583), CRSX(832341), JHMR9835251).

International Trade: Acting as legal counsel for Chinese Automobiles Industry in the Antidumping and Countervailing case against USA, the Chinese stainless steel Industry in the Antidumping case initiated by EU, the Chinese Government in the Citric Acid Administrative Review, the Chinese industry in the Oriented Electric Steel Antidumping and Countervailing case against USA.

**Education Background**

Visiting Scholar, World Trade Institution, Switzerland; LLM, University of International Business and Economics; Bachelor of Economics, University of International Business and Economics.

**Professional Associations**

Admitted to practice in P.R. China

**Publishing**

*Legal Risk and Cases of Investment in South Asia, Legal- Risk and Cases of Investment in West Asia, Legal Risk and Cases of Investment in Central Asia, Cases and Settlement of NEEQ*(China Legal Publishing House).

**Pro Bono**

The Beijing Law Society of the "Belt and Road" standing director

**Working Language**

Chinese, English, Japanese

网址：www.dhl.com.cn
详情请登录中国律师年鉴网：www.yearbooklawyer.com
— 028 —

# 崔红伟 律师

崔红伟律师是北京天达共和律师事务所资深合伙人。

崔红伟律师1989年获得中华人民共和国律师执业资格；2004年获得香港特别行政区律师执业资格；2005年获得英格兰及威尔士律师执业资格。崔红伟律师具有20多年丰富的国际、国内律师从业经验，曾在中国大陆、中国香港地区、英国等地任职。

崔红伟律师的主要执业领域包括公司投融资、跨境并购、资本市场、合规、重组、清算以及与商业诉讼相关之法律事务。凭借对中西方法律体系和商业环境的深度了解，崔律师在管理跨境项目和处理复杂合规问题的过程中为客户提供系统的法律支持和深度的全面的服务。

崔律师参与了众多的跨境投融资及并购项目，包括代表美国科氏（Koch）就壳牌公司收购其在中国境内23家公司的全部资产及业务项目；德国施耐德收购利德华福；德国威能公司中国境内投资重组；香港华润水泥境内一系列收购项目；SAF-HOLLAND GMBH收购北京柯布克科技；中国爱地公司收购非洲厄利特里亚巴伦图省Gogne金矿；联想新视界境内、外投融资项目；北京燃气境外发债项目以及众多中国境内的外资企业清算项目。崔律师也一直在为多家境内、外企业提供常年中国法律顾问服务，包括为沙特驻北京大使馆提供超过10年的常年法律服务。

崔律师好学不倦的精神，丰富的法律知识和三栖律师的多年的国际法律工作经验，使她在古老中国再次振兴的今天有机会创造其独特的法律服务空间。其对中国传统文化的尊崇以及其内心深处散发出的谦逊和自信，让她的律师执业风格散发出独特的个人魅力。

崔红伟律师1988年获得北京联合大学法学学士学位；1996年获得英国剑桥安鲁大学工商管理硕士学位；1998年获得英国剑桥安鲁大学法学专业CPE证书；2001年获得香港大学法学专业PCLL证书。

崔律师的工作语言为中文（普通话和粤语）、英文。

# Cui Hongwei(Kathryn)

Kathryn is a lawyer and partner of East & Concord Partners.

Kathryn qualified as solicitor in Mainland China (1989), Hong Kong SAR China (2004)and England and Wales (2005). Kathryn has more than 20 years of experience in legal practice and has worked in mainland China, Hong Kong China and England.

Kathryn's main areas of practice include corporate finance, cross-border M&A, capital markets, compliance, insolvency and restructuring and dispute resolution. With a deep understanding of both common law and the Chinese legal system, coupled with knowledge of commercial operations in both China and the overseas market, Kathryn is able to provide process-driven, comprehensive and unparalleled legal support to assist with clients' cross-border project management, as well as solving complex compliance issues.

Kathryn has provided legal services to numerous cross-border transactions and M&A projects, including assisting Koch Industry in the sale of its entire China business operations to Shell, Schneider's acquisition of Leader & Harvest, the restructuring of Vaillant GmbH's China business, the M&A & business expansion of China Resources Co. in China, the restructuring of Pico Denshi Group's China business; SAF Holland GmbH acquisition of Beijing Corpco, Assisting China Aidi's acquisition of mining business in Africa, Lenovo New Vision's A+ round finance project: Beijing Gas Group's debt issuing in Hong Kong China and liquidation of various foreign direct invested entities in China. Kathryn has also been rendering annual legal services to many domestic and foreign invested companies in China, including over 10 years' legal service to Royal Embassy of Saudi Arabia in Beijing.

Kathryn's timeless pursuit of excellence in her studies and legal practice, and her rich and diverse experience in international and local law has pushed her to the forefront of legal practice in China. Her Chinese heritage and culture, as well as her confident yet modest ways and her sharp wit provide her with a style of practice that is unique and charming.

Kathryn obtained a LLB degree in 1988 from Beijing Union University. Kathryn obtained a MBA in 1996 and the CPE Certificate in 1998 from Anglia Ruskin University in Cambridge, and after further study, she completed the PCLL Certificate from the University of Hong Kong in 2001.

Kathryn is a Beijing native, who is fluent in Chinese(Mandarin and Cantonese), English.

网址：www.east-concord.com

详情请登录中国律师年鉴网：www.yearbooklawyer.com

## 郭光 律师

北京光汉律师事务所主任、合伙人

### 执业领域

郭光律师主要执业领域为公司并购、金融领域、债务清收和重组、知识产权、诉讼和仲裁，尤其在代表金融机构清收债权领域经验丰富。

### 执业经历

郭光律师为众多跨国公司、国内外金融机构、内外资企业提供法律服务，行业涉及公司、银行、信托、商贸等领域；代表国内外著名公司参与项目结构设计、合同谈判、股权交易、资产收购、公司重组等法律工作；郭光律师亦具有银行业务的良好经验，包括银团贷款、风险融资、担保交易和项目融资，代理了许多重大、复杂案件的诉讼和仲裁。

### 社会职务及荣誉

郭光律师曾获得中国政法大学法学学士学位、经济法学硕士学位、波恩大学比较法学硕士学位和科隆大学法学博士学位。郭光律师曾就职于中国政法大学、德国克虏伯公司（Krupp AG）法律部和年利达律师事务所德国分所（Linklaters）。

# Dr. Guang

Founder and Managing Partner of Guo & Partners

**Fields of practice**

Dr. Guo specializes in mergers and acquisitions, banking and finance, debt collection and restructuring, intellectual property, litigation and arbitration.

**Professional Experience**

Dr. Guo provides legal service for multi-national corporations, domestic and foreign financial institutions and enterprises with domestic or foreign investment, covering areas from banking, trust, corporate governance and cross-border transactions. Dr. Guo has represented renowned domestic and overseas companies in project structuring, contract negotiation, transfer of company shares or assets, company restructuring and other transactions. Dr. Guo has particular expertise in banking related legal affairs, such as syndicated loans, venture capital, non-performing loans, secured transactions and project financing. He has successfully represented clients in a great number of complex and challenging legal proceedings.

**Education Background**

Dr. Guo obtained LL.B. and LL.M. Degree of Economic Law from the China University of Political Science and Law; a LL.M. Degree in Comparative Business Law from the Bonn University, Germany; and a Ph.D. Degree from the Cologne University, Germany.

Dr. Guo used to work for the China University of Political Science and Law, the legal department of Krupp AG and the German office of Linklaters & Alliance.

---

# 黄磊碧 律师

北京尚公律师事务所高级合伙人。

## 执业领域

海事海商、跨境并购和海外投资、重大国际活动、涉外争议解决。

## 执业经历

曾任高级人民法院法官，央企法务，在海外工作多年。对跨国公司的运作、海外投资和跨境并购、国际重大工程项目建设、国际知识产权保护、重大国际活动和涉外纠纷处理等有丰富的实践经验，与国外多家机构建立了广泛的联系和渠道，是一名具有国际化视野的优秀律师。

## 主要业绩

**海事海商：** （1）参与处理中远"TRADE WILL"轮买卖合同纠纷一案在瑞典斯德哥尔摩仲裁案；（2）为中远与三菱银行等日本银团买造船协议的合同审阅提供法律服务；（3）参与中国远洋运输的运价调整受美国301条款限制的法律风险分析及对策研究。

**跨境并购和海外投资：** （1）为中韩自贸区威海—平泽航线的跨国并购提供法律服务；（2）为"紫禁城"举办"三高"演唱会商业赞助提供法律服务；（3）为国企联合体在柬埔寨金银湾产融示范区投资项目提供法律服务；（4）为国家电网在印度、巴基斯坦和缅甸建设电网基础设施提供法律服务；（5）为瑞典NOLATO公司与英美烟草BAT的特许生产经营权纠纷提供法律服务。

**重大国际项目——2019中国北京世界园艺博览会：** （1）为世园会引进五星级国际酒店谈判、世园会知识产权保护、世园会土地一级开发信托融资提供法律服务；（2）为东盟7国参展提供法律服务；（3）为非洲15国和上合组织的参展援助提供法律服务；（4）为港澳台等展园代建提供法律服务。

**重大国际项目——2022中国北京冬奥会及冬残奥会：** （1）为连接冬奥会赛区的京张高铁拆迁纠纷处理提供法律服务；（2）为冬奥会高山滑雪及雪橇基地征地拆迁和用水提供法律咨询服务。

## 社会职务及荣誉

中国人民大学金融法学博士。北京市律师协会"一带一路"研究会副秘书长，中国法学会东盟法律研究中心研究员。获北京市律师协会颁发的"特别贡献奖"。

## 著作论文

《"一带一路"战略下高铁走出去的法律风险及应对之策》，2018年世界交通运输大会主旨演讲并收录论文集；《"一带一路"沿线六十五个国家中国企业海外投资法律环境分析报告汇编暨外国投资法律制度分析报告汇编》（合著）；《马来西亚房地产行业投资法律分析报告》（合著）；《上海自贸区细则对融资租赁业的影响》；《布鲁塞尔公约下对分包承运人直接起诉的管辖权》；《希腊海事仲裁简介》（译作）。

北京 Beijing

# Lawyer Huang Leibi

Senior Partner, Beijing S&P Law Firm

**Fields of practice**

maritime affairs, cross-border M&As and overseas investments, major international events, settlement of foreign-related disputes

**Experience of practice**

She once served as a judge of a higher people's court and a legal counsel to a central enterprise，and worked overseas for many years. As an excellent lawyer with an international vision, she has rich practical experience in operations of transnational corporations, cross-border M&As and overseas investments, major international construction projects, international intellectual property right protection, major international events, and the settlement of foreign-related disputes, and has established extensive contacts and relationships with many overseas organizations.

**Key achievements**

Maritime affairs: Participating in the arbitration of the dispute over the COSCO "TRADE WILL" liner sales contract in Stockholm, Sweden；providing legal services for the review of the ship purchase and building agreements of COSCO with Mitsubishi Bank and other Japanese consortiums；participating in the legal risk analysis and countermeasure research on COSCO's freight rate adjustment being restricted by U.S. Section 301.

Cross-border M&As and overseas investments: Providing legal services for the cross-border M&A of the Weihai-Pyongtaek shipping line in China-South Korea Free Trade Area for the Weihai Port；providing legal services for the business sponsorship for the Three Tenors Concert organized by the US-China Business Council in the "Forbidden City"；providing legal services for the investment project of a consortium of state-owned.

Enterprises in the Golden Silver Gulf Industry-Finance Demonstration Zone project in Cambodia：Providing legal services for the construction of power grid infrastructure by State Grid Corporation in India, Pakistan and Myanmar; providing legal services for the EAGLE2 franchising dispute between NOLATO Group and British American Tobacco (BAT).

Major international project——2019 Beijing International Horticultural Exhibition：Providing special legal services for negotiations on the introduction of a five-star hotel for the International Horticultural Exhibition, the intellectual property right protection of the emblem and the mascot, and the financing of primary land development; providing legal services for the participation of Pakistan, India, Yemen, Belgium, North Korea, Afghanistan, Qatar, Myanmar and Syrian, assistance for the participation of 15 African countries and the Shanghai Cooperation Organization, and the construction of the exhibition park of the Macao Civic and Municipal Affairs Bureau.

Major international project——2022 Olympic and Paralympic Winter Games: Providing legal services for the dispute of the Beijing-Zhangjiakou high-speed railway which connects the different divisions of 2022 Olympic Winter Games; providing legal advice for land acquisition, house demolition and water use for the alpine skiing and sledding base of the 2022 Olympic Winter Games.

Social titles and honors: Doctor of Financial Law, Renmin University of China; Deputy Secretary-general of the "Belt and Road" Research Council, Beijing Lawyers Association; Research Fellow at the ASEAN Legal Research Center, China Law Society; "Special Contribution Award" of the Beijing Lawyers Association.

**Papers**

"Legal Risks and Countermeasures of High-speed Rail Going Global under the 'Belt and Road' Strategy", Collection of Papers of the 2018 World Transport Convention; "Compilation of Environmental Analysis Reports on the Overseas Investment for Chinese Enterprises in 65 Countries along the 'Belt and Road' & Compilation of Analysis Reports on Foreign Investment Legal Systems" (co-authored); "Analysis Report on Investment Laws of the Malaysian Real Estate Industry" (co-authored);"Impacts of the Rules of China (Shanghai) Pilot Free Trade Zone on Financial Leading", New Zealand United News, 2013; "Jurisdiction of Direct Prosecution of Subcontracting Forwarders under the Brussels Convention" "Introduction to Maritime Arbitration in Greece" (translated), Maritime Law Newsletter, published in 1999.

网址：www.splf.com.cn
详情请登录中国律师年鉴网：www.yearbooklawyer.com
— 032 —

北京 Beijing

# 贾辉 律师

贾辉律师是北京德恒律师事务所合伙人，主要执业领域为并购和保险。贾辉律师具有美国纽约大学法学院和中国政法大学的法律硕士学历，并同时拥有美国纽约州和中国的律师执业资格。贾辉律师是商务部国际投资法律事务入库律师，还兼任"一带一路"服务机制主席助理，新能源海外发展联盟副秘书长，北京律师协会保险委员会委员，中国保险行业协会首席律师顾问团代表，中国保险资产管理管业协会法律合规委员会委员。

## 代表性项目

### 1. 跨境投资并购

（1）担任中材国际并购一家德国企业项目法律顾问（交易金额超过1亿欧元）；（2）担任中国重汽在巴基斯坦和越南的投资项目法律顾问；（3）担任中牧集团收购新西兰牛羊肉加工企业项目法律顾问；（4）担任桑德国际拟收购葡萄牙废物处理企业项目法律顾问；（5）担任中国铁路物资为其在巴西设立分公司项目法律顾问；（6）担任四川国栋建设拟并购一家意大利企业项目法律顾问；（7）担任中国烟草总公司及其子公司在巴西的并购项目法律顾问；（8）担任中国黄金集团公司在海外的重要收购项目法律顾问；（9）担任国家开发银行新疆分行在吉尔吉斯坦金矿融资项目法律顾问。

### 2. 保险涉外业务

（1）担任云南城投收购安联生命保险（韩国）公司项目法律顾问；（2）担任太古公司与美国丘博保险公司之间的第三者责任险理赔纠纷项目法律顾问；（3）担任 Zurich 保险公司就涉及境内一家中外合作企业董事责任保单问题咨询项目法律顾问；（4）担任一家外资公司国内相关保险事宜的处理制作保险手册项目法律顾问。

### 3. 公司涉外业务

（1）担任国际道路运输联盟在北京设立办事处的法律顾问；（2）担任美国 CRS 公司在中国某投资项目法律顾问；（3）担任诺基亚（中国）投资公司合同审查项目法律顾问；（4）担任韩国浦项（中国）投资公司某境内投资项目法律顾问。

## 专业著作

• 《三思而后行 —— 中国企业境外投资并购法律风险防范》，2013年1月，法律出版社；
• 《你违规了吗？保险机构合规手册》，2011年1月，人民日报出版社。

## 工作语言

中文、英语

## 执业领域

金融保险 、 跨境投资

网址：www. dhl. com. cn
详情请登录中国律师年鉴网：www. yearbooklawyer. com
— 033 —

 中国涉外律师

# Jia Hui(Harrison)

Mr. Jia Hui practices mainly in the fields of M&A and insurance. Mr. Jia is a Master of Law of both NYU and CUPL, and qualified to practice in the New York State and China. Mr. Jia is an admitted lawyer in the field of international investment legal affairs by MOFCOM. He is also the Chairman Assistant of BNRSC, Deputy Secretary of New Energy International Development Federation, Member of the Insurance Committee of Beijing Lawyer Association, Representative of Chief Lawyer Counsel of China Insurance Association, Member of Legal and Compliance Committee of China Insurance Asset Management Association.

## Representative Matters
### Cross-border Investment

•Advised Sinoma International on its acquisition of the majority shareholding of a Germany company –Hazemag, including conducting due diligence in Germany and South Africa and drafting due diligence report, negotiating transaction agreements;

•Advised China National Heavy Duty Trunk Group Co., Ltd.(CNHTC) on their investments in Pakistan and Vietnam;

•Advised China Animal Husbandry Group on its acquisition of beef and lamb processing enterprise, including conducting due diligence in New Zealand and drafting due diligence report;

•Advised Sound Global on its acquisition plan on a Portuguese waste disposal enterprise;

•Advised China Railway Materials Company to establish a branch in Brazil;

•Advised Sichuan Guodong on its acquisition of an Italian company, including conducting due diligence in Italy and drafting due diligence report, negotiating transaction agreements;

•Advised China Tobacco Group and its subsidiary on their investments in Brazil;

•Advised China Gold Group on its major outbound acquisition in Canada, including conducting due diligence and drafting due diligence report, negotiating transaction agreements;

•Advised China Development Bank Xinjiang Branch on the project financing on a gold mining project in Kyrgyzstan.

## Foreign Related Insurance Matters

•Advised YMCI on its acquisition of Allianz China Life Insurance Co., Ltd(Korea);

•Advised Swire Pacific for its commercial liability insurance claim dispute with Chubb Insurance (China) Company;

•Advised Zurich on the liabilities of a director of a foreign funded cooperative company under a D&O policy;

•Advised China Development Bank for its Cooperation Agreement with a Russian insurance company.

## Foreign Related Corporate Matters

•Advised International Road Transport Union (IRU) on registration of representative office in China;

•Advised US CRS Company on inbound investment issues and its service contracts with domestic companies;

•Advised Nokia (China) Investment Company on various contract review and drafts;

•Advised Korea Posco (China) Investment Company on various inbound investment issues.

## Publications

•"Legal Risks Prevention for Chinese Enterprises to Make Outbound Investments", January 2013, China Law Press;

•"Have you violated the rules? Compliance Handbook for Insurance Institutions", January 2011, People's Daily Press of China.

## Working Languages
Chinese, English

## Practice Areas
Finance and Insurance, Cross Border Investment

网址：www.dhl.com.cn
详情请登录中国律师年鉴网：www.yearbooklawyer.com
— 034 —

## 北京 Beijing

### 罗智愉 律师

北京市京师律师事务所境内外投融资并购部主任、互联网企业法律事务部执行主任，法治强国之路：中国改革开放40周年——向驻华商会、使馆、外向型机构推选的优秀涉外律师，司法部全国涉外律师名单入选律师。罗律师长期专注于境内外投资并购、风险投资、私募股权与基金、外商直接投资、资本市场等相关法律服务，代理了百起跨境投资案件，广泛涉及互联网相关产业及各类新兴和传统行业，业务涵盖人民币境内融资到美元离岸融资、外商直接投资到中国企业境外投资、国际红筹架构及JV架构的搭建与拆除、公司初始设立到兼并重组、境内外挂牌及上市等全流程法律服务，并为众多知名企业提供包括境内外结构搭建、公司治理、团队激励等法律服务，与商务部门、外汇管理部门、工商行政管理部门、各银行类金融机构有良好的互动关系。在加入京师之前，罗律师是大成律师事务所的律师、法律顾问。

罗智愉律师在中国互联网及各类新兴和传统行业企业通过兼并收购、战略合作"走出去"及"出海"领域拥有丰富的经验，帮助企业提供一站式法律服务，为企业整体平台化实现战略上的法律支持。

罗律师精通英美普通法系国家法律，对英国、美国、开曼群岛、英属威尔京群岛、百慕大群岛等国家以及中国香港地区的商事法律和律师实务有深入的了解，尤其擅长处理各类涉及资金出入境的国际商事投资与并购、对外投资和其他各类跨境商事业务。

#### 业务专长

国际综合、风险投资及私募股权投资、兼并重组、外商投资与境外投资、证券与资本市场、公司常年法律顾问等。

#### 教育背景

英国曼彻斯特大学国际金融法硕士学位、英国斯旺西大学普通法文凭、北京第二外国学院法学学士学位

#### 业务资质

中国律师资格、英国法律高等技能文凭、上市公司独立董事资格、中国证券从业资格、基金从业资格。

#### 工作语言

中文、英语

### 部分涉外法律服务业绩

已完成过百起境内外投资、并购重组、跨境交易项目。
（1）代表投资人。高榕资本、经纬创投、红杉资本、软银赛富、IDG资本、贝塔斯曼、乐逗投资、联想创投、梅花大航海创投、Infinity Venture Capital、丰厚资本、九合创投、不惑创投、中能华启创业投资基金、Cyber Carrier等；
（2）代表融资方（品牌）。阿里移动、中东移动、尚德教育、新浪微博基金、车来车往、36氪、考拉先生、赶集兼职、春雨医生、陪我科技、赐麓游戏、暴雨游戏、手盟游戏、明星衣橱、来来会旅游、米折网、下厨房、美食杰、优集品、社区001、百分点科技、飞碟说、淘当铺、掌星立意、秀吧、租租车、车托帮、51信用卡、蘑菇公寓、星空琴行、马展金融、辛巴达服装、易快修、千寻招聘、好好住、北京神策、老农帮、新金所、elsewhere、借啊。

中国企业"出海"典型案例。（1）中东。代表中东移动-北京米纳科技有限公司返程投资架构搭建、融资、境外再投资（投资人：梅花创投、乐逗、联想、贝塔斯曼、坚果资）；（2）巴西。代表魔宝互联境外融资，远航资本（Cyber Carrier）收购巴西Mobocity、北京魔宝互联科技有限公司；（3）南非。代表三一重工、保利集团新设持股平台对外投资并收购南非大型军工企业；（4）印尼。代表"借啊"北京慧融天下信息科技有限公司搭建中国-印尼持股结构（PT Bright Finance Indonesia）并融资（投资人：拍拍贷，纽交所上市公司）；（5）离岸。代表36氪-北京协力筑成金融信息服务有限公司返程投资架构搭建并多轮次融资（投资人：经纬、Infinity Venture Partners、蚂蚁金服等）；代表好好住——家宅一生（北京）科技有限公司返程投资架构搭建并多轮次融资（投资人：Morningside晨兴资本、GGV纪源资本、Joy Capital愉悦资本）。

境内外交易经典案例。代表徐州国资委全资公司徐州市新盛建设发展投资有限公司收购法国圣戈班（500强企业）中国境内公司；代表车来车往——世纪车来车往（北京）网络科技有限公司与开新二手车平台境内外合并；代表51信用卡——杭州恩牛网络技术有限公司境内外收购99分期——北京鼎力创世科技有限公司。

中国企业"出海"回归经典案例。代表中概股美国上市公司富尔农艺［Fuer International Inc.（0001445229）］退市并拆除境外结构，回归国内资本市场；代表尚德教育——北京尚佳崇业教育科技有限公司拆除境外结构，回归国内资本市场；代表三个爸爸——极客三个爸爸智能环境科技（北京）有限公司拆除境外结构，回归国内资本市场。

网址：www.jingsh.com
详情请登录中国律师年鉴网：www.yearbooklawyer.com
—035—

# Mr Luo Zhiyu

Luo Zhiyu is the Director of Onshore & Offshore Investment and M&A Dept. and Executive Director of Internet Enterprise Dept. of Jingsh Law Firm and the PRC Ministry of Justice Selected Lawyer of Foreign Affairs. He focus on legal services for venture capital and private equity, merge & acquisition, foreign direct Investment, outbound investment and capital markets with hundreds of onshore and offshore investment project experiences and an extensive coverage of the internet-related industries and other emerging and traditional sectors.

He is specialized in one-stop comprehensive legal services, for example from onshore RMB financing to offshore USD financing, from foreign direct investment to PRC outbound investment, from angel round financing to E round financing, from company incorporation to list in the capital markets, establishing and dismantling VIE structure/JV structure as well as employee incentive plan, corporate governance and onshore-offshore restructurings etc. He is very familiar with the local incentive and subsidy polices and maintains interactive relationship with local regulatory authorities and financial institutions.

Luo Zhiyu has a wealth of experiences in providing one-stop legal services and strategic legal support for Chinese corporations in internet-related industries and other emerging and traditional sectors in their "go global" business through merge and acquisition and strategic plans. The comprehensive understanding of the laws of Common Law Countries such as laws of U.S., UK, Cayman Islands, British Virgin Islands and other countries as well as Hong Kong China district, brings him efficiency in handling cross-border transactions onshore and offshore of PRC.

## Experiences

Up to now, Mr. Luo has represented more than hundreds cross-border investment and M&A projects. His experiences including representing Alibaba UC, Mena Mobile Inc., 36kr, 51 Credits and Chunyu and many other famous companies in their offshore financing; provide legal services for one of the Xuzhou state-owned investment company acquires Saint-Gobain (Fortune 500 company), Poly Group associated with SANY Group in their outbound investment (joint-venture) and acquisition of a large military industry enterprises in South Africa, the acquisition of Diandian Interactive Holding by Zhongji Holding (listed number 600634). In the area of VC and PE, he worked with Matrix, IDG, Banyan, BAI, Legend Capital, Idreamsky, Alibaba, JD.com and other top international PE fund and large international firms. Zhiyu Luo is also versed with "go global" one-stop legal practice and his experience including the support of numerous internet companies such as Mena Mobile, Mobocity to go out through merge & acquisition and strategy integration and extend cutting-edge businesses.

## Expertise

Comprehensive International Legal Practice, Private Equity/ Venture Capital Investment, Merger & Acquisition, Foreign

Zhiyu Luo and Ministor Mohada, the Minisher of Syria Embassy in PRC in The First Project Matchmaking Fair for Syria Reconstruction in July, 2017. Zhiyu Luo is the Executive Director of Syria Reconstruction Investment and Law Committee.

# 北京 Beijing

Direct Investment / PRC Outbound Investment, Capital Markets

## Education Background

University of Manchester (LLM in International Financial Law), University of Swansea (Common Law Diploma), Beijing International Studies University (LLB).

## Qualifications

Qualified in Attorney at Law (PRC), UK TOLES (Higher); Qualified as Independent Director of Listerd Company; Qualified in SAC and AMAC (PRC).

## Language

Chinese, English

## Part of the Foreign Legal Practice Achievements

**1.Completed hundreds of investment &financing, merge & acquisition and cross-border transactions.** (1)Representing the investors: Banyan Capital, Matrix, Sequoia Capital, IDG, Bertelsmann Asian Investment, Idreamsky, Lenovo Capital, Plum Ventures, Infinity Venture Capital, fhcapital, Jiuhe VC, Buhuo VC, Huaqi VC, Cyber Carrier etc.; (2)Representing the companies(Brands): Alibaba Mobile, Mena Mobile, Sunlands

Education, Weibo Fund, che6che5, 36Kr, Koalac, Doumi, Chunyuyisheng, Peiwo, Cilu Game, Baoyu Game, 910 APP, Hichao Net, lailaihui Net, Mizhe Net, Xiachufang, Meishijie, Ujipin, shequ 001, Baifendian, Feidieshuo, Taodangpu, Zhangxinliyi, Xiuba, Zuzuche, Chetuobang, U51, Mogoroom, Xingkong, Singbada, Yikuaixiu, Moseeker, Nice Living, Sensors Data, Laonongbang, Xinjinsuo, Stayelsewhere, Huazhi.

**2.Typical Cases of "Go Global" of PRC enterprise.** (1)Middle East: Represent Mena Mobile Inc. to organize offshore structure for its USD financing and set up business in several countries in Middle East and outbound investment in Dubai（Investor：Plum Capital, Idreamsky, Legend Capital, Bertelsmann Asian Investment, Capitalnuts; (2)Brazil：Represent Mobocity to organize offshore structure for its offshore financing and set up business in Brazil；Represent Cyber Carrier for its acquisition of Mobocity and its PRC entity; (3)South Africa：Represent Poly Group associated with SANY Group in their outbound investment (joint-venture) and acquisition of a large military industry enterprises in South Africa; (4)Indonesia：Represent PT Bright Finance Indonesia to organize PRC- Indonesia offshore structure for its USD (Investor: PPDF(NYSE listed)); (5)Offshore：Represent 36kr to organize PRC round-tripping investment structure for its series rounds of financing（investors：Matrix,Infinity Venture Partners,Ant Financial）；Represent Nice Living to organize PRC round-tripping investment structure for its series rounds of financing (Investors：Morningside, GGV, Joy Capital).

**3. Typical cases of onshore-offshore transaction：**

Represent one of the Xuzhou state-owned investment company to acquire Saint-Gobain (Fortune 500 company); Represent che6che5 merged with Carsing Group in both onshore and offshore structure; Represent 51 Credits to acquaint 99 fenqi.com in both onshore and offshore structure.

**4. The typical cases of the return of "Go Global" by PRC enterprises：**

Represent Chinese U.S. listed Company Fuer International Inc. to delist and dismantle offshore structure and return to PRC domestic capital markets.

Represent Sunlands Education to dismantle PRC round-tripping investment structure and return to PRC domestic capital markets; Represent Sangebaba to dismantle PRC round-tripping investment structure and return to PRC domestic capital markets.

网址：www.jingsh.com
详情请登录中国律师年鉴网：www.yearbooklawyer.com
— 037 —

# 邬国华 律师

金诚同达高级合伙人

## 执业领域

跨境并购、私募与风险投资、外商投资、公司合规、争议纠纷解决。

## 执业经历

邬国华律师是业界公认的从事跨境并购及私募基金业务的法律专家，她的客户包括中国及全球最大的一些基金及公司。邬国华律师定期为客户的领导层提供关键的法律意见或建议，使客户能够获得更加有利的商业条款及更完善的法律保护。

法律 500 强在其最新报道中评论道，邬国华律师作为金诚同达公司并购领域的领头律师值得力荐，同时，其在工程和能源领域的卓越表现也值得赞赏。《欧洲货币》杂志旗下的《亚洲法律概况》杂志同样高度赞赏了邬律师在公司并购领域及能源和自然资源的表现。邬国华律师还多次受到客户的好评："资深专家，卓越的客户服务，反应迅速，专注细节，拥有广泛的业务网络和国际化水准的团队。"

邬国华律师同时为跨国公司在中国的各项投资活动以日常运营事项提供全面的法律服务，其律师熟悉的行业涵盖汽车、新能源、新材料、娱乐、TMT 以及矿产资源等。邬律师在资本市场及融资领域也有广泛的经验。

## 荣誉称号

邬国华律师多次获得奖项，包括但不限于获得《亚洲法律杂志》"中国最领先的 10 名并购律师""客户首选律师 20 强"和中国"最佳女律师 15 强"等称号及"年度最佳交易律师"提名，并得到来自世界权威评级机构钱伯斯、法律 500 强、亚洲法律概况杂志的认可，涵盖的领域包括公司并购领域和工程和能源领域。

## 社会职务

北京仲裁委员会仲裁员、北京大学法学院"并购与重组"课程客座讲师、中国与全球化智库理事、康奈尔大学法学院

校友会执行委员会主席（2010～2012）、康奈尔国际律师校友联谊会（CILAN）大中华区牵头人、北京市律师协会"一带一路"法律服务研究会副主任、国家律师学院客座教授、欧美同学会 2005 年委员会理事、清华大学法学院兼职研究生导师。

## 工作经历

北京金诚同达律师事务所高级合伙人、美国普衡律师事务所北京办公室合伙人、美国凯易律师事务所芝加哥办公室顾问、美国苏利文克伦威尔律师事务所纽约办公室律师。

## 著述论文

邬国华律师曾是北京市律师协会出版的《"一带一路"沿线 65 个国家中国企业海外投资法律环境分析报告汇编》统稿人和撰稿人，担任中华全国律师协会即将出版的《"一带一路"沿线国家法律环境国别报告》的统稿人。

网址：www.jtnfa.com
详情请登录中国律师年鉴网：www.yearbooklawyer.com
—038—

# Wu Guohua (Annie)

Senior Partner at Jincheng Tongda & Neal Law Firm

### Practice Areas

cross-border M&A, private equity and venture capital, foreign direct investment, corporate compliance, dispute resolution.

### Professional Experience

A recognized authority on cross-border mergers and acquisitions and private equity transactions. Ms. Wu represents some of the largest funds and industrial companies in China and around the world. Ms. Wu works directly with her clients' leadership on a regular basis, providing critical insights and advice, which enables her clients to obtain substantially improved commercial terms and legal protections.

In its most recent report, Legal 500 noted that Ms. Wu is a leader of the JT&N Corporate and M&A practice and comes highly recommended. The report also commended Ms. Wu for her work in the firm's leading Energy and Projects practice, giving her special recognition as a "Leading Individual" in Corporate and M&A (the highest ranking). Euromoney's Asialaw likewise lauded Ms. Wu's performance in both Corporate and M&A, as well as in Energy and Natural Resources, and awarded her recognition as a "Market Leading Lawyer" in Corporate and M&A (also the highest ranking). Many of her clients commended Ms. Wu as "an experienced expert who can provide excellent legal services", and she is "always responsive" "detail-focused" and "has wide business networks as well as international team members".

Ms. Wu also provides comprehensive services to multinational companies in connection with a complete range of investment activities and daily operational matters in China. Ms. Wu's industrial expertise encompasses automotive, new energy, entertainment, TMT, and mining and natural resources sectors, to name a few. Ms. Wu also has extensive experience in capital markets and finance matters.

### Honorary Titles

Ms. Wu is an award-winning attorney. She was recognized by Asian Legal Business as a winner of the "Client Choice Top 20" Award and was named a finalist for "Dealmaker of the Year" (China). She was also ranked by Asian Legal Business as one of China's "Top 15 Female Lawyers" and as one of China's "Top 10 M&A lawyers". Additionally, she has repeatedly been recognized by renowned rating agencies like Chambers & Partners, Legal 500, and Asialaw Profiles, for her work in areas such as Corporate and M&A as well as Project Finance and Energy.

### Social Status

·Arbitrator, Beijing Arbitration Commission;
·Guest Lecturer, Merger Acquisition & Reorganization, Peking University Law School;
·Director, the Center for China and Globalization;
·President, Cornell Law School Alumni Association Executive Board (2010 ~ 2012);
·China Captain, Cornell International Lawyers Alumni Network (CILAN);
·Deputy Director, "One Belt, One Road" Research Institute, Beijing Lawyers Association;
·Guest Professor, National Lawyers College, P.R.C.;
·Director, Committee 2005;
·Adjunct Graduate Student Advisor, Tsinghua University School of Law.

### Working Experience

Jincheng Tongda & Neal Law Firm, Senior Partner; Paul, Hastings, Janofsky & Walker LLP (Beijing)，Partner; Kirkland & Ellis LLP (Chicago), Counsel; Sullivan & Cromwell LLP (New York), Associate.

### Publications

Ms. Wu publishes articles on a regular basis. She is an author and editor of *Chinese Enterprises Overseas Investment Legal Environment Report Collection of Sixty-Five Countries along the Belt and Road* published by the Beijing Lawyers Association. She is an editor of the *Legal Environment Report of the "Belt and Road" Countries*, which will be published by the All China Lawyers Association.

网址：www.jtnfa.com
详情请登录中国律师年鉴网：www.yearbooklawyer.com
－039－

# 解辰阳 博士

# Doctor Xie Chenyang

解辰阳博士是首都律师协会国际投资与贸易专业委员会副主任，ICC 气候变化争议仲裁工作组成员、ICC China 仲裁委员会、ICC China 能源与环境委员会成员、天津仲裁委员会仲裁员。解辰阳博士也是西南政法大学兼职研究员、大连大学法学院客座教授，法律 500 强上榜律师。解辰阳博士曾经担任中国专利保护协会副会长、中华商标协会理事。

解辰阳博士多年在大型企业集团服务。他担任过两家中国 500 强企业的总法律顾问；亲自主持办理了大量企业海外投资业务，包括并购和绿地投资。同时，解辰阳博士也在欧美企业集团担任过重要岗位。对跨地域的企业文化、交易文化等方面非常熟悉。

### 解辰阳博士主导的海外投资部分案例

（1）英国某老牌银行与中国某集团海外账户纠纷（英国伦敦）；（2）巴基斯坦 SECP 与中国某集团投资纠纷，该案件终审在最高法院（巴基斯坦伊斯兰堡）；（3）埃塞俄比亚、吉布提能源绿地投资，该项目是中国"一带一路"在非洲投资的标杆项目（埃塞俄比亚和吉布提）；（4）加拿大某上市公司收购（加拿大多伦多）；（5）阿根廷矿业公司并购（韩国首尔、阿根廷布宜诺斯艾利斯）；（6）美国某国际第四大半导体级硅片供应商，纳斯达克上市公司收购，当年唯一通过 CFIUS 审核的中国半导体项目（新加坡和美国）；（7）印度能源类绿地投资（印度德里）；（8）埃及能源类绿地投资（埃及开罗）；（9）越南快消品生产基地投资（越南海阳省）；（10）美国某新能源汽车项目并购（未最后交割，美国加州）；（11）某集团海外 110 个国家运营的法律支持和审计管理，时任该集团副总裁，分管法律、审计、监察和工程审计。

解辰阳博士在学术方面，也颇具造诣。凭借深厚的海外投资实践，他也是中英文两本畅销书的作者：在伦敦出版的《The Legal Regime of Chinese Overseas Investment》；在北京与北京大学、中国海洋出版社合作出版了《"一带一路"案例实践与风险防范》。

解辰阳博士获得了中国政法大学学士学位、美国宾夕法尼亚州立大学硕士及博士学位。

With a legal background of both China and America, Dr. Xie Chenyang is deputy director of International Investment and Trade Professional Committee of Capital Lawyers Association, in addition to member of ICC Climate Change Dispute Arbitration Team, member of ICC China Arbitration Committee and ICC China Energy and Environment Committee, and arbitrator of Tianjin Arbitration Committee.

Dr. Xie is also a part-time researcher at Southwest University of Political Science and Law and a visiting professor at School of Law of Dalian University. He is an on-the-list lawyer of Legal 500. Dr. Xie once served as vice president of Patent Protection Association of China and a council member of China Trademark Association.

Dr. Xie has worked in large enterprise groups for many years. He served as general counsel for two of China's top 500 enterprises. There are many overseas investment projects in these two groups and Dr. Xie personally handles numerous enterprise overseas investment affairs, including M&A and greenfield investment. Therefore, he is knowledgeable about specific requirements and risk points of enterprise overseas investment. Meanwhile, Dr. Xie worked at key positions in European and American enterprises, so that he excels at understanding cross-regional corporate culture and transaction culture.

**Partial cases of overseas investment led by Dr. XIE Chenyang**
(1) Disputes on overseas account between a certain Britain established bank and a certain Chinese group; (2)Investment disputes between Pakistan SECP and a certain Chinese group; (3)Ethiopia and Djibouti Energy Greenfield Investment, a pilot project of the Belt and Road of China investing in Africa; (4) Acquisition of a certain Canadian listed company; (5)M&A of Argentine Mining Company; (6)Acquisition of a Nasdaq-listed company that is the 4th largest semiconductor silicon wafer international supplier in America. The only China Semiconductor Project got approved by CFIUS; (7)India Energy-type Greenfield Investment; (8)Egypt Energy-type Greenfield Investment; (9)Vietnam Investment in Manufacturing Base of Fast Moving Consumer Goods; (10)M&A of a certain American New Energy Vehicle Project (without last delivery); (11)Serve as vice president of a certain group which provides state-run legal support and audit management for 110 overseas countries, and take charge of laws, audit, monitoring and engineering audit.

Dr. Xie obtained the bachelor's degree at China University of Political Science and Law and got the master's degree and the doctor's degree at Pennsylvania State University.

## 闫海 法学博士　Yan Hai

广盛律师事务所的管理委员会主任，国际贸易和竞争法法律业务的负责人。作为国际贸易领域的专家，闫海博士服务的客户包括众多世界 500 强的企业，如三井、日本电器、电通、卡特彼勒、夏普、柯达、LG、谷歌等跨国公司，并成功为客户在众多反垄断和贸易投资案件中取得利了快速和满意的结果。最近 10 年以来闫海博士在出口和进口领域获得了十几个零税率或无税结果，近年还获得了很多 10% 左右或者以下的低税率结果。2017～2018 年闫海博士为 150 多家客户在国际贸易领域提供了法律服务。2018 年 8 月又为一家知名的国内企业获得美国反倾销案件的零税率。

闫海律师在国家商务部条法司和公平贸易局担任过多年的法律官员，曾在世界贸易组织（WTO）接受专业的法律培训，参与过多起中国贸易和竞争法律案件，起草了部分反倾销法律法规，参与中国在世界贸易组织的法律谈判工作，对国际贸易、竞争法和投资法律案件的处理有着深厚的功底。闫海律师曾在美国著名的 Sidley Austin 律师事务所从事贸易法律业务，参与多起贸易和投资纠纷案件的解决。

在钱伯斯发布的 2002～2018 年度律所十几年排名中，广盛获选为中国律师事务所国际贸易法最佳团队之一。闫海律师带领的反垄断团队亦连续列入 2010～2016 年企业国际优秀反垄断律师排行，并获得美国 IFLR 的反垄断排行榜中国顶级团队的荣誉。

闫海律师毕业于在美国以贸易法和公司法著称的名牌大学乔治城大学法学院（Georgetown University），师从 WTO 之父 John H. Jackson 教授，深造期间获该校国际经济法研究所成员荣誉称号。闫律师拥有中国政法大学国际经济法学博士和硕士学位。

闫海律师带领的团队曾经服务的客户包括三井、日本电器、锦湖、陶氏化学公司、壳牌石油公司、洪博培、柯达、OFS、惠好公司、阿奇化学、古河电气工业、 三菱集团、东亚合成、日本触媒、 信越、日本出光石油化学、 大冢化学、韩国浦项制铁、 罗地亚、欧洲聚合体、 德国伍尔特集团、卡特彼勒（美国）、阿诺德、金德摩根、双日（日本）、艾萨华（德国）、LG 化学、本田、电通、谷歌等。

Hai Yan is a managing partner of Guangsheng & Partners (G&P) and the head of its international trade law practice. His practice area includes anti-dumping, countervailing duty investigations, competition and Customs Law. G&P is a pioneer of trade remedy practice in China (since 1996), represented hundreds of cases in both inbound and outbound anti-dumping and CVD law, and has been recognized as a top tier trade law firm in China for 20 years. The working team in G&P is one of the largest trade law team in Beijing during the past 18 years.

Dr Yan has successfully represented multinational companies in many trade remedy cases, including sectors such as petrochemicals, steel products, agricultural products, electronics, fine chemical products, machinery and other industries. He also represented foreign customers in merger reviews and antitrust investigations. From 2017 to 2018, he represented around 150 customers in over 50 projects. The recent cases include a zero anti-dumping duty in a US case for a well-known food additive producer, a zero CVD case for a Chemical producer, represented OFS, Mitsui and Kumho etc. in several inbound cases and got many lowest rates around or below 10% in both inbound and outbound cases. He also successfully helped clients to get exclusions of products in cases relating to steel, paper and chemical products, and non-duty results in Agricultural products.

Dr Yan has served as a senior investigation officer and legal officer in the PRC Ministry of Commerce (MOFCOM) for six years. He was actively involved in drafting MOFCOM anti-dumping and competition regulations, participating in WTO negotiations, and drafting MOFCOM anti-dumping guidelines. He also worked for a top-tier US trade law firm in international trade and antitrust practices.

Dr Hai Yan obtained his LLM from Georgetown University Law Center (U.S.) with a fellowship, and his PhD on law with distinction from China University of Politics and Law. He is also an expert on accounting issues.

Dr Hai Yan has been listed in Chambers and Partners for WTO and international trade (2010~2018), The Legal 500 for international trade (2010~2016) and Who's Who Legal (2016~2018). He is one of the "Excellent Lawyers" of the Beijing Bar Association. The working team has won high rankings in Chambers and Partners during 2001~2018, ranked by Corporate International as a top team in antitrust practice in China, and ranked by IFLR as top tier Chinese law firm in antitrust law practice.

His team has successfully represented international clients such as Mitsui, Kumho, Dow Chemical Corporation, Shell Oil Company, Huntsman, Kodak, Arnold, KMI, Sujitz (Japan), LSI (Germany), LG Chemical, Honda, Dentsu, Google, etc.

## 张晓霖 律师　Lawyer Zhang Xiaolin

北京卓海律师事务所主任、创始合伙人。曾历任海关法规处处长、武警部队秘书处处长、司法办主任，武警指挥学院助理讲师、讲师，同时兼任军队律师、海关公职律师，以及社会专职律师 20 余年。

现为中华全国律师协会国际业务专业委员会委员，北京市律师协会海商海事专业委员会名誉主任，中国房地产学会法律专业委员会副主任，中国法学会（上海）航空法研究会理事，中国科技金融研究会常务理事，中企会企业家国际俱乐部副理事长，北京赣州企业商会常务副会长；同时，兼任北京大学特约讲师，清华大学赣协会顾问，对外经济贸易大学、中央民族大学和中国政法大学硕士研究生导师。

张晓霖律师曾被武警总部授予"全国武警部队优秀律师"称号；被北京市朝阳区律协党委评为"2012 优秀律师党员""2014 优秀律师党员"；先后被盈科律师事务全球总部授予"2012 度优秀律师""2013 年优秀合伙人"称号。张晓霖律师的事迹先后入选《中国律师年鉴（2011～2012）》《中国法律年鉴（2014）》《中国商务信用年鉴（2011～2013）》《中国当代优秀律师》、国务院新闻中心中国网"时代先锋"以及《今日中国》封面人物，被《中华儿女》和《科技中国》杂志专题采访。擅长进出口贸易暨海关法律事务、海商海事、投资并购，以及军队、政府法律事务。

Lawyer Zhang Xiaolin is Director and founding partner of Beijing Zhuohai Law Office, once served as head of a customs regulations division, head of the secretariat and director of the judicial office of an armed police troop, an assistant lecturer and lecturer of an armed police command college, and has served as a military lawyer and a customs public lawyer on a part-time basis, and a social lawyer on a full-time basis for over 20 years.

He is now a member of the International Operations Committee of the All China Lawyers Association, Honorary Director of the Maritime Committee of the Beijing Lawyers Association, Deputy Director of the Legal Committee of the China Real Estate Society, member of the (Shanghai) Aviation Law Research Branch of the China Law Society, executive member of the China Science and Technology Finance Research Society, Vice Chairman of the CEDF Entrepreneur International Club, and Executive Vice Chairman of the Beijing Chamber of Commerce of Ganzhou Enterprises, and serves concurrently as a guest lecturer of Peking University, consultant to the Jiangxi Culture Association of Tsinghua University, and master supervisor of the University of International Business and Economics, Minzu University of China, and the China University of Political Science and Law.

Lawyer Zhang was awarded the title of "Outstanding Lawyer of National Armed Police Forces" by the Headquarters of the Chinese People's Armed Police Force, the titles of "2012 Outstanding Lawyer" and "2013 Outstanding Partner" by the global head office of Yingke Law Firm, and chosen as "2012 Outstanding CPC Member Lawyer" and "2014 Outstanding CPC Member Lawyer" by the CPC Committee of the Chaoyang District Lawyers Association. His deeds have been included in *China Lawyer Yearbook* (2011~2012), *China Law Yearbook* (2014), *China Business Credit Yearbook* (2011~2013), and *Outstanding Modern Chinese Lawyers*. He was "Pioneer of the Times" of the State Council Information Office, and a cover figure of China Today, and received special interviews by China Profiles and Science and Technology of China.

His practice aeras are legal affairs of import and export trade, customs, maritime affairs, investment, M&A, armed forces and government.

# 杨荣宽 律师

北京市康达律师事务所高级合伙人、香港办公室负责人，具有上市公司独立董事任职资格，担任多家上市公司独立董事，国际保护知识产权协会（AIPPI）会员、美国知识产权法律协会（AIPLA）会员，英语为其日常工作语言。

## 教育背景

中国政法大学法学博士，中国人民大学法学硕士，中南政法学院经济法学士，清华大学 EMBA，北京大学 EMBA，哈佛大学法学院访问学者。

## 专业擅长

杨荣宽律师团队具有中国、英国、美国知名院校教育背景，纽约州律师执业许可。先后为国内外诸多知名跨国公司、企业集团和民营资本提供系统优质法律服务，受到业界普遍赞誉。

杨荣宽律师团队在外商投资、知识产权、能源、邢民交叉、证券诉讼等业务方面颇有建树，尤其擅长处理疑难、繁杂法律纠纷。

杨荣宽律师先后应邀参加中国—印尼工商峰会、越南岘港 APEC 亚太经合组织工商领导人峰会、中菲经贸合作论坛、中马联合商务理事会会议、中蒙两国商务理事会成立大会、中越经贸合作论坛、新加坡与印度尼西亚法律课题研讨会、中新两国商务理事会成立大会、第六届世界工商领袖大会等，为国内外工商领袖企业提供高效法律服务，与数千计跨境企业在投资贸易、知识产权、并购、国际仲裁等方面进行深度合作，受到业界的股广泛关注。

## 代表业绩

先后为毕马威会计师事务所（KPMG）、德勤华永会计师事务所、法国国家人寿保险公司、泰国红牛家族、法国卡斯代尔·弗雷尔兄弟股份有限公司、英国 CRU、新加坡喜力集团、中化国际信息公司、中国香港新世界百货集团、中国台湾富士康科技集团、吉野家餐饮集团、中国香港中华药业生物科学有限公司、《时尚》杂志社、意大利 EMC 公司、中国台湾实联、阿斯利康投资（中国）有限公司、北京外企服务集团有限责任公司、富士康科技集团（中国总部）、北京大三元食品有限公司等数百计知名企业提供过优质的专业法律服务，以及锦州港证券虚假陈述案、爱建证券虚假陈述案、中外建南方建设有限公司合作建房纠纷案，sina 搜索引擎著作权侵权案，卡思黛乐兄弟简化股份公司（CASTEL FRERES SAS）与李道之、上海班提酒业有限公司及韦高叶、浙江优马贸易有限公司商标权侵权纠纷再审案，刘欢等被诉侵犯署名权纠纷上诉案，四川金融租赁股份有限公司与四川通信服务公司、中国建设银行成都市金河支行、四川金租实业有限公司借款纠纷法人人格混同上诉案等近千计诉讼案诉讼代理人。

北京 Beijing

# Lawyer Yang Rongkuan

Senior Partner and Hong Kong Office Director of Beijing Kangda Law Firm, qualified to be an independent director of listed companies, serving as an independent director of several listed companies, member of the International Association for the Protection of Intellectual Property (AIPPI), and member of the American Intellectual Property Law Association (AIPLA), using English as the daily working language.

## Educational background

Doctor of Laws of the China University of Political Science and Law, Master of Laws of Renmin University of China, Bachelor of Laws of Zhongnan University of Economics and Law, EMBA of Tsinghua University; EMBA of Peking University, Visiting Scholar of Harvard Law School.

## Expertise

Lawyer Yang's team has the educational background of well-known universities in China, Britain and the U.S., and lawyer practicing certificates of New York State, received extensive praises in the industry for providing systematic high-quality legal services to numerous well-known domestic and overseas transnational corporations, business groups and private enterprises.

Lawyer Yang's team is accomplished in foreign investment, intellectual property, energy, mixed criminal and civil, and securities litigations, and is particularly good at handling difficult and complex legal disputes.

Lawyer Yang is invited to participate in the China-Indonesia Business Summit, Danang APEC Economic Leaders' Meeting, China-Philippines Economic and Trade Cooperation Forum, Malaysia-China Business Council meetings, inaugural meeting of the China-Mongolia Business Council, China-Vietnam Economic and Trade Cooperation Forum, Singapore-Indonesia Legal Seminar, inaugural meeting of the China-Singapore Business Council, and 6th World Business Leaders Conference, and drawn extensive attention from the industry for providing efficient legal services to domestic and overseas leading business enterprises, and carrying out in-depth cooperation in investment, trade, intellectual property rights, M&A, international arbitration, etc. with thousands of transnational corporations.

## Representative work

Lawyer Yang has provided high-quality professional legal services to hundreds of well-known enterprises, including KPMG, Deloitte Touche Tohmatsu Certified Public Accountants LLP, CNP Assurances, RedBull Thailand, Castel Freres SAS in France, CRU in Britain, Singapore Heineken Group, Sinochem International Corporation, New World Department Store (Investment) Limited in Hong Kong China, Foxconn Technology Group in Taiwan China, Yoshinoya Fast Food Co., Ltd., China Medical and Bioscience Limited, Cosmopolitan magazine, EMC Corporation in Italy, Taiwan China Shihlien, AstraZeneca Investment (China) Co., Ltd., Beijing Foreign Enterprise Service Group Co, Ltd., Foxconn Technology Group (China Headquarters), and Beijing Dasanyuan Food Co., Ltd., and served as an agent ad litem for nearly 1 000 lawsuits, including the misrepresentation case of the Jinzhou Port stock, misrepresentation case of AJ Securities, dispute over cooperative housing construction of CCIC South Construction Co., Ltd., copyright infringement case of the sina search engine, retrial case of the trademark infringement dispute of Castel Freres SAS versus Li Daozhi (Panati Wine (Shanghai) Co., Ltd.) and Wei Gaoye (Zhejiang Youma Trading Co., Ltd.), appeal case of the authorship infringement dispute against Liu Huan, et al., and appeal case of corporate personality confusion in the borrowing dispute of Sichuan Financial Leasing Co., Ltd. versus Sichuan Communication Service Company, China Construction Bank Chengdu Jinhe Sub-branch, and Sichuan Jinzu Industrial Co., Ltd..

网址：www.kangdalawyers.com
详情请登录中国律师年鉴网：www.yearbooklawyer.com
— 044 —

上海 Shanghai

# 储小青 律师

北京金诚同达（上海）律师事务所高级合伙人。

## 教育背景

美国亚利桑那州立大学 & 上海高级金融学院全球金融工商管理博士（候选），罗兰大学访问学者，美国亚利桑那州立大学 & 上海国家会计学院金融EMBA，黑龙江大学法律硕士。

## 执业领域

并购与重组、证券与资本市场、跨境投资、诉讼与仲裁。

## 社会职务

上海市律师协会并购与重组委员会委员、广州仲裁委员会仲裁员、马鞍山仲裁委员会仲裁员、上海市杭州商会理事、上海市浙江商会理事、上海股权投资协会理事、上海市浦东新区律师青年联合会常委。

## 工作经历

2013至今，金诚同达律师事务所；2008～2013 上海中企泰律师事务所；2007～2008 上海中筑律师事务所；2006～2007 上海毅石律师事务所。

## 执业经历

储小青律师的涉外律师业务大致可以分为两个阶段：第一个阶段是为"引进来"提供法律服务，第二个阶段是为"走出去"提供法律服务。在"引进来"阶段，储小青律师曾为众多世界500强企业进入中国市场提供法律服务，这些世界500强企业包括但不限于本田、尼康、爱普生、日立、三井、欧姆龙等；在"走出去"阶段，储小青律师为众多中国企业走向世界，甚至走向欧美发达国家提供全程法律服务，包括中国人尤以为豪的中国中车及其子公司在美国的轨道交通项目，以及在加拿大的轨道交通项目等。

（1）**公司并购重组与投融资**：精通并购、重组所涉及的法律法规及相关法律实务，在并购、重组业务领域有丰富的经验，能够为客户提供并购、重组尽职调查服务、出具法律意见，协助客户进行并购谈判以及并购和重组方案设计等全方位的法律服务；经办了多起公司并购重组项目。为数个公司投融资项目提供法律服务，协助投资方和融资方就投融资事宜进行谈判、法律文件起草和审核，并就投融资交易结构设计、风险防范、税收比较等事宜提出最佳解决方案，以期实现投融资目的。

（2）**外商投资和对外投资**：曾为数件外商投资项目提供法律服务，就复杂法律问题根据中国实践，为客户提供解决方案，包括上海第一例外商以在建工程出资入股项目；为多个中国企业"走出去"提供全程法律服务，包括为中国中车及其子公司在美国的轨道交通项目以及在加拿大的轨道交通项目提供全程法律服务。

（3）**房地产与基础设施**：曾为包括保利在内的多家大型地产开发集团提供多地项目开发和收购全程法律服务，同时，在房地产建设工程纠纷的处理上，经验特别丰富；处理多起房地产和建设工程纠纷案件，并曾推翻造价鉴定报告；曾经以及正在多个国内和国际基础设施开发和建设中提供全程法律服务，尤其对跨国基础设施项目涉及跨国法律问题的处理，经验丰富。

（4）**TMT 和生物技术**：熟悉 TMT 和生物技术行业，熟练把握 TMT 和生物技术行业的法律风险，能为 TMT 和生物技术企业提出系统解决方案，协助 TMT 企业设计交易结构，提出系统法律风险解决方案；同时对 TMT 和生物技术行业的投融资有丰富的经验，包括为多个跨国 TMT 和生物技术的投资基金提供全程投融资法律服务。

（5）**商事争议解决**：在商事争议解决领域，主要针对房地产与建筑工程、金融、化工工程、知识产权等纠纷提供法律服务，曾推翻建设工程造价鉴定报告，为当事人追回工程款，代理的江苏天容集团诉湖南昊华化工不正当竞争一案获评"2016年浦东新区十大知识产权案件"。同时，还担任多个知名仲裁机构的仲裁员。

## 代表业绩

为日新制钢中国不锈钢合资项目（中方部分以在建工程出资）提供全程法律服务；作为全球牵头律师，为中国中车及其子公司美国轨道交通项目、加拿大轨道交通项目等项目提供专业法律服务；为国际自动机工程师学会（SAE）提供中国法律顾问服务；为青云资本、Magnet 风险投资基金等多个跨国美元基金提供投融资法律服务；为内资股权收购外商独资企业苏州恒光化纤有限公司项目提供全程法律服务；亚玛顿太阳能10亿规模私募基金投融资及太阳能电站收购项目；光大延安150亿规模基金投融资项目；为华信能源、世平能源、惠腾能源、弘信新能源、汉腾新能源等提供投融资

网址：www.jtnfa.com
详情请登录中国律师年鉴网：www.yearbooklawyer.com
— 045 —

## 上海 Shanghai

及风险防控法律服务；为光大资本、青云资本、逐原资本、新德股权投资基金、中悉投资、弘石股权投资等投资机构的诸多投融资项目提供全程法律服务；为上海最大的内河危险品船舶储运公司并购项目提供全程法律服务；为舜富股份股票发行项目提供全程法律服务；为浦房集团、保利房地产及其子公司提供法律服务；江苏天容集团与湖南昊华化工不正当竞争案被评为"2016年浦东新区十大知识产权案件"之一。

### 荣誉称号

第六届"浦东新区十大杰出青年律师"提名奖。

### 工作语言

中文、英语

### 著述论文

《法律思维筹划运用》（专著，法律出版社，2012年出版）

# Lawyer Chu Xiaoqing

A senior partner at Jincheng Tongda & Neal (Shanghai).

## Education background

Doctor of Global Finance Business Administration at Arizona State University & Shanghai Advanced Institute of Finance(candidate); a visiting scholar in Eotvos Lorand University; Finance Executive Master of Business Administration at Arizona State University & Shanghai National Accounting Institute; juris master at Heilongjiang University.

## Practice areas

M & A, Securities & Capital Markets, Transnational investment, Litigation and Arbitration.

## Social functions

A member of Shanghai Bar Association M & A Committee; an arbitrator of Guangzhou Arbitration Commission; an arbitrator of Ma'anshan Arbitration Commission; a council member of the Hangzhou Chamber of Commerce, Shanghai; a council member of the Zhejiang Chamber of Commerce, Shanghai; a council member of Private Equity Association Of Shanghai; a standing member of Shanghai Pudong New District Young Lawyers Association.

## Work experience

Jincheng Tongda & Neal since 2013; Zone & Chime Law Firm from 2008 to 2013; Shanghai Zhongzhu Law Firm from 2007 to 2008; Yishi Law Firm from 2006 to 2007.

## Practice experience

Lawyer Chu Xiaoqing has dealt with foreign law affairs since reform and opening-up of China, which can be divided into two phases. Phase one is providing legal service for bringing-in strategy while phase two is for going global strategy. In the phase of bringing-in strategy, lawyer Chu has provided law service for many of the world 500 strong enterprises entering the Chinese market, ones that include but are not limited to Honda, Nikon, Epson, Hitachi, Mitsui and Omron; in the phase of going global strategy, he has provided full legal service for many Chinese enterprises going global and even to developed countries, such as Europe and America. It includes CRRC and its subsidiaries winning American rail transit project and Canadian rail transit project, of which Chinese people are proud.

（1）Corporation's merging and reorganization & investment and financing: Being proficient in laws and regulations as well as related legal practice as specified in merging and reorganization and experienced in the fields of merging and reorganization, being able to provide due diligence service for merging and reorganization and issue legal opinions, and offer clients comprehensive legal service, such as assisting them for merger talks and project design of merging and reorganization,several corporation's merging and reorganization projects have been handled. Provide legal service for several corporations' projects on investment and financing, assist to negotiate on investment and financing affairs between the investor and the financer and to draft and audit legal documents, and put forward the best solution concerning transaction structure design of investment and financing, risk prevention and tax comparison to achieve the purpose of investment and financing.

（2）Foreign investment & outward investment: Provide legal service for several foreign investment projects and solutions concerning complicated law problems for clients based on Chinese practice, which includes the first case of foreign merchants investing and taking a stake in construction in progress in Shanghai; provide full legal service for many Chinese enterprises going global, which includes CRRC and its subsidiaries winning American rail transit project and Canadian

网址：www.jtnfa.com
详情请登录中国律师年鉴网：www.yearbooklawyer.com
— 046 —

rail transit project.

(3)Real estate & infrastructure: Provide full legal service concerning project of wide development and acquisition for many large real estate and investment groups including Poly, and meanwhile being experienced in dealing with disputes on real estate construction project; several cases of real estate construction project disputes have been handled and a construction cost appraisal report has been overturned; at the same time, provide full legal service for several national and international infrastructure development and construction till now, and being extremely experienced in handling transnational legal problems rising from transnational infrastructure projects.

(4)TMT & biotechnology: Being familiar with TMT and biotechnology industry and proficient in identifying legal risks in TMT and biotechnology industry. Being able to put forward system solutions for TMT and biotechnology enterprises, assisting TMT enterprises to design transaction structure and putting forward system solutions concerning legal risks; meanwhile being experienced in investment and financing in TMT and biotechnology industry, including providing full legal service concerning investment and financing for many investment funds of transnational TMT and biotechnology.

(5)Commercial disputes resolution: Provide legal service concerning disputes such as real estate construction projects, finance, chemical projects and intellectual property in the field of commercial disputes resolution. Overturn a construction cost appraisal report of construction projects and recover project funds for his client. Act as an attorney for Jiangsu Tianrong Co., Ltd which lodged an appeal against Hunan Haohua Chemical Co.,Ltd for unfair competition, a case which won Top Ten Intellectual Property Cases in Pudong New District of 2016. Moreover, lawyer Chu serves as an arbitrator of several well-known arbitration organizations.

**Outstanding performance**

Provide full legal service for a joint project of Nippon Steel and Sumitomo Metal Group and Chinese stainless steel industry (the Chinese side invests in construction in progress); provide professional legal service as a global legal initiator for CRRC and its subsidiaries winning American rail transit project and Canadian rail transit project; provide service as a Chinese legal counsel for SAE International (SAE); provide legal service concerning investment and financing for several transnational dollar foundations such as Tsing Capital, Magnet Venture Capital Investment Fund; provide full legal service concerning a project on the acquisition of a sole foreign-funded enterprise by a domestic-funded holding company for Suzhou Hengguang Chemical Fiber Co., Ltd; take part in the project of investment and financing in Almaden privately offered fund of billion solar energy and solar power station acquisition; take part in the project of investment and financing in Yanan Everbright Fund of 15 billion; provide legal service concerning investment and financing as well as risk prevention and control for China Energy Company, Sepin Energy, Huiteng Energy, Hongxin New Energy and Hanteng New Energy; provide full legal service concerning investment and financing projects for many investment organizations such as Everbright Capital, Tsing Capital, Zhuyuan Capital, Shanghai New Equity Investment Fund, Sino-Sydney Investment and Hongshi Equity Investment; provide full legal service concerning mergers and acquisitions for the largest Storage and Transportation Company for Shipping Dangerous Cargo in Inland River in Shanghai; provide full legal service concerning stock issuance projects for Shunfu Stock Company; provide legal service for Pudong Real Estate Group and Poly Real Estate and its subsidiaries; the case where Jiangsu Tianrong Co., Ltd lodged an appeal against Hunan Haohua Chemical Co.,Ltd for unfair competition won one of "Top Ten Intellectual Property Cases in Pudong New District of 2016".

**Honorary title**

Nomination Prize of the 6th "Top Ten Outstanding Lawyers in Pudong New District".

**Working languages**

Chinese, English

**Books & papers**

"Legal Thinking Projecting & Application"(which is a monograph published in 2012 by Law Press China)

# 耿亦诚 律师

北京大成（上海）律师事务所合伙人。

作为中国和美国纽约州的执业律师，耿亦诚律师在境内外跨国公司法律专业服务方面拥有丰富的经验。通过在 Dentons Rodyk & Davidson LLP 总部及上海代表处多年的执业经历，耿亦诚律师在兼并与收购、外商直接投资及跨境投融资业务领域积累了丰富的经验，并深谙诸多境内外客户的商业预期和运营模式。

耿亦诚律师在兼并与收购领域提供的专业法律服务涉及诸多行业，包括基础设施、能源、制造业、互联网、房地产、食品、高科技、汽车、快速消费品、物流、酒店与休闲业等。他协助众多客户完成许多有代表性的跨境并购及大量的境外和境内多层结构的重组及剥离业务。除了并购业务之外，耿亦诚律师在外商直接投资领域也有丰富的经验。他曾协助众多国际知名企业在中国境内进行首次绿地投资，并为外商投资企业进入中国市场后的运营涉及的公司业务提供专业法律服务。

耿亦诚律师同时还兼任美国律师协会国际法律委员会以及上海市律师协会国际投资委员会的委员。

## 代表性案例

· 代表凯德集团（一家在新加坡和中国领先的地产开发商），为其与洲际集团就中国重庆市的地标项目"朝天门广场"的合作事宜提供相关法律服务。

· 代表格罗方德（全球第二大晶圆制造商），为其在中国境内的一系列合资事宜提供相关法律服务。

· 代表新加坡樟宜机场集团，为其收购中国境内的资产以及跨境投资事宜提供全程法律服务。

· 代表腾飞房产投资信托（A-REIT），为其整体处置涉及上海、北京和嘉善的地产投资组合提供全程法律服务。

· 代表美国凯博咨询，为其在中国境内的一系列投资和合作项目提供相关法律服务。

· 代表安曼纳酒店集团，为其在中国境内的酒店及综合体项目提供相关法律服务。

· 代表辉盛国际（一家在新加坡和

中国领先的酒店管理公司），为其通过在中国境内的全资子公司收购大连凯丹广场酒店公寓的交易提供相关法律服务，该交易标的为人民币四亿八千万元。

· 代表 Santa United International，为其收购位于中国广州的一家石油贸易公司的全部股权提供相关法律服务。

· 代表星狮地产（一家在新加坡和中国领先的地产开发商），为其与金地集团在中国上海的房地产投资项目的合资事宜提供相关法律服务，该合资项目的标的为人民币十五亿元。

· 代表 Wirecard（全球领先的电子支付服务提供商），为其与环迅支付就中国境内支付结算业务的合作事宜提供相关法律服务。

· 代表 BCD Travel（全球最大的旅行管理公司之一），为其在中国境内的一系列投资及合作项目提供相关法律服务。

· 代表美邦（一家领先的电子及电脑工业注塑制造商），为其在上海外高桥保税区（现上海自由贸易区）内的项目之股权转让事宜提供全程法律服务。

· 代表丰罗（一家瑞士上市公司），为其在中国境内的投资及经营活动提供常年法律顾问服务。

· 代表永泰（一家新加坡上市公司），为其在上海美兰湖板块的房地产开发项目提供全程法律服务。

· 代表马自达（中国），为其在中国境内的投资及经营项目提供常年法律顾问服务。

· 代表丰树集团，为其涉及广东省佛山市南海怡丰城项目的股权并购交易提供全程法律服务。

· 代表腾飞集团，为其收购上海高腾大厦项目及北京某研发园区项目提供法律尽职调查等相关法律服务。

· 代表易昆尼克斯（Equinix，一家美国纳斯达克上市公司），为其在中国境内的经营活动提供常年法律顾问服务。

## 教育背景
美国南加州大学法学硕士、上海对外经贸大学法学学士。

## 执业资格
中国、美国纽约州

## 专业组织
美国律师协会
纽约州律师协会
上海律师协会国际投资委员会

## 工作语言
中文、英语

网址：www.dentons.com/zh
详情请登录中国律师年鉴网：www.yearbooklawyer.com
— 048 —

# Mr. Geng Yicheng

Partner of Beijing Dacheng Law Offices, LLP (Shanghai).

As a lawyer qualified in both China and New York State of the United States of America, Mr. Geng is an invaluable resource for many multinational corporations within and out of the territory of China. Through his years of practice in the headquarter and Shanghai representative office of Dentons Rodyk & Davidson LLP, he is experienced in structuring and providing reliable legal expertise in the areas of mergers and acquisitions, foreign direct investment and cross-border investment and financing. He is very familiar with the expectations and business operations of both foreign and domestic clients.

Mr. Geng has provided professional services in the areas of strategic mergers and acquisitions involving a wide variety of industries, including infrastructure, energy, manufacturing, TMT, real estates, foods, high-technologies, automobiles, FMCG, logistics, hotel and leisure industry, etc. He has assisted numerous clients in consummating many high-profile cross-border mergers and acquisitions, as well as restructurings and disposals with onshore and offshore structures.In addition to mergers and acquisitions, Mr. Geng is also very experienced in foreign direct investments. He has represented numerous multinational companies in their green field investments in China, and provided professional advice to foreign invested enterprises on general corporate matters involved in the day-to-day operations after the entry into China market.

Mr. Geng also serves as the committee member of the International Law Committee of American Bar Association and International Investment Committee of Shanghai Lawyer's Association.

## Noticeable Cases

· Acted for Capitaland Group, a leading real estate developer in Singapore and China, in its cooperation with Intercontinental Group in respect of the landmark development of "Chaotianmen Square" in Chongqing, China;

· Acted for Global Foundries, the second largest wafer fabrication group in the world, in its series of joint venture investment in China;

· Acted for Changi Airport Group, in its acquisition of relevant assets in China and cross-border investment matters;

· Acted for Ascendas Real Estate Investment Trust (A-REIT), in its divestment of the China portfolio of properties in Shanghai, Beijing and Jiashan;

· Acted for Amara in its hotel and mixed-use development project in China;

· Acted for Frasers Hospitality Group Pte Ltd, a serviced apartments operator in Singapore and China, in its acquisition of a serviced apartment building of Europark Dalian through its wholly-owned subsidiary in China for a purchase consideration of RMB 480 million;

· Acted for Santa United International in its acquisition of a 100% stake in a petroleum trading company in Guangzhou, China;

· Acted for Frasers Centrepoint Limited, a real estate developer in Singapore and China, in its joint venture with Gemdale Group in respect of a real estate project for an investment value of RMB 1.5 billion in Shanghai, China;

· Acted for BCD Travel, one of the world's largest travel management companies, in its series of investment and cooperation matters in China;

· Acted for Meiban, an electronic and computer industry mold making manufacturer in Singapore, in a share transfer transaction of its projects located in Shanghai Wai Gao Qiao Free Trade Zone (Now Shanghai Free Trade Zone);

· Acted for Von Roll, a Switzerland listed company amd Mazda Motor (China) Co., Ltd. by providing retainer legal services in respect of its investment and operation projects in China;

· Acted for Wing Tai, a real estate developer in Singapore and China, in its real estate development projects in Mei Lan Hu Area in Shanghai;

· Acted for the Chinese subsidiary of Mapletree in its share acquisition deal in respect of Vivo City in Foshan, Guangdong Province;

· Provided legal due diligence and other relevant services for the Ascendas Group in its acquisition of Cross Towers in Shanghai and a research and development zone in Beijing;

· Acted for Equinix, a company listed in NASDAQ, by providing retainer legal services in respect of its operation projects in China;

## Educational Background

University of Southern California (Master of Laws); Shanghai University of International Business and Economics (Bachelor of Laws)

## Bar Admission

China; New York State, the United States

## Professional Associations

American Bar Association, New York State Bar Association, International Investment Committee of Shanghai Lawyer's Association

## Working Language

Chinese, English

网址：www.dentons.com/zh
详情请登录中国律师年鉴网：www.yearbooklawyer.com
－ 049 －

上海 Shanghai

## 陈振生 律师

上海泛洋律师事务所创始合伙人、主任。

### 工作经历

1982 年毕业于大连海事大学，留美学者。曾任上海海事法院高级法官、审判委员会委员、海事庭庭长、英国某律师事务所中国法顾问。现兼任中国国际经济贸易仲裁委员会仲裁员、中国海事仲裁委员会仲裁员，上海财经大学、上海海事大学校外硕士生导师。

### 执业经验

　　陈振生律师在处理商事、海事、金融保险和对外贸易纠纷中有着近 30 年的丰富经验，曾办理过众多重大的国际货物买卖、融资租赁、保险、水上水下工程、海上货物运输、船舶买卖及租用、船舶碰撞、海上油污染案件。陈振生律师观点独到犀利，其代理的多起案件判决书被"中国涉外商事海事审判网"全文登载。

　　陈振生律师曾于 2015 年作为中国法专家在英国高等法院出庭。被上海市律师协会评为涉外专业律师、金融保险专业律师。他还担任多家公司的法律顾问，为航运、贸易、保险等公司提供全方位、专业的法律服务，其扎实的法律功底和严谨负责的工作态度赢得了众多当事人的信任。

# Mr. Chen Zhensheng

Founding Partner and Director of Polaw & Co. Shanghai.

## Work experience

He graduated from Dalian Maritime University in 1982, who is a Scholar staying in U.S. He used to be a Senior Judge of Shanghai Maritime Court, a Commissioner of the Judicial Committee, a Chief of the Maritime Court and an Advisor to the Chinese law of the Law Office of Samuel R. Terry, P.C. Now he holds the concurrent posts of an Arbitrator of China International Economic and Trade Arbitration Commission, an Arbitrator of China Maritime Arbitration Commission and an extramural master tutor of Shanghai University of Finance and Economics and Shanghai Maritime University.

## Practice experience

 Lawyer Chen has nearly 30 years of rich experience in handling commercial affairs, maritime affairs, financial insurance and foreign trade disputes. He has handled many major cases such as international cargo transactions, finance lease, insurance, above and under water engineering, maritime cargo transportation, ship trading and leasing, ship collisions and oil pollution at sea. Lawyer Chen has unique and sharp viewpoints, and many judgments of cases he acted on have been published with the full text by China Foreign-related Commercial and Maritime Trial.

Lawyer Chen once appeared in a UK High Court as a Chinese law expert in 2015. He was named by Shanghai Bar Association as a professional foreign-related lawyer and a professional lawyer on finance and insurance. He also serves as a legal advisor to many companies, providing comprehensive and professional legal services for shipping, trade and insurance companies, etc. His solid legal knowledge and rigorous and responsible work attitude have won the trust of many parties.

网址：www.polaw.net
详情请登录中国律师年鉴网：www.yearbooklawyer.com
－ 050 －

上海 Shanghai

# 王正超 律师

　　王正超律师是香港注册外国律师、竞天公诚律师事务所的高级国际法律顾问，主要在上海和香港办公室工作。

　　王正超律师的主要执业领域为企业收购与兼并、私募股权与风险投资融资、外商直接投资、证券法及国际商业交易。长期以来，王正超律师作为各类知名跨国公司及国际和中国的顶尖私募股权基金、风险投资基金投资者的法律顾问，协助其在大中华地区完成投资、并购以及退出。所涉及的业务领域包括房地产与不良资产交易及电信、传媒、科技、生物科技、生命科学、制药及消费品等行业的交易。

　　王正超律师在国际交易领域尤其是在代表财富 500 强企业诸如通用汽车和陶氏化学等在中国进行直接投资的业务领域具有非常丰富的经验。同时，王正超律师还在代表国际承销商和亚洲证券发行商发行跨国股票与代表中国企业进行境外投资的业务领域具有相当的经验。

　　在加入竞天公诚前，王正超律师曾作为高级国际法律顾问长期在上海市锦天城律师事务所工作。在此之前，王正超律师作为专职律师任职于一家著名的美国律师事务所和一家顶级的英国律师事务所。1999 ～ 2000 年间，他在香港担任凤凰卫视的法律顾问。1989 年，王正超律师由福特基金会支持赴美进行法律深造。此前，他曾作为研究人员任职于一家上海知名的政策研究机构，专事研究美国经济与政治制度。与此同时，他也作为兼职律师在一家知名的中国律师事务所执业。

　　王正超律师连续多年持续被法律界知名刊物诸如钱伯斯亚洲、国际金融法律评论连续评选为中国顶尖的企业并购与私募股权律师。

　　王正超律师于 1984 年毕业于复旦大学，获法学学士学位；于 1987 年毕业于上海社会科学院法学研究所，获法学硕士学位；此后，王正超律师于 1991 年毕业于美国爱荷华大学法学院，获法学硕士学位；于 1996 年毕业于美国圣母大学法学院，获法律博士学位。

　　王律师的工作语言是英语和中文。

# Wang Zhengchao(Victor)

Mr. Wang is a registered foreign lawyer in Hong Kong China based in Shanghai and Hong Kong China, and a Senior International Legal Counsel at Jingtian & Gongcheng focusing on mergers and acquisitions, private equity and venture capital financing, foreign direct investment, securities law, and international business transactions.

Mr. Wang regularly advises leading international and Chinese private equity/venture capital investors and multinational corporations, on their investments, acquisitions and divestments in the Greater China region. These exercises range from real estate and distressed asset deals to transactions in the telecommunications, media, technology, biotech and life science, pharmaceutical and consumer product industries. Mr. Wang has had significant experience in cross-border transactions, particularly in representing many Fortune 500 companies with respect to their direct investments in China. He also has considerable experience in representing international underwriters and Asian issuers in their global share offerings, as well as acting for Chinese companies in their outbound investments.

Prior to joining Jingtian & Gongcheng, Mr. Wang was a senior international legal counsel at AllBright. Prior to that he worked in Hong Kong with a major New York law firm and a top UK "magic circle" firm, where he represented many multinational corporations and investment funds in establishing joint venture companies and making acquisitions in the PRC and other Asian countries. Prior to a career in the private law firm sector he was in-house at a major Asian TV and media group where he oversaw all legal affairs arising from the company's Hong Kong IPO and global placement exercises.

Mr. Wang is consistently recognized by legal industry publications such as Chambers Asia and IFLR as one of the leading M&A, corporate and private equity lawyers in China.

Mr. Wang received an LL.B. from Fudan University (1984), an LL.M from the Shanghai Institute of Law (1987), an LL.M. from the University of Iowa Law School (1991) and a J.D. from the University of Notre Dame Law School (1996).

网址：www.jingtian.com
详情请登录中国律师年鉴网：www.yearbooklawyer.com
— 051 —

中国涉外律师

上海 Shanghai

# 李见刚 律师

北京盈科（上海）律师事务所高级合伙人、律师、盈科全国国际投资与贸易专业委员会主任。

## 职务与荣誉

2016 年度英国大律师公会中国赴英专项工作培训律师；2014 ～ 2017 年盈科全国国际法律服务领域十佳律师、2015 年度最佳法律服务奖获得者。

## 教育背景

国际经济法硕士。

## 专业领域

国际投资、国际贸易、跨境并购与风险管控；境外民商事争议处理；跨国债务催收，复杂疑难个案处理；涉外合同起草审查，法律尽职调查及相关事宜；合同纠纷、经济纠纷处理及公司法律事务顾问等。

## 工作语言

中文、英语，及简单的日语、韩语和意大利语交流。

## 工作经历

担任过多年大型合资企业总经理等职务；为多家中国大中型公司及上海主板上市公司进行跨境战略并购提供全程法律服务；代表国内公司赴美国爱达荷州、科罗拉多州、新泽西州等进行多回合的商务及法律谈判等；代表客户处理在西班牙、希腊、德国、荷兰、比利时、法国、捷克、意大利、英国、挪威、罗马尼亚、保加利亚、波兰、美国、加拿大、澳大利亚、阿联酋、印度、马来西亚、柬埔寨、印度尼西亚、斯里兰卡等国家和中国香港地区的贸易与投资纠纷案件；代表国内公司在荷兰、德国、西班牙、英国、加拿大等国家与当地律师配合进行国际诉讼或者国际仲裁；代理了数量较多的复杂涉外商事案件的国内诉讼和国内仲裁；委托人对处理结果均表示满意。

## 代表案例

• 为上海证券交易中心某上市公司进行跨境战略并购提供完整的并购交易法律服务，为主板上市公司跨越 4 国的并购提供全程法律服务，北京某生物科技公司股权投资美国生物医药研发公司的协议谈判、尽职调查和医药法律以及监管制度的研究，某央企上海子公司收购德国一家著名智选假日酒店的并购提供全程法律服务，美国某著名化学公司并购内蒙古化工厂提供全程法律服务，德国公司 1.2MW 光伏电站的收购提供全程法律服务等。

• 代表香港公司与希腊公司、荷兰物流仓储公司等在荷兰鹿特丹和海牙法庭进行的扣货禁令的程序诉讼和国际贸易与知识产权及海运纠纷混合的实体诉讼进行上诉审，最终全胜诉并且使所有被扣押的集装箱货物返回上海港，进而在希腊等执行诉讼判决的赔偿款项；上海某能源公司与希腊公司等 10 家公司之间的合同纠纷、担保纠纷、债权纠纷处理；国内某制造商与希腊公司、荷兰公司等的合同纠纷、专利侵权以及海运和仓储纠纷；为黑龙江一食品公司解决与迪拜、伊朗公司的贸易纠纷并追回 400 万货款，代表深圳上市公司处理与加拿大 AK-PAK 公司之间的国际贸易纠纷。

• 上海某食品原材料进出口贸易公司与印度 AVT Natural Products Ltd. 买卖合同纠纷，国内某制造商与保加利亚 EPC 总包商的合同以及质量纠纷，德国 Rinovasol GmbH 与国内某光能股份的销售合同之诉，上海某食品原材料进出口贸易公司与印度公司买卖合同纠纷，某央企华东公司向美国公司的索赔纠纷，某著名外资信息服务有限公司与某科技公司数据库著作权侵权纠纷，浙江某汽车零部件制造有限公司与英国公司以及丹麦公司的研发纠纷，德国公司与国内某光电股份公司（上市公司）的产品质量索赔纠纷，代表台湾公司处理与西班牙知名运动品牌的国际贸易以及授权纠纷，代表江苏某光伏电池厂处理与荷兰 Heerlen 公司的破产案件等。

• 德国慕尼黑赛马场太阳能电站投资项目的尽职调查与谈判，江苏公司投资意大利成套设备集成商的跨境法律交叉研究、尽职调查、增资扩股、协议谈判等的全程法律服务，国内某知名海洋工程装备及工程公司与印度尼西亚本地公司的合资、股份转让、合作运营、架构设计等全程法律服务，捷克公司 40MW 光伏项目涉及的光伏组件入股及变现协议等的谈判、草拟签署、股权质押、股权转让、解除质押的全程法律服务，与美国硅料生产商的债转股谈判及诉讼，国内某知名化妆品公司收购欧洲公司的前期谈判、当地法律调查、协议起草协商修改等法律服务等。

• 为上市供应链管理股份公司提供新加坡公司法律尽职调查报告（大宗货物交易商），为国内某信息科技公司提供境外架构设计以与美国公司及其律师的对接服务，为德国公司提供控股架构设计以及投融资协议和日常法律顾问服务，为法国赛车经销商提供法律服务和支持等，为多家境内外公司提供法律咨询和法律顾问等。

## 学术研究

在《人大报刊复印资料》《中国外汇》《中国行政》《当代经济》等专业杂志上发表多篇关于公司运营管理、风险控制、国际贸易投资并购及国际应收账款处理等方面的论述。

网址：www.yingkelawyer.com
详情请登录中国律师年鉴网：www.yearbooklawyer.com
— 052 —

## 沙海涛 律师     **Sha Haitao**

山东曲阜人，北京金诚同达（上海）律师事务所高级合伙人。

沙海涛律师具有丰富的法律实践经验，主要从事公司、知识产权、外商投资领域内的诉讼及非诉讼业务，代理了大量诉讼案件，其中多起在中国具有较大影响。如代表上海宝钢集团参与美国国际贸易委员会（USITC）对中国钢铁企业输美碳钢与合金钢产品钢铁发起的"337调查"；代表上海耀宇文化传媒股份有限公司诉广州斗鱼网络科技有限公司侵害著作权及不正当竞争纠纷上诉案（2016年中国法院知识产权司法保护50个典型案例）；代表雅培制药（美国）有限公司诉雅培乳业（南昌）有限公司商标侵权及不正当竞争纠纷案（福建省2011年知识产权十大案例）；代表雅培制药（美国）有限公司诉汕头雅培商标侵权及不正当竞争案（2010年中国法院知识产权司法保护50件典型案例）；代表首诺（美国）公司诉香港龙膜公司等商标侵权及不正当竞争案；代表微芯科技（美国）公司诉上海海尔集成电路有限公司计算机软件著作权侵权案（中国首例计算机微程序软件著作权侵权案）。

沙海涛律师曾为Pasonic、夏普、东芝、F1、卡夫、3M等众多世界500强企业在知识产权保护等方面提供过专业法律服务。从事律师职业前，沙海涛律师曾在法院工作，任助理审判员。

沙海涛律师于2018年获得强国知识产权论坛颁发的"十佳专利律师"，于2015年、2016年、2018年作为团队带头人获得中国知识产权杂志与中国日报知识产权颁发的"中国杰出知识产权诉讼团队"奖，并于2012年、2014年入选《中国律师年鉴》之"年度优秀知识产权专业律师"和"经典案例"，曾于2013年入选《中国当代优秀律师》（法律出版社2013年12月出版）和《中国当代涉外律师》（法律出版社2013年9月出版）之"向驻华商会、使馆、外向型机构推荐的100位优秀涉外律师"。

沙海涛律师先后获得上海大学知识产权学院法学硕士学位、美国芝加哥肯特法学院国际知识产权法法学硕士学位和武汉大学软件工程硕士学位，具有专利代理资格，现为澳门科技大学法学博士研究生。曾至夏礼文（英国）律师事务所香港分所和贝克·麦坚时（美国）国际律师事务所华盛顿特区分所作为访问律师，参与普通法和美国知识产权法及国际贸易法的法律实践。

沙海涛律师的工作语言为中文和英语，并具备日语基本知识。

Mr. Sha Haitao, who was born in Qufu Shandong, is a senior partner at Beijing Jincheng Tongda & Neal Shanghai Law Office. Mr. Sha has tremendous legal practice experience, focusing on contentious and non-contentious cases related to corporate law, intellectual property, international investment. He has dealt with many intellectual property cases with influence in China, such as representing Baosteel Group in a Section 337 investigation on certain carbon and alloy steel products manufactured by China steel companies exported into US, Guangzhou Douyu Network Technologies Co., Ltd. v. Shanghai Yao Yu Culture Media Co., Ltd. copyright infringement and unfair competition case (Supreme People's Court in 2016 China's court of intellectual property protection of 50 typical cases), Microchip(US) Technology Incorporated v. Shanghai Haier IC., Ltd. software copyright infringement case (The first microcode software copyright infringement lawsuit in China).

Mr. Sha has provided legal opinions regarding intellectual property protection and corporate law to many Fortune 500 companies (Pasonic, Sharp, Toshiba, F1, Kraft, 3M). Before being a lawyer, Mr. Sha had been a judge in China People's Court.

In 2018, Mr. Sha was awarded the "Top Ten Outstanding Patent Lawyer in China" by China Intellectual Property Forum. He, as the team leader, was also awarded the "China Outstanding Intellectual Property Litigation Team" in 2018, 2016, and 2015 by the China Intellectual Property Journal and China Daily. He was selected in 2014 and 2012. "China's Lawyers Yearbook" "Excellent Intellectual Property Lawyers of the Year" and "Classic Cases" were selected in 2013 as "China's Contemporary Outstanding Lawyers" (Legal Press, December 2013) and "China Contemporary Foreign Lawyers"(Law The publishing house published in September 2013) "100 outstanding foreign-related lawyers recommended to the Chamber of Commerce, Embassy and Export-oriented Organizations in China".

Mr. Sha holds master's degree in law from Chicago-Kent College of Law (IIT) and Shanghai University, and the master's degree of Software Engineering from International School of Software of Wuhan University, admitted in China Patent Bar. Now, Mr. Sha is a candidate of JD at Macau University of Science and Technology. Besides, he took part in common law professional training in Holman Fenwick & Willan law firm in Hong Kong and Washington D.C. office of Baker & McKenzie LLP as a Chinese intellectual property lawyer.

Mr. Sha's working language are both Chinese and English. And he has basic knowledge of Japanese.

网址：www.jtnfa.com
详情请登录中国律师年鉴网：www.yearbooklawyer.com
— 053 —

## 上海 Shanghai

### 赵平 律师

北京金诚同达（上海）律师事务所高级合伙人。

### 执业领域

争议解决、国际贸易、知识产权。

### 执业经历

赵平律师作为律师和仲裁员，办理了大量涉及金融投资、房地产、知识产权和国际贸易方面的诉讼和仲裁案件。赵平律师拥有 8 年的法院审判工作经验，加之严密的法律逻辑思维能力，对民商事争议案件有精深的理解和把握。赵平律师长期致力于知识产权方面的法律研究和纠纷解决，在企业知识产权保护体系构建和知识产权战略方面有丰富的经验；此外，赵平律师还在国际贸易方面有较深的造诣。

### 代表业绩

上海世纪联华超市发展有限公司系列仲裁和诉讼纠纷案，上海恒积大厦包租纠纷案，上海汽车工业（集团）总公司与平安保险公司买方信贷保险纠纷，上海电信知识产权全套合同模板制订，上海卫星通信公司改制案，上汽集团资产经营公司债务处置及改制事宜，上海石化下属杭州金山大酒店和新金山大酒店改制、重组案，华融资产管理有限公司资产重组、债权合并处置案，上海电气集团债转股案件等。

### 社会职务

上海市人民政府行政复议委员会委员，中国仲裁法学研究会常务理事、房地产仲裁研究专委会主任，中华全国律师协会仲裁委员会委员，中国国际经济贸易仲裁委员会仲裁员，中国海事仲裁委员会仲裁员，北京仲裁委员会仲裁员，上海国际经济贸易仲裁委员会仲裁员，上海仲裁委员会仲裁员，香港国际仲裁中心仲裁员，亚洲国际仲裁中心仲裁员，青岛、广州、武汉、深圳、哈尔滨等地仲裁机构仲裁员，上海市律师协会国际贸易业务委员会主任，中欧校友国际贸易和知识产权保护协会秘书长，中国政法大学上海校友会会长。

### 荣誉称号

被中共上海市司法局直属律师事务所委员会评为"2005 ～ 2007 年优秀共产党员"，2012 年被中国政法大学评为"优秀校友"。

### 工作经历

2010.1 至今，北京金诚同达（上海）律师事务所；2002.7 ～ 2009.12，上海市世代律师事务所；1999.7 ～ 2002.7，上海市国耀律师事务所；1991.7 ～ 1999.7，河北省邢台市中级人民法院法官。

### 教育背景

美国芝加哥肯特法学院国际比较法学硕士，中欧国际工商学院 EMBA，中国政法大学研究生院民商法硕士，中国政法大学法律系法学学士。

### 著述论文

（1）《仲裁裁决是如何作出的》（《北京仲裁》，2017 年第 99 辑）；

（2）《"一带一路"国家战略对中国仲裁的挑战和对策》（《仲裁视点》，2016 年 10 月）；

（3）《以自贸区制度创新为契机 推动中国仲裁与国际接轨》（《上海律师》，2015 年第 12 期）；

（4）《上海律师办理境外商事仲裁法律业务操作指引》（主笔人）；

（5）《上海律师办理外国仲裁裁决承认和执行法律业务指引》（协调人，2012 年）。

### 媒体报道

赵平律师接受新华社采访 —— 谈"一带一路"走出去企业的法律风险防范。

网址：www.jtnfa.com
详情请登录中国律师年鉴网：www.yearbooklawyer.com
— 054 —

# Mr. Zhao Ping

Senior Partner of Jincheng Tongda & Neal Law Firm

## Practice Areas

dispute resolutions, international trade, intellectual property.

## Professional Experience

As a senior lawyer and an arbitrator, Mr. Zhao has dealt with a large number of litigation and arbitration cases in relation to financial services, investment, real estate, intellectual property and international trade. Mr. Zhao has a deep understanding of civil and commercial disputes with his eight years' experience as a judge in the PRC court and meticulous legal logic reasoning ability. Mr. Zhao is dedicated to the best interests of clients with his excellent overall skill and strategy in litigation and arbitration. Mr. Zhao has particular expertise in representing cross-regional and international cases, and has insightful understanding on the nature and key issues of such cases.

## Representative Cases

Acted as legal counsel for Shanghai CenturyMart Development Co., Ltd. in a series of arbitration and litigation cases; Acted as legal counsel in Shanghai Hengji Mansion charter dispute case, credit insurance dispute case between SAIC Motor Corporation Limited and Ping An Insurance Limited, the establishment of a complete set of model intellectual property contracts for Shanghai Telecom, the corporate reorganization of Shanghai Satellite Communication Limited, the debt disposal and restructuring of SAIC Assets Management Limited, the restructuring and reorganization of Hangzhou Jinshan Grand Hotel and Xin Jinshan Hotel under Shanghai Petrochemical Limited, Huarong Asset Management Limited in the assets reorganization and merger of creditor's rights, Shanghai Electric Limited in debt to equity swap case.

## Social Membership

Member of Shanghai Municipal Administrative Reconsideration Committee; Executive Council Member of China Academy of Arbitration Law; Director of Professional Committee on Real Estate Arbitration of China Academy of Arbitration Law; Member of Arbitration Commission of All China Lawyers Association; Arbitrator of CIETAC, HKIAC, AIAC, CMAC, BAC/BIAC, SHIAC, SHAC, and Wuhan, Qingdao, Guangzhou, Shenzhen, Harbin Arbitration Commission; Director of Research Commission on International Trade of Shanghai Bar Association; Secretary-general of the International Trade and IP Protection Association of CEIBS; Executive member of the council and Vice Secretary-general of the Alumni Association of China University of Political Science and Law; President of the Shanghai Alumni Association of China University of Political Science and Law.

## Work Experience

2010.01-Present, Senior Partner of JT&N Shanghai Office; 2002.07-2009.12, Founding Partner of Shanghai Eternal Law Firm; 1999.07-2002.07, Lawyer at Shanghai Guo Yao Law Firm; 1991.07-1999.07, Judge at the Intermediate People's Court of Xingtai City, Hebei Province, China.

## Honorary Titles

Outstanding Communist Member for 2005-2007 awarded by The Committee of the law office directly under the Shanghai Municipal Judicial Bureau; Excellent Alumni of China University of Political Science and Law.

## Education Background

Chicago Kent College of Law, L.L.M. of International Comparative Law, 2008; China Europe International Business School, EMBA, 2008; China University of Political Science and Law, Master of Law, 1997; China University of Political Science and Law, Bachelor of law, 1991.

## Publications

(1)"How Is Arbitration Award Made"(author, *Beijing Arbitration*, 2017 Vol. 99); (2)"The Challenge and Countermeasure of China's Arbitration in the National 'Belt and Road' Strategy"( author, *Arbitration Viewpoint*, 2016.10); (3)"Promoting China's Arbitration and International Practice by Taking the Innovation of Free Trade Zone System as an Opportunity"( author, *Shanghai Lawyers*, 2015 Vol. 12); (4)"Guidelines for Shanghai Lawyers on Foreign Commercial Arbitration"( lead writer); (5)"Guidelines for Shanghai Lawyers on the Recognition and Enforcement of Foreign Arbitration Awards"( Coordinator, *Shanghai Bar Association*, 2012).

## Media Report

The Legal Risk Prevention of Chinese Enterprises under the "Belt and Road" Strategy, interviewed by the Xinhua News Agency.

网址：www.jtnfa.com
详情请登录中国律师年鉴网：www.yearbooklawyer.com
— 055 —

# 赵宁宁 律师

# Ms. Zhao Ningning

赵宁宁律师毕业于中国政法大学，硕士学位，现为北京金诚同达（上海）律师事务所合伙人。赵宁宁律师执业领域为涉外民商事诉讼与非诉讼法律服务，主要擅长涉外家事法律、包括但不限于婚姻财产与子女问题、遗产与继承、家族财富传承、家族信托等领域，代理家事诉讼与非诉讼案件，为各国法院、使领馆等机构就跨国家事案件出具专家意见书，长期担任《法律与生活》特约撰稿人。

Ms. Zhao Ningning is one partner of Jincheng Tongda & Neal Law Firm, one of the top and most respected law firms in China. Ms. Zhao is an eminent expert in international family laws. With over ten years of experience in international family laws, she deals with the cross-border family cases involving in divorce, child custody, asset division, wealth succession and private legal counsel as well as pre or post-marital agreements and she also deals with cross-border civil and commercial cases for

## 社会职务

国际家事律师协会（IAFL）会员、亚太法律协会（LAWASIA）会员、中国国际私法学会理事、上海市律师协会民事业务研究委员会委员、东方调解中心特邀调解员、中国传媒大学法律硕士诉讼与仲裁课程授课教师、上海外事翻译工作者协会会员、上海市律师协会"巾帼志愿团"成员。

## 著述文集

（1）《涉外婚姻家庭案件律师实务》（独著，2015年4月，法律出版社）；（2）《民事诉讼律师实务》（合著，2014年1月，法律出版社）；（3）《家事法学》（合著，2016年3月，法律出版社）；（4）《拳王阿里的财富传承猜想》（2016年8月《法律与生活》特约撰稿）；（5）《德肖维茨的"命运逆转"》（2015年5月《法律与生活》特约撰稿）；（6）《践行人身保护令》（2013年11月《法律与生活》特约撰稿）；（7）涉外离婚案件中法律适用与管辖冲突问题研究》（2013年中国国际私法学会论文集）；（8）《家庭暴力防治体系的构建与完善》（2013年"家庭暴力受害者人身安全保护措施及实施问题"研讨，并获"优秀论文奖"）；（9）《聚焦"美国式离婚"》（2013年7月《法律与生活》特约撰稿）；（10）《富二代"接班"》（2013年3月《法律与生活》特约联合撰稿）；（11）《涉外婚姻诉讼制度之完善》（2012年中国国际私法学会论文集）；（12）《IPO与婚变》（2012年6月《法律与生活》特约撰稿，荣获全国普法办公室与中华全国法制新闻协会共同举办的2012年度全国法制好新闻深度报道类二等奖）；（13）《聚焦跨国婚姻》（2012年4月《法律与生活》特约撰稿）；（14）《推开涉外家事法律服务之门》（2011年"全国涉外婚姻家庭律师实务论坛"主题演讲并发表于《上海律师》杂志）；（15）《离婚后夫妻扶养制度的对比研究》（收录于2008年中华全国律师协会民事法律研究会编著的《婚姻家庭法律师实务》）；（16）《民事诉讼法律研究》（在2007年上海市诉讼法学研究会和上海市高级人民法院主办的上海市诉讼法学研究会上被评为"优秀论文"）。

the individuals or companies from various jurisdictions. She is the fellow of IAFL (International Academy Family Lawyers), member of LAWASIA, member of China Law Society, director of China International Private Law Society, Instructor of Communication University of China, a mediator of Oriental Mediation Centre in Shanghai, member of Civil Law Research Committee of Shanghai Bar Association. Ms. Ningning Zhao published the books at *China-Law Press*, they are "Legal Practice of International Family Cases" "The Lawyer Practice in Civil Litigation" and "Family Law". And she also published over 30 professional articles. Exchanging and sharing with practitioners, judges or law professors from various legal jurisdictions at kinds of international conferences is also one part of Claudia's practicing experience.

# 郑蕾 律师

上海市协力律师事务所高级合伙人。

### 执业领域
争议解决、国际贸易、航运物流。

### 执业经历
　　在 20 年的律师执业经历中，郑蕾律师曾任多家国内外知名进出口贸易公司、金融机构、融资租赁公司、航运物流企业、船舶修造企业、大型国内外企业和上市公司的法律顾问，为重大国际贸易、船舶买卖融资、海事物流非讼项目及诉讼和仲裁业务提供法律服务，兼具扎实的理论功底和丰富的实践经验，被业界誉为专家型律师。郑蕾律师同时为多家机构的仲裁员，在国际和国内仲裁方面具备丰富经验。

### 代表业绩
　　其经手的丹麦供油有限公司申请扣押"星耀"和"海芝"轮船抵押融资合同纠纷案已入选最高人民法院 2015 年公布的全国海事法院船舶扣押和拍卖十大典型案例；
　　受中国海事仲裁委员会委托起草《船舶融资租赁合同标准文本》，为目前业界使用的唯一一份船舶融资租赁格式合同；作为专家参与《中华人民共和国船舶登记办法》的制定；作为专家参与"《海商法》修改"课题研究。

### 社会职务
　　上海海事大学客座教授、华东政法大学法律硕士研究生校外导师、上海海事大学法律硕士研究生校外导师、上海海事大学经管学院工商管理硕士授课专家、中国仲裁法学会海事仲裁研究中心研究员、中国海事仲裁委员会仲裁员、上海国际仲裁中心（即上海国际经济贸易仲裁委员会）仲裁员，深圳国际仲裁中心（即华南国际经济贸易仲裁委员会）仲裁员，交通部国际海事委员会船舶登记分委会专家顾问，上海市律师协会海事海商业务委员会委员。

### 荣誉称号
2008 年长宁区优秀律师和长宁区律师代表；
2010 年起入选首批上海市律协青年律师人才库成员；
2018 年荣获上海市优秀女律师提名奖。

### 工作经历
2014.11 至今，上海市协力律师事务所；
2000.1 ～ 2014.10，上海市耀良律师事务所；
1999.1 ～ 2000.1，北京市金杜律师事务所上海分所。

### 教育背景
大连海事大学国际法专业法学博士，上海海事大学国际经济法专业法学硕士。

### 著述论文
　　已在各类法学专业期刊公开发表论文并参编著作 30 余篇，其中《如何认识海上保险中的"保证"—— 兼谈对我国海商法第 235 条的理解》荣获中国海商法协会优秀论文评选优秀论文奖；《实际承运人制度在航次租船合同中的适用》荣获中华律师协会论文评选二等奖。

网址：www.co-effort.com
详情请登录中国律师年鉴网：www.yearbooklawyer.com
— 057 —

上海 Shanghai

# Zheng Lei(Grace )

Senior Partner of Co-Effort Law Firm

## Practice Areas

Dispute Resolution, International Trade, Shipping and Logistics

## Professional Experience

During the practice of almost two decades, Grace Zheng has gained extensive experience in handling maritime claims, charter party disputes and shipbuilding & repair contracts disputes. She handles a variety of arbitration and litigation cases, representing domestic clients in international and domestic arbitration and litigation proceedings and representing international clients in arbitration and litigation proceedings taking place in China. She also has in-depth experience in advising on ship sales and financial leasing transactions.

She is the legal counsel of a number of China state-owned trading companies, shipyard, shipping companies, financial institutions and leasing companies. She is also retained by international companies and law firms to provide legal services in relation to Chinese law.

## Social Membership

Grace Zheng is the arbitrator of China Maritime Arbitration Commission, Shanghai International Arbitration Center and Shenzhen International Arbitration Center, which are the most reputable international arbitration centers in China. She also is the professor and part time tutor of Shanghai Maritime University and East China University of Politic and Law.

## Honorary Titles

Changning District Outstanding Lawyer and Lawyer Representative, 2008;

Member of First Young Lawyer's Talent Pool of Shanghai Bar Association, 2010;

Award Nomination of Shanghai Outstanding Female Lawyer, 2018.

## Work Experience

2014.11 ~ Present, Senior Partner of Co-Effort Law Firm;

2000.1 ~ 2014.10, Partner of Yao Liang Law Firm;

1999.1 ~ 2000.1, Lawyer at King & Wood Shanghai Office.

## Education Background

LLM of International Economic Law, Shanghai Maritime University, PhD of International Law, Dalian Maritime University.

## Publications

Grace has published more than 37 pieces of articles and books in many reputable legal journals in China. Being a legal expert and senior lawyer in maritime and arbitration, Grace is frequently invited to speak at the seminars held in China, Singapore, Norway and other countries focusing on development of maritime law and arbitration practice in China.

# 刘尔婵 律师

### 简介

刘尔婵律师是天津华盛理律师事务所高级合伙人，持有中国及美国纽约州律师执业资格并拥有多年海外从业经验。先后被司法部评为中华全国律师协会涉外领军人才并入选全国千名顶尖涉外律师人才库。工作语言是中文、英语。

### 擅长领域

刘尔婵律师尤其擅长国际、国内重大疑难商事争议解决、跨境收购、海外投融资等相关法律事务。凭借其对中西方法律体系和商业环境的深度理解，刘尔婵律师在管理跨境项目和解决复杂争议的过程中为客户提供了系统、全面的法律支持。

在复杂商事争议解决领域，刘尔婵律师的客户服务偏好尤为突出。不同于传统律师的"对人"服务模式，即为某一客户提供综合法律服务，其多年来倡导专业精分，一直以来仅为商事"疑难杂症"提供高效的法律解决方案，尤其擅长在常规案件中探索出独特的诉讼思路，代理企业客户扭转僵局反转成败。刘尔婵律师还特别擅于在诉讼环境中辅以精准的商业谈判策略，适时地打破法律规定给当事人带来的局限性。执业以来其特有的"对事"服务理念及专业品质受到了业内广泛好评，吸引了大量面临败诉风险的客户慕名而来。

刘尔婵律师常年活跃在国际诉讼和仲裁领域，目前是英国皇家御准仲裁员协会（CIArb）中级会员、伦敦国际仲裁院青年仲裁员协会会员。执业期间多次与美国、新加坡、中国香港的律师联手参与完成国内客户的跨境争议解决并获得胜诉判决。刘尔婵律师的跨境服务优势不仅在于其与各国、各地区不同领域的专业律师成功搭建起了高密度的合作网络，更重要的是其丰富的国际执业经验可以高效地帮助国内客户将经济效益向域外延展。

自国家提出"一带一路"倡议以来，刘尔婵律师在众多的跨境投融资及并购项目中发挥了专业优势，成功地帮助越来越多的国内企业"走出去"。前不久司法部牵头发布的最新一期的"一带一路"国别报告，刘尔婵律师受邀作为波斯尼亚和黑塞哥维那的撰稿人，在该报告中刘尔婵律师全面分析了该国的投资环境和"走出去"所面临的法律、商业及政策风险，可供相关企业参考。

# Liu Erchan

## About Ms. Liu

Ms. Liu Erchan is a senior partner of Wisely Law Firm based in Tianjin. She is qualified as a lawyer in China and State of New York and has many years' overseas experiences. She has been named by the Ministry of Justice as the National Outstanding International Lawyer and selected by the National Top 1000 Foreign Lawyers' Pool. Her working Language is Chinese and English.

## Practice Aeras

Ms. Liu particularly focuses on legal matters relating to international and domestic complex commercial dispute resolutions, cross-border acquisitions, overseas investment and financing., etc. With her deep understanding of the legal system and business environment in China and the West, Ms. Liu is famous in the industry by providing systematic and comprehensive legal solutions to clients in managing cross-border projects and resolving complex disputes.

Ms. Liu's customer service preference is particularly prominent in the field of complex commercial dispute resolution, which is different from the traditional lawyers' "person-to-person" service mode, that is to provide clients with comprehensive legal services. On the contrary, she has been advocating professional fine division for many years, and has only provided efficient legal solutions for commercial "difficult and complicated problems". She is especially good at exploring unique litigation ideas in conventional cases, and acting corporate clients to reverse the deadlock of failure. Ms. Liu is used to introducing precise business negotiation strategy in litigation environment, and timely breaking the limitations of legal regulations to reach a "win-win" solution for clients. Her profession has been widely praised by the industry and has attracted a large number of clients who face risk of loss and are badly in need of legal services.

Ms. Liu is also active in international litigation and arbitration area. She is currently a member of the Chartered Institute of Arbitrators (CIArb) and of the Young Arbitrators' Association of the London Court of International Arbitration. During practice, she joined hands with lawyers from the United States, Singapore, Hong Kong, China and other countries (regions) on a series of cross-border dispute resolutions. The outstanding advantage of Ms. Liu's cross-border services is not only that she has successfully established a high-density network of cooperation with lawyers from various countries, regions, and different fields. More importantly, her own rich experience in the West can better educate domestic clients how to wisely extend economic benefits abroad.

Since China initiated the "Belt and Road" policy, Ms. Liu has played a professional role. Now small and medium-sized enterprises going abroad are also increasing proportionately. Recently, the Ministry of Justice led the release of the latest issue of the "Belt and Road" country report, in which Ms. Liu was also invited to write articles about Bosnia and Herzegovina. In this report, Ms. Liu comprehensively analyzed the country's investment environment, regulations, business and policy risk, which is a bible for Chinese enterprises.

# 姜晋衔 律师

姜晋衔律师 1989 年毕业于上海复旦大学法律系，中国社会科学院研究生院经济法硕士研究生。1990 年取得中华人民共和国律师资格，2006 年获一级律师职称。曾执业于北京天达律师事务所，现为天津泰达律师事务所创始合伙人。

### 主要业务领域

姜晋衔律师从事专职律师工作近 30 年，擅长国际投资、国内公司与投资、企业并购及重组、房地产开发、建筑工程、基础设施等领域的法律业务，知识渊博，经验丰富，业绩卓著。

自 20 世纪 90 年代初始，姜晋衔律师先后参与美国美孚、英国珀金斯、丹麦诺和诺德、韩国三星、美国劳特、瑞士 NESTLE、香港南丰集团、香港嘉里集团、泰国正大集团等众多国际跨国公司在中国投资的法律事务。

姜晋衔律师尤其积累了基础设施建设项目和房地产项目法律服务的丰富经验，服务对象包括政府机构、中央企业、项目投资商、建筑承包商、设备和材料供应商等，参与了水电、高速公路、铁路、轨道交通、化工、环保、房地产等诸多大型项目的法律事务，熟悉 BOT、BT 等融资模式和其他投资、融资方式，先后担任过数十家大型企业的法律顾问，兼任过中央企业的总法律顾问职务。

在诉讼和仲裁代理方面，姜晋衔律师凭借深厚的法律专业功底和超群的辩才，先后代理超百件国际跨国公司或国内大型集团公司在中国的重大、棘手案件，是民事诉讼经验丰富的律师之一。

# Lawyer Jiang Jinxian

Lawyer Jiang Jinxian graduated from the Department of Law, Fudan University, and got a master of commercial law from Chinese Academy of Social Sciences in 1989. He became a lawyer of the People's Republic of China in 1990, and a Grade 1 lawyer in 2006. He once worked at East Associates Law Firm, and is a founding partner of Tianjin Teda Law Firm.

### Main business areas

Since the early 1990s, lawyer Jiang has handled legal affairs for investment in China for numerous transnational corporations, including US-based Mobil and Lawter, UK-based Perkins, Denmark-based Novo Nordisk, Korea-based Samsung, Switzerland-based Nestle, Hong Kong-based Nan Fung Group and Kerry Group, and Thailand-based Chia Tai Group.

In the nearly 30 years that lawyer Jiang has been working as a full-time lawyer, he built up solid expertise in legal operations in international investment, domestic corporate affairs and investment, business M&A and restructuring, real estate, construction, infrastructure.

In particular, lawyer Jiang has rich experience in legal services for infrastructure and real estate construction projects, and serves government agencies, central enterprises, project investors, construction contractors, equipment and material suppliers, etc. He has participated in legal affairs of numerous major hydropower, expressway, railway, rail traffic, petrochemical, environmental and real estate projects, and served as a legal adviser to tens of major enterprises, and chief legal adviser to central enterprises, and is familiar with such investment and financing modes of BOT and BT.

Lawyer Jiang has successfully handled over 100 major or difficult cases in China for transnational corporations and large domestic groups thanking to his profound legal knowledge and his outstanding eloquence. He is also experienced in civil litigation.

中国涉外律师

天津 Tianjin

### 袁伟明 律师

　　北京中伦文德（天津）律师事务所高级合伙人、副主任。袁伟明律师毕业于大连海事大学国际海事（法学）专业。之后在天津及北京的数家知名海事律师事务所工作。于 2018 年作为高级合伙人加入北京中伦文德（天津）律师事务所。袁伟明律师担任天津律师协会海事海商专业委员会副主任职务。曾被推选参加全国青年律师领军人才训练营，并被司法部列选入全国千名涉外律师人才拟入选名单，被知名评级机构钱伯斯 2017 年榜单列为中国北部受认可海事律师。

　　袁伟明律师擅长争议解决（诉讼与仲裁）业务，主要专业方向包括海事海商、保险、物流、国际贸易、银行与金融等，此外袁伟明律师的重点执业领域还包括跨国海事及贸易欺诈以及追赃案件处理。

　　袁伟明律师所处理的案件涉及各地海事法院、高级法院、最高人民法院等司法机关，以及国际、国内机构仲裁及临时仲裁。其中多起案件在国际上享有广泛影响。其工作语言为中文、英语。

Mr. Yuan is the Senior Partner and Deputy Director of Beijing Zhonglun W&D (Tianjin) Law Firm and he graduated from Dalian Maritime University with LL.B in International Maritime Affairs (Law), and then has worked in several shipping law firms in Tianjin and Beijing. He joined Beijing Zhonglun W&D (Tianjin) Law Firm as a senior partner in 2018. Mr. Yuan is serving as the deputy director of the seventh Maritime Committee of Tianjin Lawyers Association. He was elected to participate in National Youth Lawyer Leading Talent Training Camp, and was named and listed in the One Thousand Foreign-Related Lawyers Talents by Ministry of Justice of the P. R. China. He was also rated as "Recognized Practitioner in Shipping and Maritime Practice in Northern China" by Chambers & Partners 2017.

Mr. Yuan specializes in dispute resolution (litigation and arbitration), and his primary practice areas include shipping, insurance, logistics, international trade, banking and finance. Additionally, Mr. Nick Yuan also has rich experience in handling cases involving cross-border maritime and trade fraud as well as cross-board crime assets recovery.

Mr. Yuan handled litigation cases before various local maritime courts, high courts, the Supreme People's Court and other judicial authorities, as well as the arbitration cases covering the international and domestic institutional arbitration and ad hoc arbitration, some of which are internationally well-known and influenced. His working language is Chinese and English.

广东 Guangdong

### 谢沁洋 律师

　　广东华商律师事务所资深合伙人。国际经济法和国际金融学士、民商法学硕士。具有上市公司独立董事任职资格。深圳市律师协会"一带一路"及涉外法律业务委员会委员、业务创新与发展委员会委员。

　　业务领域包括涉外民商事诉讼或仲裁代理、国际科技人才及技术项目引进法律服务、涉外投融资项目法律服务、跨境并购、法律尽职调查服务、国际贸易法律服务、涉外知识产权法律服务、企业法律顾问服务等诉讼和非诉讼法律服务领域。

　　谢沁洋律师在深圳从事法律专业服务工作 20 多年，具有丰富的涉外法律服务经验，特别擅长处理复杂、疑难的法律事务。为国内外众多知名企业、集团提供优质而高效的法律服务，以其扎实的法律专业功底、卓越的服务质量，以及良好的沟通技巧，获得了广大客户的赞誉。工作语言为中文（普通话、粤语）和英语。

Senior Partner of China Commercial Law Firm.

LLM of Civil & Commercial Law; LLB of International Economic Law and International Finance; Qualified to be an independent director of listed companies; Member of the Belt and Road Initiatives & Foreign-Related Legal Services Committee of Shenzhen Lawyers Association. Member of the Business Innovation & Development Committee of Shenzhen Lawyers Association.

The lawyer's team provides legal services in the fields of litigation and arbitration, international talent and technology cooperation, International investment and financing projects, cross border M&A, due diligence, settlement of disputes of international trade and commerce, Intellectual property protection, corporate counsel.

Lawyer Xie has been engaged in legal professional services in Shenzhen for more than 20 years, and has rich experience in foreign-related legal services, especially in solving complex legal issues. She has provided professional and efficient legal services to numerous well-known enterprises and groups around the world. With her solid professional foundation, high-quality service and good communication skills, lawyer Xie has won praises from the clients.

Lawyer Xie has good language communication skills. She can communicate with clients well in Chinese(Mandarin, Cantonese) and English.

## 黄晖 律师　　Lawyer Huang Hui

广东恒运律师事务所高级合伙人，国际法学＆海商法硕士，广东省涉外律师领军人才，广州市律师协会海商海事法律业务专业委员会副主任，广东省航运法学研究会常务理事，中华全国律师协会海商海事专业委员会委员，广东省律师协会海商海事法律业务专业委员会委员，广东省律师协会港澳台和外事工作委员会委员，广东省第十一次律师代表大会代表，中国广州仲裁委员会仲裁员，中国人民财产保险股份有限公司、中国太平洋财产保险股份有限公司、中国船东互保协会及广州港集团有限公司律师库入库律师，广州市律师协会调解中心调解员。

黄晖律师自2003年专职海商海事及涉外法律事务以来，代理近千起各类型海商海事案件，不少案件是我国海事司法历史上重大和颇具影响力的案件，其中最高人民法院公开开庭审理并同步现场直播的"加百利"轮海难救助合同纠纷再审案被最高人民法院评和中央电视台选为"2016推动法治进程十大案件"以及"2016年中国海事审判十大典型案例"，该案还同时入选广州海事法院服务保障"一国两制"下香港回归20周年十大典型案件，以及成功入选国际权威专业法律经典文献《劳氏法律报告》2016年第7卷。黄晖律师因为该起案件的成功代理还接受了《东方时空》《今日说法》《法制日报》《中国审判》《庭审现场之大法官开庭》等媒体的采访和报道。

黄晖律师富有涉外案件处理经验，除在国内法院及仲裁机构代理涉外案件外，还参与处理了数起国外商事案件及国际海事仲裁案件。黄晖律师多次作为中国法律问题的专家证人到纽约、伦敦、中国香港、新加坡和巴拿马等地法院和国际仲裁庭出庭，均取得了令委托人满意的诉讼及仲裁结果。

黄晖律师2011～2018年连续被钱伯斯评选为"年度顶尖海商海事律师"，黄晖律师还因数起涉外案件的成功代理而多次荣获广州市律师协会"业务成果奖"。

Senior Partner of Huang & Huang Co. Law Firm, LL.M.; international law & maritime law; member of the "Leading Lawyers in International Work Talent Pool of Guangdong Province; deputy Director of the Maritime Law Committee of Guangzhou Lawyers Association; standing Director of the Maritime Law Research Institute of Guangdong Law Society; member of the Maritime Law Committee of All China Lawyers Association; member of the Maritime Law Committee of Guangdong Lawyers Association; member of the Hong Kong China, Macao China, Taiwan China and Foreign Affairs Committee of Guangdong Lawyers Association; deputy to 11th Annual Meeting of Guangdong Lawyers; certified arbitrator in China-Guangzhou Arbitration Commission; member of the Lawyers Database of PICC Property and Casualty Company Limited, China Pacific Property Insurance Co., Ltd., China Shipowners Mutual Assurance Association, and Guangzhou Port Group; mediator of Mediation Center of Guangzhou Lawyers Association

Since 2003, Huang Hui has represented numerous international and domestic clients in China, including Nanhai Rescue Bureau of the Ministry of Transport of the People's Republic of China v. Archangelos Investments E.N.E. where an open hearing was held by the Supreme People's Court of the People's Republic of China and was broadcast live on the Internet. The high-profile salvage case was selected by the Supreme People's Court of China and published by China Central Television as one of the "10 Landmark Court Cases of 2016" and one of the "10 Typical Maritime Cases of 2016". It was also one of the "Top 10 Typical Court Cases on the Twentieth Anniversary of Hong Kong's Return" selected by Guangzhou Maritime Court and was included in *Lloyd's Law Reports* (2016, Vol7). Huang Hui was invited to interview by China Central Television news programs including *Oriental Horizon*, *Legal Report* and *Court Hearing Scene* and law journals such as *China Trial Journal* for successfully handling the case.

Huang Hui has extensive experience in international commercial dispute resolution. He has been to courts or arbitration tribunals in regions such as New York, London, Hong Kong China, Singapore and Panama as expert witness in Chinese law and assisted his clients in obtaining very satisfactory results.

From 2011 to 2018, Huang Hui has been consecutively recommended as a "Leading Lawyer" in Shipping in Southern China by Chambers Asia-Pacific Guide. He has also won a couple of "Annual Achievement" awards presented by Guangzhou Lawyers Association.

网址：www.hnhlawfirm.com
详情请登录中国律师年鉴网：www.yearbooklawyer.com
— 063 —

## 广东 Guangdong

### 吴国权 律师

北京德恒（广州）律师事务所主任。吴国权律师擅长于贸易与投融资、并购、基建工程与房地产开发、金融证券保险、知识产权、产品责任等领域的诉讼与非诉讼及仲裁业务。

吴国权律师毕业于西南政法大学（法学本科）和中国政法大学研究生院（法学硕士），并曾在中国法律服务（香港）有限公司工作和培训。吴律师于 2007 年作为合伙人加入德恒律师事务所广州办公室，现担任管理合伙人、主任。在此之前曾供职于中国国际经济贸易促进委员会广东省分会（1987～1995 年）、广东至信忠诚律师事务所（1995～2007 年）。

吴律师曾担任中国国际经济贸易仲裁委员会仲裁员，现担任上海国际经济贸易仲裁委员会（上海国际仲裁院）、华南国际经济贸易仲裁委员会（深圳国际仲裁院）、深圳仲裁委员会和珠海仲裁委员会仲裁员。工作语言为中文、英语。

Director of Beijing Deheng Law Offices (Guangzhou).

Mr. Wu specializes in litigation and arbitration. His experience covers a wide variety of area, including trade and investment, M&A, infrastructure and real estate development, financial instrument, insurance, intellectual property and product liability.

He got LLB in Southwest University of Political Science and Law (1985), LLM in China University of Political Science and Law (1987); He Studied and worked in China Legal Service (H. K.) Ltd.. Mr. Wu has joined in Deheng Law Office (Guangzhou) in 2007 as Managing Partner and director. Prior to joining the firm, Mr. Wu served in China Council for the Promotion of International Trade (CCPIT) from 1987 to 1995, and Guangdong ZhiXinZhongCheng Law Office from 1995 to 2007.

Lawyer Wu served as Arbitrator for Shanghai International Economic and Trade Arbitration Commission (Shanghai International Arbitration Commission), South China International Economic and Trade Arbitration Commission (Shenzhen International Arbitration Commission), Shenzhen Arbitration Commission; Arbitration for Zhuhai Arbitration Commission.

### 吴凯 律师

广东恒益律师事务所合伙人。吴凯律师先后毕业于国内中山大学、英国格拉斯哥大学，并获得国际法硕士、反垄断法硕士学位。

吴凯律师长期从事跨境投资、并购、境外上市、公司法、反垄断法、商业诉讼、仲裁等法律事务，执业经验丰富。

2013 年，吴律师获全国律师协会选为"涉外律师领军人才"，先后被派往德国、美国等地进行跨国投资并购法律培训及交流。2017 年，吴律师入选全国律师协会"一带一路"跨境律师库。

吴律师现亦兼任广东省律协竞争与反垄断委员会副主任、广州市律师协会公平贸易法律专业委员会副主任、广州市政府下属的国际投资促进中心的外聘专家顾问等社会职务。

吴律师的工作语言为中文（普通话、粤语）、英语。

Mr. Raymond Wu is a senior partner of GFE Law Office in Guangzhou, China, which has been recommended by Legal 500 as one of the leading law firms in Guangzhou. Mr. Wu graduated from Sun Yet Sen University in China and Glasgow University in UK respectively with Master Degree of International Laws and Master Degree of International Competition Laws and Policies.

Mr. Wu mainly practices corporate and commercial laws. His specializations include cross-border investment and transaction, overseas listing, antimonopoly legal affairs, general corporate legal affairs, commercial litigation and arbitration.

Mr. Wu was elected as one of the leading Chinese lawyer talents practicing foreign related legal affairs by All China Lawyers Association (ACLA) and assigned to Germany and US for professional training and exchange program for Chinese lawyers in 2013 and 2016 respectively. In 2017，he was enrolled to the "Cross-border Transaction Lawyers Pool for China's 'Belt and Road' initiatives" by ACLA.

Currently, Mr. Wu is the vice director of Competition and Anti-monopoly Committee under Guangdong Lawyers Association, vice director of Fair Trade Laws Committee under Guangzhou Lawyers Association, and external expert counsel for International Investment Promotion Center under Guangzhou Municipal Government.

Mr. Wu's working languages are Chinese(Mandarin, Cantonese) and English.

网址：www.dhl.com.cn　网址：www.gfelaw.com
详情请登录中国律师年鉴网：www.yearbooklawyer.com

— 064 —

# 谭岳奇　律师

谭岳奇律师先后于西南政法大学法律系、武汉大学法学院、荷兰海牙国际法学院学习进修，于 2002 年取得法学博士学位。目前为北京市中银（深圳）律师事务所（简称"中银"）主任、高级合伙人，并担任深圳市律师协会涉外法律专业委员会主任、中国国际经济贸易仲裁委员会仲裁员、中国国际私法学会理事、华南国际经济贸易仲裁委员会仲裁员、深圳仲裁委员会仲裁员、武汉大学韩德培法学基金会理事、深圳市律师协会前海发展战略工作委员会委员。曾在香港特别行政区高等法院作为内地法律专家证人出庭。

公开出版《创业板上市法律事务及典型案例分析》（主编，法律出版社 2011 年 7 月出版）、《中小企业介入式团队法律服务》（主编，法律出版社 2009 年 7 月出版）、《内地与香港的法律冲突与协调》（副主编，湖北人民出版社 2001 年版）、《法官能断家务事——现代法律实务丛书之二》（与人合著，湖北人民出版社 1997 年版）等专业著作，在《现代法学》《政法论坛》《法学评论》《律师与法制》等国内法学核心期刊上发表论文 20 余篇，多次接受《深圳商报》《深圳晚报》《晶报》《深圳法制报》等多家媒体采访，就多个热点法律问题在上述媒体公开发表法律意见。

## 处理的涉外诉讼类案件

谭岳奇律师代理在香港国际仲裁中心审理的国内某公司与国外某著名投资机构之间标的逾十亿人民币的 PE 纠纷案件，代理国外某风投机构与国内某公司之间标的为五亿人民币的投资纠纷案件，代理香港太平洋通讯设备有限公司与美国摩某某某公司通讯事业部、美国摩某某某公司国际贸易合同纠纷；代理德国 Opotinova 公司与香江国际集团（香港）有限公司国际贸易合同纠纷；代理深圳市牧人电器有限公司与创阁实业有限公司（香港）和骏基实业有限公司（亚洲）国际贸易合同纠纷；在香港高等法院审理的李知徕（Li Chiloi）遗产继承案件担任被告方内地法律专家证人；ABB 阿西亚·布朗·勃法瑞有限公司诉深圳市深北开电器有限公司知识产权纠纷；代理萨尔国际保险公司处理与浙江吉利汽车销售有限公司的汽车经销协议纠纷；代理珠海广通汽车有限公司解决与 Sarl BSL Location 的汽车买卖合同纠纷；代理深圳市南岭玩具制品有限公司解决非法售卖 CAT 品牌玩具的纠纷；代理盖帝图片有限公司（美国）系列图片著作权侵权案件等。同时，作为仲裁员处理了大量国际贸易纠纷、外商中国投资纠纷。

## 处理的非诉讼类涉外案件

为中国建筑国际集团（香港）、安宁控股有限公司收购石家庄勒泰房地产公司提供法律服务；为深圳市海斯比船艇科技股份有限公司引进 PTP 的技术签订合同提供法律服务；为 Cyrium 技术有限公司与深圳安泰科建筑技术有限公司合作提供法律服务；为利达制造有限公司（深圳）与东芝移动显示有限公司之间的交易提供法律服务；为湖北香江电器股份有限公司与深圳市爱思杰电子有限公司、深圳市远特信电子有限公司、香港香江国际集团、美国 Weighmax 集团跨境并购重组提供法律服务；为东莞某东电子有限公司与香港某东电子有限公司跨境并购重组提供法律服务。

## 中银介绍

中银成立于 1993 年 1 月，2008 年与成立于 2003 年的证泰律师事务所合并后，进入了快速发展的轨道。中银是经司法部门批准的我国最早的合伙制律师事务所之一。目前可在金融证券、法律风险管理、公司业务、建筑与房地产、知识产权、国际业务、诉讼与仲裁业务等领域提供全面的法律服务，是国内领先的规范化、专业化、规模化、国际化的大型综合性律师事务所。

中银总部设在北京，目前已在上海、天津、重庆、深圳、贵阳、成都、南宁、济南、福州、长沙、银川、南京、杭州、沈阳、西安、合肥、南昌、厦门、鸡西、台州、苏州、青岛、泉州、赣州、珠海等 25 个城市设有分支机构，现有律师和工作人员超过 2000 人。大部分律师获得国内外著名学府的硕士或博士学位，多数律师兼有专利代理人、注册会计师、高级工程师、经济师、房地产评估师、税务代理人、教授、研究员等专业技术职称或资格。另有多名国内外著名法学专家担任中银律师高级顾问。

中银积极开拓境外市场，构建全球法律服务体系，在实践中促使各领域业务水平处于领先地位。中银与美国、德国、法国、加拿大等十几个国家的律师机构建立了战略合作关系，培养的大量国际化律师人才能以英语、法语、日语、韩语、德语等多国语言为客户提供法律支持，保障了中银的客户在全球范围内迅速获得全面、高效的法律服务。卓越的业务水平让中银成为客户最认可、最信赖的伙伴。近年来，律所的客户数量、市场份额、总收入等均有显著提升。

中银始终秉持"客户至上、专业合作、勤勉尽责、优质高效"的服务理念，坚持以客户的需求为核心，充分发挥中银全球化法律服务体系的优势，整合各分所全体律师及部门资源，在为客户提供优质高效的法律服务的同时，还可为客户提供商业信息，促进客户间的商业合作。中银紧跟国家政策法规，与中国人民银行、中国证监会、中国保监会、国资委、发改委、财政部、商务部、工信部等政府部门保持着良好的工作关系，与各级司法部门、仲裁机构有着良好的业务关系和交流渠道。

网址：www.zhongyinlawyer.com
详情请登录中国律师年鉴网：www.yearbooklawyer.com
— 065 —

# 中国涉外律师

## 广东 Guangdong

### Mr. Tan Yueqi

Lawyer Tan Yueqi has successively pursued his study at Law Department of Southwest University of Political Science and Law, Law School of Wuhan University, Hague Academy of International Law of Netherlands, and obtained his Juris Doctor in 2002. For now, he not only serves as director and senior partner in Beijing Zhong Yin (Shenzhen) law firm, but as director of Foreign Legal Professional Committee of Shenzhen Lawyers Association, arbitrator of China International Economic and Trade Arbitration Commission, council member of Chinese Private International Law Society, arbitrator of South China International Economic and Trade Arbitration Commission, arbitrator of Shenzhen Arbitration Commission council member of Han Depei Law Foundation of Wuhan University, vice-chairman of Shenzhen Alumni Association of Law School of Wuhan University as well as the committee member of Qianhai Development Strategy Working Committee of Shenzhen Lawyers Association. He once entered an appearance in High Court of Hong Kong Special Administrative Region as a mainland legal expert witness.

His four professional publications such as "Legal Practice of Listing Affairs on China Growth Market and Analysis of Cases of Example "(Chief editor, Law Press, July 2011 Version), "How to Provide Team legal service for Small and Medium-sized Enterprises"(Chief editor, Law Press, July 2009 Version), "Legal Conflict and Coordination of Mainland and Hong Kong"(Deputy Editor, Hubei People' s Press, 2001 Version), "Judges Can Settle Household Chores the second book of Modern Legal Practice Series"(co-author, Hubei People' s Press,1997 Version)are released publicly. In the *Modern Law*, *Political and Legal Forum*, *Law Review*, *Lawyer and legal System* and other domestic core journals of law, he has published more than 20 articles. Being interviewed by multiple media agencies, including *Shenzhen Commercial Daily*, *Shenzhen Evening Paper*, *The Crystal*, *Shenzhen Legal Daily*, etc., he expresses his views on multiple legal hotspots in the aforementioned media.

### Foreign litigation Cases

To act for a domestic company in the dispute regarding Private Equity at the amount of a billion RMB with a Foreign prestigious investment company in Hong Kong International Arbitration Center, to act for a Foreign venture capital for an investment dispute at the amount of 500 million RMB with a domestic company, to handle the international trade contract disputes of Hong Kong Pacific Communications Equipment Co., Ltd. with MX Inc. Communications Department and MX Inc.; to handle the international trade contract disputes between Opotinova Gmbh (German Corporation) and Xiangjiang International Group (Hong Kong) Limited; to handle the international trade contract disputes among Shenzhen Muren Electric Corporation, Inno-Corner Industrial (HK) Limited Company and Chun Kit Industrial (Asia) Limited Company; to serve as the mainland legal expert witness in Li Chiloi's inheritance case heard by the High Court of Hong Kong Special Administrative Region; to resolve the disputes concerning intellectual property between ABB Asea Brown Boveri Limited Company and Shenzhen Shen Beikai Electric Co., Ltd.; to resolve the automobile distributorship agreement disputes between Sarl C.I.M.A and Zhejiang Gonow Automobile Sale Limited Company; to act as an attorney in the disputes arising from the sale contracts of automobiles between Zhuhai Guangtong Automobile Co., Ltd. and Sarl BSL Location; to act as an attorney on behalf of the Shenzhen Nanling Toy Products Co., Ltd. to handle the disputes regarding illegal sale for brand toys; to participate in the serial cases of pictures copyright infringement concerning Getty Images, Inc.(USA), etc.. As an arbitrator, he handled many arbitration cases involving international trade, foreign investment in China,etc..

### Foreign Non-litigation Cases

Providing legal services to China State Construction International Holdings and ENM Holdings Limited for their merging with Letai Real Estate Development Corporation in Shijiazhuang; providing the legal services for Shenzhen Hispeed Boats Science and Technology Joint Stock Company on signing contracts of introducing PTP technology, offering legal services for the cooperation between Cyrium Technologies Co. Ltd. and Shenzhen Atec Building Technology Co., Ltd., offering legal services for the transaction between Leader-Tech Electronics (Shenzhen) Co., Ltd. and Toshiba Mobile Display Co., Ltd, providing legal service for cross-border Merger and Acquisition project between X.J.Electrics(Hubei)Co., Ltd, Huanggang(CN) and Shenzhen Aisijie Electrics Co.,Ltd, Shenzhen Yuantexin Electrics Co.,Ltd, X.J Group Limited and WEIGHMAX Group, providing legal service for cross-border Merger and Acquisition project between Dongguan Xdong Electrics Co., Ltd and Hongkong Xdong Electrics Co., Ltd.

**Introductions of Beijing Zhong Yin Law Firm**

Founded in January 1993, Zhongyin Law Firm is one of the first private partnership law firms in China approved by Ministry of Justice. As a recognized leading comprehensive law firm, the firm provides services in a whole spectrum of areas such as finance and securities, legal risk management, company business, construction and real estate, intellectual property, international business, litigation and arbitration.

In addition to the headquarter in Beijing, Zhongyin operates branches in 25 cities in China including Shanghai, Tianjin, Chongqing, Shenzhen, Guiyang, Chengdu, Nanning, Jinan, Fuzhou, Changsha, Yinchuan, Nanjing, Hangzhou, Shenyang, Xian, Hefei, Nanchang, Xiamen, Jixi, Taizhou, Suzhou, Qingdao, Quanzhou, Ganzhou, and Zhuhai with a team comprised of more than 2 200 lawyers and staffs.

Zhong Yin Law Firm is committed to providing efficient legal service in a whole spectrum worldwide by actively expanding overseas market, building a global legal service system and promoting professional skills to take the leading position in all fields. Zhong Yin Law Firm has developed strategic cooperation with law firms in more than 10 countries such as U.S., Germany, France and Canada and trained a large amount of international lawyers to provide legal support to clients in English, French, Korean and German. Excellent professional skills turn Zhong Yin Law Firm into a most reliable partner recognized by clients. In recent years, the amount of law firm's clients, market share and gross income have significantly grown.

Adhering to the principle "client first, professional cooperation, diligence and responsibility, quality and efficiency", Zhong Yin Law Firm persists in focusing on the demands of clients, takes full advantage of global legal service system and integrates resources of all lawyers and departments to provide top-quality and efficient legal service to clients, as well as commercial information to promote business cooperation. Zhong Yin Law Firm forges ahead and follows a trend with national policies and regulations, maintaining a sound friendly relationship with The People's Bank of China, China Securities Regulatory Commission, China Insurance Regulatory Commission, State-Owned Assets Supervision and Administration Commission of the State Council, National Development and Reform Commission, Ministry of Finance, Ministry of Commerce, Ministry of Industry and Information Technology and other government departments as well as judicial departments and arbitration institutions at all levels.

中国涉外律师

山西 Shanxi

# 王志萍 律师　lawyer Wang Zhiping

全国优秀律师、山西省优秀律师、太原市仲裁委员会仲裁员、山西法学会理事、山西省律师协会常务理事、山西省律师协会涉外专业委员会主任、太原市律师协会副会长、山西省国资委法律顾问、山西省发展与改革委员会法律顾问、山西省财政厅法律顾问、太原市民政局法律顾问。

Outstanding Lawyer of China; Outstanding Lawyer of Shanxi Province; Arbitrator, Taiyuan Arbitration Commission; Director, Shanxi Law Society; Executive Director, Shanxi Lawyers Association; Director, Foreign-related Committee, Shanxi Lawyers Association; Vice President, Taiyuan Lawyers Association; Legal advisor, Shanxi Provincial State-owned Assets Supervision and Administration Commission; Legal advisor, Shanxi Provincial Development and Reform Commission; Legal advisor, Shanxi Provincial Finance Department; Legal advisor, Taiyuan Municipal Civil Affairs Bureau.

## 主要业绩

1991 年毕业于西北政法学院经济法系，1993 年通过律师资格考试，1994 年取得律师执业资格，在太原市资格最老的一家国办律师事务所执业 13 年后，2008 年成为山西省创办个人律师事务所第一人，经历了聘用律师、合伙人、个人律师事务所发起人的身份变化。

擅长涉外法律服务、政府法律服务、顾问单位服务、大型项目法律事务。在山西省一家兵工企业与外国公司 6 亿多元的项目谈判中，王志萍律师作为外方律师在中国的合作伙伴，成功地促成项目合作；作为山西省党纪教育基地的项目法律顾问，在长达两年的时间里，全面、全程提供专业建设法律服务，起草、审查合同达 40 余份；多次参加省、市政府信访案件大接访，充分发挥律师的专业优势，引导当事人正确理解相关政策和法律，为稳定事态、化解矛盾起到重要作用，达到从根本上息诉息访；在太原市城中村改造以及在太原市重点工程项目法律服务中，为改变过去被动接受咨询和服务要求的习惯做法，主动策划、设计法律服务方案，极力推行法律服务项目组制度，并且积极为参与主体提供政策解读和法律指导。

## 学术研究

商品房开发地下空间权属法律问题探讨、城中村改造中农村宅基地权属研究。

### Key Achievements

She graduated from the Economic Law Department, Northwest University of Political Science and Law in 1991, passing the lawyer qualification examination in 1993, obtaining the practice qualification in 1994, and founding the first private law firm in Shanxi Province in 2008 after working at the oldest state-run law firm of Taiyuan City for 13 years. She has experienced identity changes from an engaged lawyer, a partner to a founder.

She is good at foreign-related, governmental, organizational and project-based legal services. In negotiations for a project of over RMB600 million between a military industry company in Shanxi Province and a foreign company, she promoted mutual cooperation successfully as the partner of the foreign lawyer in China; as legal advisor to the Shanxi CPC Discipline Education Base Project, she offered professional legal services on construction in all aspects, drafted and reviewed over 40 contracts; she participated in complaint cases of the provincial and municipal governments, where she guided parties to understand relevant policies and laws, and played a crucial role in stabilizing the situation and settling conflicts; in legal services for Taiyuan City's "urban village reconstruction" and key projects in Taiyuan City, instead of receiving inquiries and service requests passively, she prepared a legal service plan actively, practiced the task force system vigorously, and provided policy interpretations and legal guidance to participants.

### Academic Research

Discussion of legal issues on the ownership of underground spaces in commercial housing development, study on the ownership of rural housing land in urban village reconstruction.

**工作语言**
中文、英语

### Working Languages
Chinese, English

网址：www.allan365.cn

详情请登录中国律师年鉴网：www.yearbooklawyer.com

# 迟菲 律师

## 基本信息与学历

迟菲，男，1973年生，1996年取得中国政法大学国际经济法专业法学学士学位，2003年取得首都经贸大学产业经济专业硕士学位。

## 工作经历

1996年起从事律师工作，1996～2000年，在北京信义德律师事务所担任律师兼行政主管，主要从事北京市市属外贸企业的法律顾问工作及8家外贸企业的国际贸易仲裁与诉讼。其间主持《国际商报》的《信义德律师信箱》栏目，回答全国各地外贸企业的法律咨询。2000年回太原加盟山西华晋律师事务所，任合伙人、副主任，代理了大量在山西省有影响力的大案要案，并担任多家房地产开发企业、能源企业、银行等金融机构及政府、事业单位的法律顾问。2012年起牵头成立山西恒驰律师事务所，并任该所主任，除继续代理各类大案要案外，还对信息网络与电子商务法律服务进行了深入专项研究，成功代理多个电商项目的专项法律顾问服务。

## 社会兼职（先后兼任）

中华全国律师协会信息网络与高新技术专业委员会研讨员；

山西省律师协会信息网络与电子商务专业委员会主任；
山西省律师协会业务指导委员会委员；
太原市律师协会教育培训与对外交流专门委员会主任；
太原仲裁委仲裁员；
太原市迎泽区农村土地仲裁委员会仲裁员；
太原市人民检察院人民监督员；
天权律师联盟（山西）主席。

## 荣誉

（1）迟菲律师2001年当选太原市第二届十大杰出青年律师并荣立市级二等功；（2）自2009年起连续4年被收录入中华全国律师协会主编的《中国律师年鉴》；（3）3次被收录入中华全国律师协会主编、中国法律出版社出版的《中国涉外律师》；（4）多次被收录入中国法律出版社出版的《中国当代优秀律师》以及中国法学会出版的《中国法律年鉴》；（5）2015年，被山西省律师协会评选为"诚信执业、坚守法治"主题教育实践活动先进律师。

## 主要学术著作（仅列举全国范围发行杂志或书籍文章）

（1）《数据库之法律保护》，中国知识产权网；（2）《山西省计算机软件侵权第一案代理心得与评析》，中国司法；（3）《电子商务平台法律关系研究》，信息网络与高新技术法律前沿；（4）《非典型P2P网贷平台法律框架搭建实务分析》，中国律师；（5）《大数据法律保护之困》，第九届中国西部律师论坛获二等奖；（6）参与了全国律协《律师办理高新技术领域法律尽职调查业务操作指引》的编写，收录在《中华全国律师协会律师业务操作指引（3）》。

## 经典案例

### 1. 重大诉讼案件

（1）代理太原市通过诉讼解决一等残废功臣某某诉太原市公安局国家赔偿第一案，案件最终调解解决；（2）代理山西省第一起计算机软件侵权纠纷案件的二审，最终该案依法改判；（3）担任山西省最大虚开增值税发票案16名被告中第7名被告辩护人；（4）担任太原市打黑第一案中两名被告人辩护人；（5）担任太原市劳动监察大队单位受贿罪辩护人；（6）担任太原市多起非法集资类重大案件多名被告辩护人；（7）代理寿阳某房地产公司诉寿阳县政府破产拍卖纠纷案。

### 2. 担任法律顾问的重点企业

北京7家进出口公司、法国福奈特洗衣（全国连锁）总部、山西和路雪冷食有限公司、中国农业发展银行山西省分行、山西双明房地产开发公司、山西太和远景房地产开发公司、山西成城房地产开发有限公司、山西星光矿业有限公司、太原市住房公积金管理中心、太原市企业养老保险中心等。

### 3. 重大非诉讼案件

（1）太原市旅游招商年暨建城2500年庆典系列活动法律框架设计及全程法律服务；（2）太原市住房公积金贷款线上线下流程的法律框架搭建及有关法律文件审核，太原市公积金有关规范性文件的合法性审查；（3）中国农业发展银行山西分行的贷款合法性审核业务（两年）；（4）太原市公积金贷款的合法性审核业务（4年）；（5）太原市民营经济开发区内2000亩土地的一级开发法律顾问服务；（6）太原市五龙湾阳光海岸房地产项目的开发专项法律顾问服务；（7）太原市杨家峪村城中村改造项目全程法律顾问服务；（8）长治市长治林业局棚户区改造全程项目法律顾问服务；（9）太原市多家企业的改制业务；（10）多家计划经济时期挂靠企业的个人国有资产产权界定法律顾问服务；（11）通过PE方式完成的信托计划法律顾问服务；（12）一般信托计划法律顾问服务等。

网址：www.hengchilawyer.com
详情请登录中国律师年鉴网：www.yearbooklawyer.com
— 069 —

**律** 中国涉外律师

香港　Hong Kong

# 邝家贤 律师

### 学历

中国政法大学中国民商法博士（2008 年），中山大学中国经济法律硕士（1999 年），修读由中国人民大学及香港树仁学院共同开设的中国律师培训班（1994 年），英国萨里法律学院法律学士（L. S. F）（1986 年），英国布里斯托尔工学院通过普通法律专业考试（C. P. E）（1984 年）香港大学历史及政治学士（1980 年）。

### 专业资格

香港执业律师，香港注册财务策划师，认可调解员，婚姻监礼人。

### 现任职位

亚太法律协会会长、 邝家贤专业顾问公司总裁、 陈叶苏律师行顾问律师、香港中小企业国际交流协会的创会会长、香港公民协会中常委、香港董事学会资深会员、香港中国企业协会会员、香港台湾工商协会董事法律顾问等。

### 获得荣誉

2011 创业中国年度十大杰出女性、十佳创业新锐人物、中国行业最具影响力人物、2009 年度中国企业创新优秀人物。

品牌中国海外维权、师团联合发起单位、中国民营企业发展促进会副会长单位、全国 AAA 级信用律师事务所、100 家最具投资潜力品牌企业（中国经济贸易促进会）金典奖——全国法律服务公众满意最佳典范品牌。

### 执业理念范围

20 多年来邝家贤律师秉承"扎根香港、服务中华"的服务理念，致力为中国企业提供优质、严谨、务实而有效的专业服务。

### 业务范围

粤港澳大湾区发展 、"一带一路"商机、企业合并收购、跨境直接投资、调解仲裁、金融科技、 企业法律顾问。

# Lawyer Kwong Ka Yin Phyllis

## Educational Background

Doctor of Chinese Civil and Commercial Laws, China University of Political Science and Law (2008); Master of Chinese Economic Law, Sun Yat-sen University (1999); Chinese lawyer training course offered by Renmin University of China and Hong Kong Shue Yan University jointly (1994); Law Society's Final, College of Law, Surrey, UK (L.S.F) (1986); passing the Common Professionl Examination (C.P.E) at the Bristol Polytecnic (1984); Bachelor of History and Politics, University of Hong Kong (1980).

## Professional Qualifications

Hong Kong Practicing Lawyer, Hong Kong Registered Financial Planner, Accredited Mediator, Civil Celebrant of Marriages.

## Current Positions

President of the Asia Pacific Law Association; Consultant, Phyllis Kwong Professional Consulting Limited, Legal Consultant to Messrs. J. Chan Yip So Law Firm, Founding President of Hong Kong Association of International Co-operation of Small & Medium Enterprises, member of the Central Standing Committee of the Hong Kong Civic Association, fellow member of the Hong Kong Institute of Directors, member of the Hong Kong Chinese Enterprises Association, director and legal advisor of the Taiwan Business Association (Hong Kong), etc.

## Honors

Top 10 Outstanding Woman Entrepreneur of China in 2011, Top 10 New Entrepreneur, Most Influential Industry Person of China, New Elitist in Business Innovation of China in 2009；Joint sponsor of the Brand China Overseas Rights Protection Lawyer Team, Vice President of China Private Enterprises Development Promotion Association, National AAA Credit Rating Law Firm, Top 100 Branded Enterprises with the Greatest Investment Potential (China Economic Trading Promotion Agency) Jindian Award——National Exemplary Brand with the Best Public Satisfaction in Legal Services.

## Practice Philosophy

For more than two decades, Lawyer Kwong Ka Yin Phyllis has been offering high-quality, rigorous, practical and effective professional services to Chinese enterprises under the service philosophy of "being rooted in Hong Kong and serving China".

## Practice Scope

Guangdong-Hong Kong-Macao Greater Bay Area Development, "Belt and Road" Strategies, Mergers & Acquisitions, Cross-border Direct Investment, Mediation & Arbitration, Fintech, Corporate Legal Advisory.

浙江 Zhejiang

## 陈嗣云 律师

武汉大学法学学士，英国伦敦大学亚非学院和美国休斯顿大学访问学者。现为浙江六和律师事务所高级合伙人，国际法律事务部主任。

陈嗣云律师 2004 年在香港易周律师行（Chartons）进行交流。2005 年 6 月至 2006 年 4 月参加英国司法大臣中国青年律师赴英培训项目，在伦敦大学进修英国法律及律师实务；在伦敦罗森泊律师行（Rosenblatt）实习；在伦敦 No.24 Old Building 出庭律师行实习。2006 年 5 月至 6 月，在中国香港胡百全律师行（PC Woo & Co）进行交流。2011 在美国休斯大学作为访问学者，研究和学习美国知识产权法及实务。

陈嗣云律师主要从事国际投资和国际贸易法律事务、公司法律事务，工作语言为英语、中文。现担任浙江医药股份有限公司、杭萧钢构股份有限公司、浙江物产金属集团有限公司、浙江物产物流投资有限公司、浙江省五金矿产进出口有限公司、浙江中大技术进口有限公司等上市公司和国有大型进出口公司的常年法律顾问。曾经为中国进出口银行浙江省分行、泰隆银行等金融机构提供法律服务。

## Mr. Chen Siyun

Bachelor of Law, Wuhan University; Visiting scholar to the School of Oriental and African Studies, University of London and the University of Houston; currently Senior Partner and Head of International Legal Affairs of Zhejiang Liuhe Law Firm. Lawyer Chen made exchanges at Charltons in Hong Kong in 2004, studied British legal and lawyer practices at SOAS London, under the Lord Chancellor Training Scheme for Young Chinese Lawyers, and practiced at the Rosenblatt and No.24 old building chamber in London from June 2005 to April 2006, made exchanges at P.C. Woo & Co. in Hong Kong China during May-June 2006, and studied U.S. intellectual property law and practiced as a visiting scholar to the University of Houston.

Lawyer Chen deals mainly with legal affairs on international investment, international trade and companies, and works in English and Chinese. Currently, he serves as permanent legal adviser to listed companies and major state-owned import and export companies, including Zhejiang Medicine Co., Ltd., Hangxiao Steel Structure Co., Ltd., Zhejiang Metals and Materials Company, Zhejiang Materials Logistics Investment Co., Ltd., Zhejiang Metals and Miners import and export co. ltd., and Zhejiang Zhongda Technical Import Co., Ltd. He once provided legal services to financial institutions such as the Zhejiang Branch of the Export-Import Bank of China, and Zhejiang Tailong Commercial Bank.

黑龙江 Heilongjiang

## 张晓美 律师

张晓美律师毕业于黑龙江大学法律系、北京第二外国语学院，1994 通过全国律师资格考试。1996 年执业。现担任中国法学会会员，齐齐哈尔市法学会专家委员会委员。

张晓美律师擅长办理涉外案件。英语水平专业八级（TEM-8）。曾经在北京系统地学习法律英语，能够熟练地用英语进行交流和翻译，和全国优秀涉外律师团队的律师合作共赢，并在多家公司担任翻译工作和非诉讼业务，具有扎实的理论基础和实践经验。

张晓美律师曾在多家贸易公司担任法律顾问，对涉外合同有非常深入地研究；对民商法、国际经济法等领域进行了深入透彻地研究；对合同纠纷、劳动人事管理及争议、国际贸易纠纷、外商投资、股权转让等诉讼与非诉讼业务具有丰富的经验和实际操作技能。2018 年 1 月 1 日受到邀请参加了由中国西北政法大学和抱柱大学主办的中美法庭庭审实战技能突破高级训练班的学习。张晓美律师还获得全球投资移民律师协会认证的移民律师资格。在 2018 年金牌律师网络投票中获得第一名。

## Lawyer Zhang Xiaomei

Graduated from the Law Department of Heilongjiang University and Beijing International Studies University, Zhang Xiaomei passed the national lawyer qualification examination in 1994 and began practice in 1996. Now, she serves as a member of China Law Society, as well as a member of Qiqihar City Law Society Expert Committee.

She is particularly good at handling foreign-related cases. Since she studied legal English systematically in Beijing with the English proficiency level of TEM-8 (Test for English Majors-Band 8), she has been able to make communication and translation in English well. Besides, she has worked in many companies as a translator, laying a solid theoretical foundation.

As a legal advisor, she has engaged in in-depth and thorough studies on foreign-related contracts, civil and commercial laws, international economic laws, contract disputes, labor and personnel management issues and disputes, international trade disputes, foreign investment, equity transfer and other litigation and non-litigation business. Currently, she serves as a permanent legal advisor and translator for several large and medium-sized companies.In 2018, she got the first gold medals on the Internet voting.

# 彭焰 律师

彭焰，刑法学硕士、国际经济法学博士、英国牛津大学博士后。恒合律师事务所主任、一级律师、CIETAC仲裁员。影视传媒、量子科技、生态农业、女性类文化公司的创始合伙人。中国政法大学博士校友会专家顾问、中华博士会双创校园行创业导师、世界华人文化名人协会常务副会长。彭焰律师执业30多年，一直在实践与理论的前沿深度探究不曾停歇，倾其一生的专业磨砺，锻造出一把无可比拟的专业神剑，在法学及其交叉领域游刃挥洒，为国家、社会和中国的法治文明建设竭尽绵薄之力，作出了突出的贡献。

## 职业特征

法学功底深厚、律师实务经验丰富，具有法律人精神和良好的职业修养；执业风格独特，办案注重程序切选、案情透析、证据运用，作法律判断时能综合适用法律规范与政策及立法精神，力求案件结果客观公正、法理与事理的适度平衡；执业语言规范，善用准确语汇、语体结合辩证法规律与逻辑思维定律，清晰、准确地论证表达代理或辩护意见。公正、冷静、理性、文明和敏锐迅捷的应变反应是外界对其公认的职业形象。

## 专业领域

先后担任市政府、国有大中型企业和集团公司、民营企业、中外合作合资和外商独资企业、专业银行和商业银行、风投、上市和私募基金等公司法律顾问；深度参与或独立操作国企改制、外商投资、多类项目落地策划与风控、企业并购、资产重组、产权交易、知识产权保护、国际贸易、BOT项目运作、房地产和国际工程项目、金融、证券、境内外上市、投融资及新型的经济刑案等法律事务；成功处理上百件在各省市及国际国内具有重大影响的民商事刑案，尤其是在公司上位治理、大宗土地交易、高端房地产开发、投融资领域的金融资本代币、多层次资本市场之场外交易等多发违规涉众的大型要案，具有很强的协调处理、组织维稳、化解危机、消除隐患的综合治理能力。

## 业务覆盖

新加坡、印尼、日本、韩国、美国、德国、英国等国家和中国香港、中国台湾地区。

## 业绩概览

曾为六部委联合通报之抢劫杀人重案和多个省市重大涉黑刑案主犯、多个重大杀人绑架大案和其他经济犯罪要案辩护，获得无罪释放或减轻判决的良好效果；代理国企跨五省六区之连环合同巨款被骗案，踏破几省地力挽狂澜追回损失，化解企业破产风险；代理数宗大型建设工程项目案件，因熟知招投标、工程定额及概预结决算等法律和建设工程专业知识每获胜诉；为多家跨国公司（包括西门子、丰田公司）在华投资进行优化设计、拆分组合、资股并购或资股置换，低成本低风险实现投资经济目标。多年来，为外商投资、外资并购，中资海外投资、股权置换和产权交易，为外资参与国企改革、资产剥离、人员分流、股份制改造、资产重组、企业并购，为外商进入西部投资教育、医疗、能源、水力、电力等提供全程法律服务，从项目的法律架构到各阶段程序的操作控制，都是在平衡各方利益前提下消除和避免任何法律风险的产生。完成了两所大学三个独立学院开办设立的全程法律服务；一所国有建工医院改制、收购、重整为国际现代化医院；完成两个电站的收购及都江堰某藁干大型项目的综合性开发建设；为能源项目、环保项目、绿色循环经济项目的开发、推广进行法律架构和保护，负责策划、设计和推进。数年坚持不懈地为遭受重大权利损害而无力救济的弱势群体无偿甚至投入巨资为他们提供有效的法律援助，在保护他们合法权益的同时为他们建立起对社会法治、公平正义的信心。处理全国多省市重大投融资涉众的刑事要案，具有很强的商业风险、法律风险、社会和政治风险化解能力以及维权维稳并重的实务经验和技巧；成功代理多桩民商事知名要案，获得法益公平正气，彰显危机消弭的良好社会效果；坚持不懈地做非官方的法律援助，以济民权。

## 社会活动与专业理论文化修养

曾参加第十四届世界法律大会、第四届世界妇女大会、世界优秀华人联谊会、GATT和WTO中国最高端研修，经常性参加国际国内所涉政经、文化、法治等关乎社会文明进步改良命题的高端论坛或峰会。独撰和与他人合作发表专业文章、论文，并在国家级出版社出版，如《非刑事法规中的刑事立法》《刑法修改管见》《第三性征与婚姻解体初探》《行政复议与行政诉讼案例选析》《贪污、挪用与玩忽职守罪案鉴析》《保安处分刑事立法论》《中国金融改革与立法》《中国刑事和解制度架构》等。

## 社会声望与荣誉

从20世纪80年代末期，彭焰律师便进入社会公众视野，其业绩被编入《中国律师辞典》《中国百科专家学者经典》《中国专家大辞典》《中国人才世纪献辞》《中国国情报告·专

全国精英律师竞选获公司和公益律师风采奖

做客 CCTV《华人频道》

CCTV《影响力》访谈

家学者卷》《中国人才辞典》《世界优秀专家人才名典·中华卷二》《世界华人杰出专家名典》《世界妇女大会·中华巾帼画册》《中国名律师大典》《中国律师在线》《中国涉外律师》《法律门》《中国律师年鉴》《人物辞海》《红色金典》《时代人物》《中国领导科学文库》《CHINA TODAY》等。获得多届中国市级"优秀律师"荣誉。获得国家级杂志"人物专访""法界明星"和"十佳女律师"荣誉；获中国国际经济（香港）研究院、世界文化名人交流协会、世界文化艺术研究院、建设功臣评审委员会建党九十周年"党旗下的建设功臣－奉献奖"；获中华杰出爱国华商联合会、中华英模文化促进会、华商英才国际文化传媒中心"推动中国社会进步突出贡献人物"重点提名；曾受邀中央电视台《华人频道》和《影响力对话》节目访谈、《今日中国》杂志栏目专访。2014 年入编《今日中国》两会特刊封面人物及荣登官方权威存书封面人物，与柳传志、马云等名家同刊出版；获"中华爱国先进模范人物"荣誉，所抒爱国宣言镌刻幕墙，先进事迹载入《中华爱国国典》。

法律之光，她秉持法律人的本色，不哀不弃、不畏权贵、追求正义、崇尚人权、维护秩序、热爱祖国、热爱和平，坚守在法律框架内渐进法治的理念，既仰望星空，又脚踩大地，以一位优秀法律人的理论探索与实务经验，办理了一系列令人称道的案件，为推动行业发展和法治建设，融入了自己的智慧与力量。

彭焰热爱生命、酷爱学习、博览群书，喜读世界名著，做读书笔记，在政法学院曾获书法、绘画三等奖。作诗填词、吹拉弹唱，情趣广泛。20 世纪 80 年代中期，《中国律师》《法学研究》《法学杂志》《法学译丛》等法学刊物，在她微薄工资的支出中一本也不能少。这些专业刊物伴她一路走来，为她专业发展、实务操作和学业升级提供了丰沛的养分和理论支撑。除法学本业外，对文学、政经、哲学、形式逻辑辩证逻辑、心理学、星相学、易学等方面知识有很浓厚的兴趣，同时对现实世界的政经人文等国际国内时事十分关注，并将这些知识和信息在工作、学习中善加融通应用，以使其看待问题和判断事物更理性、更客观、更全面和准确。

## 人生价值观与生活态度

彭焰有着全球化的视野，有民主、自由、公平、正义的价值观，对法律人的精神与律师职业的使命感有宗教般的情怀和执着。有热爱祖国母亲的情怀，热爱生命和生活、爱亲人、朋友、同学、同事；感恩给过她引领、帮助和服务的生命相遇者。

从拿到律师执业证的那一刻，她就意识到了自己肩负的责任和义务。她认为自己是一个法律的守护者、是法制环境中的一名保洁工，无论什么情形和条件，都会恪尽职守、力所能及地推出相对公平的结果并保持职业的精神和荣誉。正是这种以荣誉、责任、勇气、自律等系列价值为核心的职业精神元素，让她每每感受到心里充满爱和责任。在彭焰律师的执业生涯中，成功的案例不计其数，每个案件都折射出她对职业的忠守和法律人的执着。她时常感受到生命被使命所引领，心里充满爱和肩上压满责任。因为她执着于律师的神圣职责，而对功名利禄十分淡泊。执业 30 余年，一以贯之地坚守着对职业的挚爱，永远追逐的是内心那道永不熄灭的

## 彭焰的职业感言

彭焰律师的星座是天秤座。传说天秤座是古代罗马正义女神的化身阿斯拉雅女子手中所持的一杆称，实公正的衡器。正如她的感言："在中国社会力求摆脱几千年封建意识进入现代文明社会的历史进程，我们选择的律师职业，就像一个拓荒者，高擎公平正义的火炬，穿越充满荆棘的历史森林，经纬白度伤痕斑驳，一如既往百折不挠，这就是我们的使命！

"几十年的律师生涯，我对律师职业的热爱和对法律正义公平的秉持从未减淡，我用一生捍卫着律师职业的崇高荣誉，践行了一个党员律师的执业誓约。'衣带渐宽终不悔，为伊消得人憔悴'，瑰红剑影，春华不在，我心依旧，钟爱无悔。我将继续秉持法律人的本色，不哀不弃，不畏权贵、追求正义，崇尚人权、维护秩序，热爱祖国、热爱和平，坚守在法律框架内渐进法治的理念。

我希望通过我们的执业经历，向世人披露在历史浮尘中不失这样传承自由、平等、公平、正义基因的优秀律师，一代一代，禅竭青春和生命，化人类历史文明发展之人权保护

律 中国涉外律师

四川 Sichuan

和权力制衡的脉道于无形。

"作为具有法律人精神的律师，我们细胞每一次泵压，都是为了平抑权力对公平的伤害。我们竭尽毕生的努力为世人换取一片蓝天、一朵白云，我们以并不强壮的身躯为社会挚起公平正义的火炬，给世人以希望、信心和定力。

"作为几十年跻身法律实践与理论前沿的、具有很深法律人情结的律师，我时常陷于职业的深度思考中，深感谋求实现社会公平正义的价值目标必须以法治理念取代国家本位、官本位、行政本位及公民义务本位的理念和法制观，以最高阶位的价值理念驱动宪法和法律的运行，逐渐促进法治文明的社会氛围，引导公民社会自发生成'公民、国家、责任、荣誉'感，实现公民与国家的自然连接和中国社会心理完全符合现代法治的理性要求。"

君未看花时，花与君同寂。君来看花日，花色一时明。彭焰律师闲庭信步地与法律伴行，从容而快乐。她做律师如火纯青而纯粹，她把执业信仰融入到了法治环境的需要和人生追求，并嵌入到了灵魂深处。

### 彭焰如是说

如果生命可以重复，将重操律师这个良知之王的职业，在潜命中认真履行这个万物尺度的神职！

### 媒体报道

百度 baike.baidu.com/view/9841712.htm?fr=aladdin

《中国律师年鉴》www.yearbooklawyer.com/sites/lawyer/detail_201204250552591806_c_6.html

《华人会客厅》v.ifeng.com/vblog/others/201303/40cb0633-91e6-e26e-8067-6eef598a904c.shtml

《影响力对话》xiyou.cntv.cn/v-a3c85d6e-57de-11e3-8b06-e60566ef7fac.html

榜样的力量 www.gx.chinanews.com/2014/1502_0604/95732.html

出访瑞典英德国最高法院和国际仲裁院 cn.cietac.org/NewsFiles/NewsDetail.asp?NewsID=1382

主持首届中国国际商事仲裁高修班结业典礼和法学院长与中国国际经济贸易仲裁委主任秘书长的高端对话 www.law.ruc.edu.cn/article/?47005.html

# Lawyer Peng Yan

Peng Yan, female, is Director of Henghe Law Firm, Class A Lawyer, CIETAC Arbitrator, Master in Criminal Law, Doctor in International Economic Law, Postdoctoral Fellow of the University of Oxford, founding partner of movie and media, quantum technology, ecological agriculture and women's culture companies, Expert Advisor to the Alumni Association of China University of Political Science and Law, business startup tutor of the "Double Creation" Campus Tour of the Association for China's Doctors of Philosophy, and Executive Vice President of the World Association of Chinese Cultural Celebrities. Lawyer Peng has been making in-depth explorations at the forefront of practice and theory in her practice for over 30 years. This experience has given her unrivaled expertise to play freely in the science of law and related fields, and enabled her to make prominent contributions to the country, society, and China's legal system building and civilization.

## Professional identity

She has a solid foundation of law knowledge, rich practical experience as a lawyer, and good professional ethics. With a unique practicing style, she focuses on procedure selection, case analysis and evidence application when handling cases, and can make objective and fair legal judgments based on applicable laws, regulations and policies, and by striking an appropriate balance between legal principles and facts. She uses a normative practicing language and chooses wording accurately by combining dialectics and logics to demonstrate and express agency or defense opinions clearly and accurately. Fairness, calmness, rationality, civility and agility summarize her generally recognized professional image.

## Specialties

She has served as legal advisor to municipal governments, large and medium state-owned enterprises and group companies, private enterprises, Chinese-foreign joint venture and wholly foreign-funded enterprises, specialized and commercial banks, venture capital, listed and private equity companies successively, and deeply participated in or independently handled legal affairs, such as state-owned enterprise restructuring, foreign investment, project implementation planning and risk control, enterprise M&A, asset restructuring, property transactions, intellectual property protection, international trade, BOT project operation, real estate and international projects, finance, securities, domestic

接受《今日中国》专访

访问英国最高法院

与瑞典著名律所律师交流

and overseas listing, financing, and new-type economic cases. She has handled over one hundred influential civil, commercial and criminal cases both at home and abroad, especially major cases involving corporate governance, bulk land transactions, high-end real estate development, financial capital tokens in investment and financing, and over-the-counter transactions on the multi-level capital market, and has strong capabilities in conducting coordination, maintaining stability, solving crises and removing potential perils.

## Business coverage

China (Hong Kong, Taiwan), Singapore, Indonesia, Japan, Korea, U.S., Germany, Britain, etc.

## Performance overview

She defended a severe crime of robbery and murder jointly notified by six states ministries and commissions, major gang crimes, murders and kidnappings, and other economic crimes in many provinces and cities, and got desirable results of acquittal or lenient sentence. She handled a serial fraud involving a huge contract amount across five provinces and six regions for a state-owned enterprise, and managed to retrieve the losses and prevent the enterprise from going bankrupt. She handled several major construction project cases, and won the cases because she was familiar with legal and construction expertise in bidding, quota calculation, budgeting, final settlement, etc. She conducted optimal design, splitting and reorganization, M&A or capital-equity replacement for Chinese investment by a number of transnational corporations (including Siemens and Toyota), realizing their investment objectives at low costs and risks. Over these years, she has provided whole-process legal services for foreign investment, M&A by foreign investors, overseas investment by Chinese investors, equity replacement, property transactions, foreign investors' participation in state-owned enterprise reform, divestiture, staff reassignment, joint stock system reform, asset restructuring, and enterprise M&A, and foreign investors' investment in the educational, medical, energy, hydropower and electricity sectors in western China, and managed to avoid any legal risk while balancing interests of all parties through legal framework design and procedure control. She provided whole-process legal services for the establishment of three independent schools of two universities, the acquisition and restructuring of a state-owned engineering hospital into an international modern hospital, the acquisition of two power stations, and the integrated development of a major project of the Dujiang Dam. She conducted legal framework design and protection for the development and promotion of energy, environmental protection and green circular economy projects through her personal planning, design and implementation. She has been providing effective legal assistance to vulnerable groups who have suffered great damages but are unable to get relieved, even at her own expense, thereby helping them build up confidence in rule by law, fairness and justice while protecting their lawful rights and interests. In handling major crimes in many provinces and cities, she has shown strong capabilities and practical skills in mitigating commercial, legal, social and political risks, protecting rights and maintaining stability. By handling many well-known major civil and commercial cases successfully, she has realized favorable effects in upholding social fairness and justice. She has been offering unofficial legal assistance to protect people's rights.

## Social activities and theoretical accomplishments

She once attended the 14th Congress on the Law of the World, the 4th World Conference on Women, the Global Outstanding Chinese Sodality, and GATT and WTO advanced studies in China, and often takes part in international and domestic high-level forums or summits on politics, economy, culture, rule by

与斯德哥尔摩商会仲裁院主席 Ulf Franke　　　　参观瑞典最高法院　　　　与梵蒂冈红衣大主教

law, and other topics on social civilization and progress. She has written independently or co-authored professional articles and papers, which were published at state-level publishing houses, such as *Criminal Legislation in Non-criminal Laws*, *Opinions on the Amendment of the Criminal Law*, *A Preliminary Study on Tertiary Sexual Characters and Marital Disintegration*, *Selected Cases of Administrative Reconsideration and Litigation*, *Analysis of Corruption, Embezzlement and Malpractice Crimes*, *Discussion on Criminal Legislation on Security Measures*, *Chinese Financial Reform and Legislation*, and *Framework of the Chinese Criminal Reconciliation System*.

### Social reputation and honors

Lawyer Peng entered the public vision in the late 1980s, and her name was included in *Chinese Lawyers Dictionary*, *Classic of Chinese Encyclopedia Experts and Scholars*, *Chinese Experts Dictionary*, *Chinese Talent Century Dictionary*, *Report on China's Conditions • Experts and Scholars*, *Chinese Talent Dictionary*, *Collection of Global Outstanding Experts • China Volume 2*, *Collection of Outstanding Chinese Experts*, *World Conference on Women • Chinese Women Album*, *Collection of Famous Chinese Lawyers*, *Chinese Lawyers Online*, *Chinese Foreign-related Lawyers*, *Access to Law*, *Yearbook of Chinese Lawyers*, *Dictionary of Figures*, *Red Golden Dictionary*, *Figures of the Times*, *Chinese Library of Leadership Science*, *China Today*, etc. She has won many city-level "Excellent Lawyer" titles, state-level "Exclusive Interview" "Law Star" and "Top 10 Female Lawyer" titles, the "CPC Contributor – Dedication Award" at the 90th anniversary of CPC founding conferred by China International Economy (HK) Institute, World Cultural Celebrities Association, World Culture & Art Institute, and the Contributor Review Committee, and "Outstanding Contributor to China's Social Progress – Key Nomination" by China Outstanding Patriotic Chinese Merchants Federation, Chinese Model Culture Promotion Association, and Chinese Elite

Merchants International Culture & Media Center. She was once interviewed by the Chinese Channel and Dialogue of Influence programs of CCTV, and the China Today magazine. In 2014, she was chosen as the cover star of the Special Issue of the Two Sessions of China Today, and was included in the official book together with Liu Chuanzhi, Ma Yun and other celebrities. She won the "Chinese Advanced Patriotic Model" honor, her patriotic statement was inscribed, and her meritorious deeds were included in Chinese Patriots Catalogue.

### Values and attitude to life

Peng Yan has a global vision, the values of democracy, freedom, fairness and justice, and a sense of mission and dedication for the law spirit and the lawyer profession. She loves the motherland, life, and her family, friends, schoolmates and colleagues, and is always grateful to those who have led, helped and served her.

From the moment she received the lawyer's license, she realized her duties and obligations. She thinks that she is a law protector and a cleaner in the legal environment, and would do her best to pursue fair results and professional ethics in whatever case. It is this professional spirit of glory, courage and self-discipline that makes her always feel love and responsibility. Her career is filled up with successful cases, each of which reflects her dedication to the lawyer profession. She often feels that her life is led by the holy duties of a lawyer, and cares little about personal honors and interests. For over three decades of practice, she has been pursuing the eternal brilliance of law with a deep love for the profession. It is such pursuit that makes her devoted to her duties in protecting justice, order, peace and human rights. She always practices the philosophy of rule by law within the legal framework, and has handled a number of admirable cases, and contributeing to industry development and legal system building with her own wisdom and power.

Peng Yan loves life and learning, likes to read world classics, take reading notes, write poems and lyrics, and play musical instruments, and once won calligraphy and painting prizes at the political science and law. In the mid 1980s, law journals like *Chinese Lawyer*, *Chinese Journal of Law*, *Law Science Magazine and Law Translation* were her must-reads despite of her slender salaries. These journals have helped her a lot in career development, and practical and academic upgrading. In addition to her own specialty, she is also strongly interested in literature, politics, economy, philosophy, formal logic, dialectical logic, psychology, astrology, Yi Jing studies, etc., and highly concerned about international and domestic current events. She has applied such knowledge and information to her work and study, enabling her to view and judge things more rationally, objectively, comprehensively and accurately.

### Career feelings

Lawyer Peng's constellation is Libra, which is said to be a scale——a fair weighing instrument in the hands of Lady Justice Astraea in ancient Rome. As she felt, "In the historical process that Chinese society attempts to cast off thousand-year-old feudal ideology and become a modern civilized society, we lawyers are pathfinders who hold a torch of fairness and justice, and run through a historical forest full of thistles and thorns. Despite of countless wounds, we remain indomitable. This is just our mission!"

In my lawyer career that has lasted for decades, my love for the profession, and persistence for legal fairness and justice have never diminished. I have been defending the glory of the profession with my life, and honored my professional pledge as a CPC member. In spite of so many difficulties, I never regret my original choice. I will keep performing my duties in protecting justice, order, peace and human rights earnestly, and practicing the philosophy of rule by law within the legal framework.

I hope to make people know through our practicing experiences that there do be excellent lawyers with the DNA of freedom, equality, fairness and justice who have been devoting their efforts to human civilization and development.

As lawyers with the law spirit, we make every effort to protect fairness from powers, create a fair and just world for all people, and give everyone hope and confidence.

As a lawyer having worked at the forefront of practice and theory for decades, I'm often obsessed by in-depth profession thinking. I think that social fairness and justice must be realized by replacing the old legal system based on bureaucracy and citizenship

with the philosophy of rule by law, driving the operation of the Constitution and laws with the highest values, developing a social atmosphere of law-ruled civilization gradually, guiding people to develop a sense of citizenship and responsibility, and build inherent connections with the country, and aligning the social psychology with the modern requirements of rule by law.

Lawyer Peng has always been working work law leisurely, happily, proficiently and purely, because her practicing faith has been integrated deeply into her lifelong pursuit and soul.

Peng Yan said, "If the life could be repeated, she would resume this profession of conscience and perform her holy duties extremely carefully!"

### Media Report

baike.baidu.com/view/9841712.htm?fr=aladdin (Baidu.com)

www.yearbooklawyer.com/sites/lawyer/detail2012042505 52591806c6.html (*Chinese Yearbook of Lawyers*)

v.ifeng.com/vblog/others/201303/40cb0633-91e6-e26e-8067-6eef598a904c.shtml (*Chinese Parlor*)

xiyou.cntv.cn/v-a3c85d6e-57de-11e3-8b06-e60566ef7fac.html (*Influence Dialog*)

www.gx.chinanews.com/2014/15020604/95732.html (*The Power of Example*)

cn.cietac.org/NewsFiles/NewsDetail.asp?NewsID=1382 (visit to supreme courts and international arbitration tribunals of Sweden, Britain and Germany)

www.law.ruc.edu.cn/article/?47005.html (high-level dialog with the Dean of the Law School, and Secretary-general of the China International Economic and Trade Arbitration Commission when hosting the closing ceremony of the First China Advanced Studies Course on International Commercial Arbitration)

中国涉外律师

## 江苏 Jiangsu

# 陈发云 律师

### 简介

国浩律师（南京）事务所高级合伙人，一级律师，全国律协首届"涉外律师领军人才""一带一路"项目跨境律师人才库"律师、司法部"涉外律师人才库"律师。国际商会中国国家委员会仲裁委员会委员，新加坡国际仲裁中心、香港国际仲裁中心及中国国际经济贸易仲裁委员会等知名仲裁机构仲裁员，香港仲裁司学会资深会员。江苏省人大常委会立法咨询专家库专家，江苏省欧美同学会常务理事、法律委员会会长。曾在美国马里兰大学、德国汉堡大学、英国利物浦大学留学与访学，并在英国律所 DLA Piper 及美国律所 Jones Day 见习工作过。被中华全国律师协会、法制日报社、中国律师网、法制网评为"2016 年度中国律师行业最受关注新闻人物"，被江苏省司法厅、江苏省商务厅、中国国际贸易促进委员会江苏省分会、江苏省律师协会评为"江苏省十佳涉外律师"。《法制日报》首届"中国律师故事"专栏以"陈发云：帮中国企业打赢国际官司"为题对他做过专题报道。

### 执业领域

执业 24 年，积累了丰富的涉外非诉与诉讼仲裁的经验。曾为投资总额过百亿元人民币的英国捷豹路虎合资项目提供全程法律服务。代理过美国联邦及州法院、伦敦海事仲裁员协会、国际商会仲裁院、新加坡国际仲裁中心、香港国际仲裁中心、香港高等法院等机构审理的民商事案件，其中，成功代理中国企业应诉美国联邦地区法院、香港国际仲裁中心审理的中企海外诉讼仲裁第一大案，涉案金额高达 150 亿美元；成功代理中国企业在伦敦应诉见索即付退款保函纠纷 LMAA 仲裁案，使业界公认的"死案"起死回生，为企业避免了巨额经济损失。

### 教育背景

英国利物浦大学法学院毕业，获国际商法硕士学位。在此之前，他先后获得复旦大学法学学士学位和安徽师范大学文学学士学位。作为访问学者，他在马里兰大学学习 WTO 和美国贸易法，并在汉堡大学接受跨国并购方面的培训。他曾在众达律师事务所华盛顿办事处和欧华律师事务所汉堡办事处实习。

### 著作

牵头编写全国普法办、中华全国工商业联合会联合出版的七五普法教材《非公有制企业经营管理法律知识及风险以案释法读本》并担任副编审；连续 4 年主编由中华全国律师协会资助出版的《涉外律师在行动》系列丛书；著有《外资在华并购：法律与实务》（Cross-Border Mergers & Acquisitions in China: Law and Practice, LexisNexis 2009 年香港版）等，并在国内外专业刊物上发表中英文论文多篇。

网址：www.grandall.com.cn
详情请登录中国律师年鉴网：www.yearbooklawyer.com
— 078 —

# Chen Fayun(Walter)

## About Chen Fayun

Chen Fayun is a Senior Partner and Senior Counsel of Grandall Law Firm (Nanjing), Mcmber of the "Leading Chinese Lawyers Dealing with Cross-Border Legal Affairs" of All China Lawyers Association and Member of the "Pool of Lawyers Engaged in Foreign Related Legal Matters" of the Department of Justice of P.R.China.  He is arbitrator of China International Economic and Trade Arbitration Commission (CIETAC), Singapore International Arbitration Center (SIAC), Hong Kong International Arbitration Center (HKIAC) and a number of other top arbitration institutions. He is a member of ICC China Arbitration Committee and fellow of Hong Kong Institute of Arbitration (FHKIArb).

## Practice Aeras

Being in legal practice for 24 years, Walter Chen has accumulated abundant practical experience in non-litigation, litigation and arbitration matters, especially in handling complicated cases in the United States, Britain, Singapore and other countries as well as Hong Kong China and mainland China. He has represented Chinese clients in numerous civil and commercial cases heard by the US federal district courts, London Maritime Arbitrators Association(LMAA), ICC International Court of Arbitration, Singapore International Arbitration Center(SIAC), Hong Kong International Arbitration Center(HKIAC), Hong Kong High Court, and other overseas judicial and arbitration institutions, inter alia, he once successfully represented a well-known Chinese automobile enterprise in a huge case first tried in a US federal district court, then after the proceedings being stayed, heard in HKIAC. The amount claimed in such case was over USD 15 billion. The case was supposedly the largest case against Chinese business sued overseas. He also successfully represented a Chinese bank in responding to a refund guarantee case brought in London in accordance with the LMAA Rules. The claimed amount was over USD 20 million. In this case, a rarely seen defence of public policy was used which rendered the underlying shipbuilding contract unenforceable. As a result, the case was won. He once provided legal services for the automobile joint venture project between Jaguar Land Rover and Chery Automobile, the total investment of which was as high as RMB 10.9 billion. The project was rated the "Best Deal of the Year 2012" by China Business Law Journal, Hong Kong China.

## Education

Chen Walter graduated from the Faculty of Law of the University of Liverpool with a degree of master of laws in international business law. Before that, he graduated from Fudan University with a Bachelor Degree of Laws and from Anhui Normal University with a Bachelor Degree of Arts. He pursued WTO and US trade law studies in the University of Maryland as a visiting scholar, and got trained as well on cross-border M&A in the University of Hamburg. He interned at Washington D.C. Office of Jones Day and Hamburg Office of DLA Piper.

## Honors

He was rated by All China Lawyers Association together with other legal media as the "Lawyer of the Year 2016", and Jiangsu Provincial Department of Justice, Jiangsu Provincial Department of Commerce, Jiangsu Provincial Bar Association and Jiangsu Sub-Council of China Council for the Promotion of International Trade as one of "Ten Top Lawyers Involved in Foreign-Related Legal Matters". The prestigious newspaper *Legal Daily* once published a feature report titled "Walter Chen: Helps Win an International Lawsuit for Chinese Business".

## 江苏 Jiangsu

# 刘惠明 律师

刘惠明，江苏省靖江市人。1985 年毕业于河海大学工程力学系并取得工学学士学位；1989 年毕业于南京大学法学院第二学位班，获得法学第二学士学位；1995～2001 年在日本留学、工作，就读于日本著名的一桥大学法学院攻读民商法学，获得法学硕士学位；2001～2002 年曾在美国加州大学进修，后获得南京大学法学博士学位。

现担任江苏钟山明镜律师事务所主任、河海大学法学院教授，南京仲裁委员会委员，中华全国律协涉外律师领军人才，江苏省十佳涉外律师，江苏省律师协会涉外专业律师人才库成员，南京市留学归国人员联谊会副会长，留日博士总会副会长。

### 擅长业务领域
国际经济贸易、外商投资、知识产权、房地产、重大劳动纠纷。

### 主要经历
刘惠明律师 1985 年起在河海大学任教，从事法学教育工作多年。1990 年取得律师资格并开始从事律师工作。留学日本期间，曾在日本著名的律师事务所工作两年，担任过日中律师联合会和留日江苏同学会秘书长。精通中日两国法律，主责民商、对日业务。

刘惠明律师凭借深厚的法学理论功底、杰出的辩护能力和高超的外语水平，曾为肯德基、本田技研、日产汽车、三洋电器、丸红株式会社、日立金属、三菱商事等著名跨国公司提供过公司并购、国际投资、国际贸易、知识产权、劳务管理等方面的法律服务，现担任住友化学、理光公司、尼康公司、大塚化学、横河电机、卫材药业、八乐梦床业、王子橡胶等著名日资企业的法律顾问。

刘惠明律师处理过多起有影响的疑难案件，其代理的美国最大的化工企业与日本著名化工企业之间的专利纠纷案、日本著名商社与美国企业间的钢材买卖纠纷案等均是标的额巨大的案件，其代理的余一中名誉侵权案、经典公司文物拍卖案也曾受到广泛关注，有的被刊登在《最高人民法院公报》上。并且刘惠明律师积极参与援助对日本国政府的细菌战赔偿诉讼、南京大屠杀受害者李秀英名誉权诉讼案的代理及各项研究翻译工作。

刘惠明律师在河海大学法学院讲授过多门法律课程，现主要讲授公司法、票据法、知识产权法等，在这些领域有较高的学术造诣。

### 著述
留日期间，刘惠明律师曾以中日两国文字发表过多篇论文，并出版过日文专著和译著。主要论文有《论人权的实现与法制保障》《论拍卖行为的法律性质及形成之法律关系》"试论确定专利保护范围的等同原则"《WTO 加盟后中国法律的变化》《WTO 加盟后中国涉外投资法律的调整》《中国的工程建设项目招标范围和规模标准规定》《中国物权法试论中国现行不动产法制的主要问题及对策》《中国的招标投标法》（日文），《中国不动产法制的问题点》（日文），《中国的劳动合同的解除》（日文），《违法行为与董事责任》《日本公司法上的法人人格否认法理》《等同原则》《董事的内部控制义务探析》《股权回购的弊端及防范制度研究》《数字时代复制权各方利益平衡研究》《对赌条款法律效力辨析》。参加编写《经济法教程》《经济法案例评析》《中国水事案选》《中国水法教程》《经济法学》等教材。出版专著《流动动产让渡担保的对外效力》（日文），译著《日本公司法典》。

### 工作语言
中文、日语、英语

### 为中日经济保驾护航
近年来，中国经济高速发展，经济总量不断扩大，且拥有大量的贸易盈余，外汇储备逐年增加，有实力到海外投资的企业也逐年增多，对日投资也在不断扩大。作为曾留学日本、了解日本经济、日本文化的刘惠明律师自然要为中国企业赴日投资和活动提供法律帮助，保驾护航。

网址：www.zsmjlawyer.cn
详情请登录中国律师年鉴网：www.yearbooklawyer.com
— 080 —

# Mr. Liu Huiming

Liu Huiming, borned in Jingjiang City, Jiangsu Province, was graduated from the Department of Engineering Mechanics, Hohai University with a bachelor degree in engineering in 1985, and the Second Degree Course of Law School of Nanjing University with a second bachelor degree in law in 1989. From 1995 to 2001, he studied and worked in Japan. During the period, he studied civil and commercial law at the Law School of Hitotsubashi University, a famous university in Japan, and received a master degree in law. Furthermore, he engaged in advanced study at the University of California in the United States from 2001 to 2002. Later, he received a doctorate of philosophy in law from Nanjing University.

At present, he is a director of Jiangsu Zhongshan Mingjing Law Firm, a professor of Hohai University School of Law, a member of Nanjing Arbitration Commission, a leading foreign-related lawyer of All China Lawyers Association, one of top ten foreign-related lawyers of Jiangsu Province, a member of the foreign-related professional lawyer talent pool of Jiangsu Provincial Lawyers Association, vice president of Nanjing Returned Scholars Association, and vice president of Japanese Association for Doctorates.

## Specialized field

International economic and trade, foreign investment, intellectual property, real estate, and major labor dispute

## Main experience

Mr. Liu was a teacher in Hohai University since 1985 and had engaged in legal education for many years. In 1990, he won the qualification for lawyer and began practice as a lawyer. During study in Japan, he worked in a famous Japanese law firm for two years and served as secretary general of the Japan-China Lawyer Association and Jiangsu Reunion for Students in Japan. He is proficient in Chinese and Japanese laws and is mainly responsible for civil and commercial affairs, as well as Japanese related businesses.

With solid legal theory foundation, excellent defense capability and proficient foreign language skills, Mr. Liu has provided company merger and acquisition, international investment, international trade, intellectual property, labor management and other legal services for many renowned transnational corporations, such as KFC, Honda Motor, Nissan Motor, Sanyo Electric, Marubeni Corporation, Hitachi Metals and Mitsubishi Corporation. Now, He serves as legal advisor of many well known Japanese companies, such as Sumitomo Chemical, Ricoh Corporation, Nikon Corporation, Otsuka Chemical, Yokogawa Electric, Eisai Pharmaceutical, Paramount Bed and Prince Rubber.

Mr. Liu has handled a number of influential and difficult cases. For example, the patent dispute case between American largest chemical company and Japanese famous chemical company, and the dispute between Japanese famous trading company and American company on steel transactions are all large cases with huge subject amount. Besides, the reputation infringement case of Yu Yizhong and the classic case of company cultural relic auction received extensive attention, and even some cases were published in the *Gazette of the Supreme People's Court*. Moreover, Mr. Liu actively provided assistance to the bacterial warfare compensation lawsuit against the Japanese government, acted as an agent for the reputation case of Li Xiuying, a victim of the Nanjing Massacre, and in addition, took charge of research translation work.

网址：www.zsmjlawyer.cn
详情请登录中国律师年鉴网：www.yearbooklawyer.com
— 081 —

律 中国涉外律师

## 江苏 Jiangsu

Mr. Liu has taught many legal courses in the Hohai University School of Law. Now, he mainly teaches company law, negotiable instrument law, and intellectual property law, because he has high academic achievements in these fields.

**Writings**

During study in Japan, Mr. Liu published many papers in Chinese and Japanese language, as well as monographs and translations in Japanese. The main papers include "Realization of Human Rights and Protection of Legal Systems" "Legal Nature of Auction Behavior and Legal Relationship Formed" "Discussion of Equivalent Principles For Determining the Scope of Patent Protection" "Changes in Chinese Laws After WTO Accession" "Adjustments in the Foreign-related Investment Laws of China After WTO Accession" "Regulations on the Standards of Bidding Scope and Scale for China's Engineering Construction Projects" "Law of Chinese Property" "Discussion on the Main Problems and Countermeasures of Existing Real Estate Legal System in China","Law of the People's Republic of China on Tenders and Bids" (Japanese), "Problems of Chinese Real Estate Legal System" (Japanese) "Removal of Chinese Labor Contract" (Japanese), "Unlawful Acts and Responsibilities of Directors" "Denying Principle of the Personality of Legal Person in Japanese Company Law", and "Equivalent Principles" "Analysis of Internal Control Obligations of Directors" "Research on the Equity Repurchase Disadvantages and Prevention" "Research on the Balance of Interests of All Parties in Reproduction Rights in the Digital Age" and "Analysis on the Legal Effects of Gambling Clauses". He participated in the compilation of many textbooks, such as Economic Law Course, Analysis of "Economic Law Cases" "Selection of China Water-related Case" "Chinese Water Law Course" and "Economic Law", published the monograph "Foreign Effect of Alienation Guarantee of Current Movable Property" (Japanese) and translated the "Japanese Company Code".

**Working language**

Chinese, Japanese and English

**Guarantee of China–Japan economy**

In recent years, China's economy has developed at top speed, and the economic aggregate has continued to expand with large trade surplus. Besides, foreign exchange reserves have been increasing year by year and the same goes for the enterprises capable of overseas investment. The investment in Japan has also been expanding. As a lawyer who studied in Japan and understood the Japanese economy and Japanese culture, it is certain that Mr. Liu provides legal assistance and guarantee for investment and activities in Japan by Chinese companies.

网址：www.zsmjlawyer.cn
详情请登录中国律师年鉴网：www.yearbooklawyer.com
— 082 —

# 劉 恵明　弁護士

　劉　恵明弁護士は江蘇省靖江市の出身で 1985 年に河海大学工学部を卒業し、1989 年に南京大学法学部第二学位を取得した。1995 年から 2001 年まで日本で留学して就職した。その間、一橋大学大学院法学研究科民商法専攻をし、法学修士学位を取得した。後に南京大学法学部で法学博士学位を取得した。

　劉　恵明弁護士は現在河海大学法学部教授、南京仲裁委員会仲裁員、中華全国弁護士協会渉外　弁護士リーダ人材、江蘇省ベスト 10 渉外弁護士、江蘇省弁護士協会渉外弁護士人材バンクメンバーであり、そして江蘇鐘山明鏡法律事務所所長、南京市留学帰国　人員親睦会副会長と留日博士協会副会長を担任する。

## 得意の業務分野
　国際経済貿易、外商投資、知的財産権、不動産、労務紛争処理。

## 主な経歴
　1985 年から河海大学の教師として法学教育に携わった。1990 年に弁護士資格を取得し、弁護士としての仕事を始めた。日本に滞在する間に、日本有名な弁護士事務所に 2 年間勤め、在日中国弁護士連合会、留日江蘇同窓会事務局長を歴任した。劉　恵明弁護士は中国と日本の法律を精通し、民商法関する業務と日本業務を主に担当している。2001 年に帰国してから、江蘇鐘山明鏡法律事務所所長に就任し、江蘇省及び安徽省における数少ない日本での留学経験を持ち、日本語及び日本の民法・商法などを精通する弁護士として活躍している。

　本田、東芝、三洋電機、丸紅、日立金属、三菱商事など有名な会社に M ＆ A、国際投資、国際貿易、知的財産権、労務管理にかかる法律サービスを提供したことがある。現在、住友化学、ニコン、大塚化学、横河電機、衛材、王子ゴムなどの日系企業の法律顧問を担任している。また、数多くの大きな事件を処理した経験はある。

　劉恵明弁護士は河海大学法学部で多くの法律科目の講義を行った。現在、主に会社法、手形法、破産法、知的財産法を教えて多くの研究成果をあげている。

## 著作
　劉　恵明弁護士は中国語、日本語で多数の論文と著作を出版した。例えば「特許の保護範囲における均等論」「中国における不動産法制の問題点」「流動動産譲渡担保の対外的効力」「中国における入札と入札法」「WTO 加盟に伴う中国法律の整備」「中国における労働契約の解除」「中国の物権法」「違法行為と取締役の責任」「日本の法人人格否認法理及び実践」「日本会社法訳文」「取締役の内部統制責任」などである。

## 仕事言語
　中国語、日本語、英語

## 中国及び日本の経済発展のため
　労働問題、債権回収をはじめ、新規事業の立上げ、国内営業網の企画立案、知的財産権、立退問題処理、企業の解散・清算、訴訟・仲裁などのトラブル解決等々の分野で、お客様に全面的かつ迅速で効率のよい法律サービスを提供する。

网址：www.zsmjlawyer.cn
详情请登录中国律师年鉴网：www.yearbooklawyer.com
— 083 —

江苏 Jiangsu

## 秦华平 律师

江苏国瑞律师事务所主任。张家港市政府法律顾问、张家港市政协法律顾问、张家港市法律专家咨询委员会成员。

### 经历

秦华平律师 1989 年毕业于中国政法大学国际经济法系，1995 年开始从事律师职业，1995 ～ 1996 年工作于张家港市对外经济律师事务所，1997 ～ 1998 年工作于苏州合力律师事务所，1998 年合伙设立江苏国瑞律师事务所并担任主任。张家港市律师协会第三届副会长，第四、五届会长；苏州市律师协会第五届副会长。

### 业务专长

国际投资和贸易、国内企业并购改制、政府法律业务、金融证券、清算破产、并购重组、疑难民商案件等方面的诉讼与非诉讼业务。

### 主要业绩

在 20 多年的职业生涯中，秦华平律师为中外客户提供过大量的诉讼和非诉讼法律服务，包括项目投资过程中的全程法律服务，企业规章制度等内部治理构建，并购、股权转让、清算、破产重组，策划和制订企业知识产权保护制度，策划和制订企业的节税制度，策划和制订企业劳资制度。常年担任张家港市区域内十多家企业集团和地方政府的法律顾问，其中包括江苏沙钢集团、江苏永钢集团、长江润发集团等本地区规模企业。

近年来被人民法院指定担任管理人处理的企业破产重组案件：江苏龙马纺织集团有限公司破产清算案、江苏华邦物流有限公司破产重整案、张家港市色织厂有限公司破产清算案、张家港新丰纺织破产清算、飞腾集团及泰普奇装饰材料公司、庆顺贸易公司破产清算案、华显光电破产清算案。

### 荣誉

2016 年江苏省优秀律师、2008 ～ 2009 年度苏州市先进律师事务所主任、张家港市首届十佳律师、首届十佳法律服务工作者。多次被评为张家港市司法行政先进工作者。

### 著作

《公司董事的义务和失责追究》《论民事诉讼中的自认》《律师的诚信建设》《律师在破产改制企业群体事件中的作用》《有限责任公司章程限制股权转让效力效力研究和实证分析》。

# Lawyer Qin Huaping

Director of Jiangsu Guorui Law Firm, legal adviser to the Zhangjiagang Municipal Government and the Zhangjiagang Municipal Peoplemedia report's Political Consultative Conference, member of the Zhangjiagang Municipal Legal Experts Advisory Committee.

## Experience

Lawyer Qin Huaping graduated from the Department of International Economic Law of the China University of Political Science and Law in 1989, began to practice as a lawyer in 1995, worked at Zhangjiagang Foreign Economic Law Firm during 1995 ～ 1996 and at Suzhou Heli Law Firm during 1997 ～ 1998, and established Jiangsu Guorui Law Firm jointly as Director in 1998. He was the third vice chairman, the fourth and fifth chairmen of Zhangjiagang Lawyers Association, the fifth vice chairman of Suzhou Lawyers Association.

## Expertise

Litigious and non-litigious operations in international investment and trade, domestic enterprise M&A and restructuring, government legal affairs, finance and securities, liquidation and bankruptcy, M&A and reorganization, difficult civil and commercial cases, etc..

## Key achievements

In his over-two-decade career, lawyer Qin Huaping provided extensive litigious and non-litigious services to Chinese and overseas customers, including legal services throughout the project investment process; internal governance building inclusive of corporate rules and regulations; M&A, equity transfer, liquidation and bankruptcy reorganization; planning and development of corporate intellectual property protection systems; planning and development of corporate tax avoidance systems; and planning and development of corporate labor-management systems.

He serves as legal adviser to over ten business groups and local governments in the jurisdiction of Zhangjiagang City on a long-term basis, including local large-scale enterprises such as Jiangsu Shagang Group, Jiangsu Yonggang Group and Changjiang Runfa Group. The corporate bankruptcy reorganization cases handled by him as designated by people's courts in recent years include the bankruptcy liquidation cases of Jiangsu Longma Textile Group Co., Ltd., Zhangjiagang Yarn-dyed Mill Co., Ltd., Zhangjiagang Xinfeng Textile, Feiteng Group, Taipuqi Decorative Materials Co., Ltd., Qingshun Trading Co., Ltd. and China Display Optoelectronics Technology Holdings Limited, as well as the bankruptcy reorganization of Jiangsu Huabang Logistics Co., Ltd..

## Honors

Excellent Lawyer of Jiangsu Province in 2016；

Leading Law Firm Director of Suzhou City in Year 2008 ～ 2009, First Top 10 Lawyers of Zhangjiagang City；

First Top 10 Legal Workers of Zhangjiagang City；

Outstanding Judicial and Administrative Worker of Zhangjiagang City (many times).

## Works

"Obligations and Investigation of Defaults of Corporate Directors"；

"Self-confession in Civil Actions"；

"Integrity Building of Lawyers"；

"Role of Lawyers in Group Events of Bankrupt and Restructured Enterprises"；

"Study and Empirical Analysis on the Validity of Equity Transfer Restriction by Articles of Association of Limited Liability Companies".

网址：www.grsws.com
详情请登录中国律师年鉴网：www.yearbooklawyer.com
— 085 —

# 三、优秀涉外律师访谈

# 宣传知识产权保护意识，为知识产权保驾护航

## ——访"北京市十佳知识产权律师"、北京罗杰律师事务所主任、

## 法学博士罗正红律师

在全球经济一体化程度日益加深的今天，知识产权已成为企业参与市场竞争的重要武器，而"世界未来的竞争就是知识产权的竞争"已成业界共识。

今天我们要采访的主人公就是一位在知识产权领域，尤其在涉外知识产权保护方面，已深耕27个春秋的法律人，他就是北京罗杰律师事务所主任、法学博士罗正红律师。

罗正红律师是一位学者型律师。笔者了解到，1991年罗正红律师自中国人民大学知识产权法专业第二学士毕业后，即开始在一家中美合资公司从事知识产权保护及其他法务工作。1999年，他在中国"青年律师培训项目"全国选拔中胜出，受中国司法部选派、英国政府资助前往英国伦敦大学深造，学习欧洲法律，并在英国律师事务所学习律师实务；同时，他也获得中国国家留学基金委员会访问学者奖学金，在伦敦大学以访问学者身份进行知识产权学习和研究。2000年取得英国伦敦大学国王学院知识产权法学硕士学位；2002年，考取中国人民大学知识产权法专业法学博士，师从刘春田教授，2008年获得法学博士学位。其博士论文《商标权刑事保护研究》更是从国际视野对比研究中、英、美知识产权刑事保护的理论和实践，更是对其多年知识产权刑事保护实务的总结，对同业者具有重要的参考价值。即使10年后的今天，其博士论文仍具有非常重要的现实指导意义。

罗正红律师执业经历丰富，2008年起开始担任英国鸿鹄律师事务所权益合伙人。在全国30多万名执业律师中，曾担任过外国律师事务所知识产权权益合伙人的中国律师屈指可数。罗正红律师曾担任北京市律师协会商标法律专业委员会主任（2012～2015年），国际商标协会反假冒委员会中国区主席（2010～2011年），中国外商投资企业协会优质品牌保护委员会（QBPC）副主席（2008～2010年，QBPC现有近200家国际跨国公司会员），摩托罗拉北亚区知识产权总监（2007～2008年），北京市仲裁委员会仲裁员五年（2007～2012年），美国贝克·坚时律师事务所知识产权律师（2000～2007年）等，同时他还担任着最高人民法院知识产权案例指导研究（北京）基地专家咨询委员专家。

罗正红律师的客户几乎都是世界500强公司。若百度搜索"罗正红"，他的名字经常与路易威登（Louis Vuitton）、香奈儿（Chanel）、古驰（Gucci）、普拉达（Prada）、博柏利（Burberry）、迈克高仕（Michael Kors）、韩国MCM（MCM）、杰尼亚（Zegna）、阿玛尼（Armani）、花花公子（Playboy）、微软（Microsoft）等世界级企业及众多国际高知名度品牌联系在一起。多年来，罗正红律师也成为了国际高知名度品牌企业权益的保驾护航者。

国际法律评级机构"钱伯斯"这样评价：罗正红律师通晓法律，及时回复客户咨询，能为客户提供务实、有建设性的法律建议。众所周知，罗正红律师在知识产权诉讼及与国际品牌公司合作的经验方面非常著名。罗正红律师为团队带来宝贵的国际律所经验，特别在商标保护领域，他是国外客户的优先选择。

"法律500强"（Legal 500）：罗杰律师事务所以商标诉讼闻名。主任合伙人罗正红博士在商标诉讼方面享有盛誉。

"世界商标评论"：罗正红律师因其代理众多著名奢侈品公司进行不倦的打假维权而受到钦佩。

国际法律评级机构"Legal Band"：罗正红律师，知识产权诉讼领域的优秀从业者，具有广泛的商标诉讼经验，其专业性及出众的商务技能在知名奢侈品牌企业中享有盛誉……

### 为知识产权保驾护航

作家最美丽的语言是作品，那么律师最美丽的语言就是案例了。一直致力于代理国际高知名度品牌企业维权的罗正红律师带领团队每年提起数十件涉及侵害商标权、著作权、不正当竞争民事诉讼案件。自2009年担任北京罗杰律师事务所主任以来，他带领团队办理了一大批具有里程碑意义的案件，例如，（1）代理最高人民法院审理的"竹家庄避风塘及图"注册商标争议再审案并胜诉，该案被最高人民法院评选为"2014年中国法院10大知识产权案件"，同时该案也成为对知识产权的权利边界做出认定的典型案例；（2）代理最高人民法院审理的"Too Faced及图"商标异议再审案并胜诉，商标评审委员会被责令重新作出裁定。该案被最高人民法院收录于"2017年最高人民法院知识产权年度报告"中；（3）代理最高人民法院审理的"花花公子图标"（Playboy ICON）商标侵权案并胜诉；（4）代理路易威登马利蒂（Louis Vuitton）诉安徽白马商贸城侵害商标权纠纷案胜诉，该案被最高人民法院评为"2014年中国法院50件典型知识产权案例；（5）代理香奈儿股

罗正红博士访问德国时与德国律所合伙人在一起

罗正红与人民大学同学毕业 20 周年后再聚首

份有限公司（Chanel）诉文大香、广州凯旋大酒店有限公司等侵害商标权纠纷案以及勃贝雷有限公司（Burberry）诉陈凯、鲁秋敏侵害商标权纠纷案均被最高人民法院列入2015 年 9 月 9 日公布的"北京、上海、广州知识产权法院审结的典型案例"；（6）代理路易威登马利蒂（Louis Vuitton）、香奈儿股份有限公司（Chanel）、勃贝雷有限公司（Burberry）和普拉达有限公司（Prada）在广州法院联合提起的市场管理单位侵害商标权纠纷系列案件，被中国外商投资企业协会优质品牌保护委员会（QBPC）评为"2015至 2016 年度知识产权保护十佳案例"；（7）代理勃贝雷有限公司（Burberry）诉宁波中轻进出口公司定牌加工商标侵权案获 QBPC"2017 至 2018 年度知识产权保护十佳案例"。

此外，罗正红律师及团队代理的多个案件还曾被辽宁省高级人民法院、安徽省高级人民法院等列为所属辖区的十大知识产权典型案例。

### 宣传知识产权保护意识，锲而不舍

多年来，罗正红律师还经常受邀参加各种国际知识产权高峰论坛及研讨会，进行现场演讲或接受媒体采访，宣传知识产权保护意识，例如，（1）应邀为中美商会、欧盟商会、国际反假冒联盟、日本贸易振兴机构等协会讲授知识产权保护策略及执法实务；（2）应英国《知识产权管理》杂志邀请，在 2007 年 12 月小型知识产权圆桌会议上讲授知识产权保护和管理经验；（3）多次应邀参加美国大使知识产权圆桌会议；（4）2012 年 5 月，在"2012 年中美知识产权司法审判研讨会"上用英文演讲"帮助侵权的法律责任"，1000 多位中美知识产权专业人士参会，其中 200多位中国知识产权法官参会；（5）2012 年 10 月，应美国伯克利大学法学院邀请，与最高人民法院法官及中国人民大学教授等代表团成员，共同讲授中国著作权保护及存在的法律问题；（6）2013 年 5 月，应美国商会、美国联邦上诉律师协会邀请，作为中国代表团成员，在华盛顿举行的中国知识产权保护会议上用英文讲授"中国知识产权司法保护的进展"；（7）2013 年 12 月，应邀在"知识产权法律应用高层论坛"中演讲，讲授"中国知识产权损害赔偿及市场管理单位法律责任"等议题，超过 700 多位知识产权法官及其他知识产权专业人士参会；（8）应美国富兰克林皮尔斯法学院邀请，多次用英文在清华大学法学院为来自美国、加拿大等国家法学院的学生讲授中国知识产权保护中的法律问题及策略；（9）应香港浸会大学、中国人民大学、北京大学、复旦大学及华东政法学院的邀请，为MBA 及法律硕士生讲授中国知识产权保护中的法律实务；（10）2013 年 11 月 25 日，中国之声 CNTV 对罗正红律师进行访谈，主题为"创新型国家的诞生需要知识产权的保护"；（11）2015 年 4 月，在首届中国知识产权法院论坛上作为律师代表发表演讲；（12）2015 年 7 月，华人频道 HRTV 对罗正红律师进行英文访谈，主题为"罗正红律师——知识产权的保驾护航者"。罗律师也曾接受中央电视台英文频道《对话》的专访。

这样的履历、经历和业绩已足以诠释罗正红律师对知识产权事业的热爱，他深爱着知识产权的建设与保护工作，数十年如一日坚守至今，可谓持之以恒、始终如一，锲而不舍、矢志不渝。

### 为中国企业"走出去"保驾护航

近年来，随着中国企业"走出去"战略和"一带一路"建设的深入推进，各个行业、各个领域的有识之士皆在为中国经济实现全球化布局建言献策、竭尽所能。鉴于罗正红律师在国际知识产权保护领域的从业经验和贡献，2017年，罗正红律师被中华全国律师协会知识产权委员会选拔为"一带一路"及国际业务组组长。罗正红律师深感自豪，同时更觉责任重大。"我做知识产权工作已有 27 年，可以说是中国知识产权保护工作发展的一个见证者和推动者。我希望在未来的岁月里，可以利用自身海外工作经历和涉外知识产权维权经验为更多的中国企业实现海外布局和参与国际竞争保驾护航，贡献自己的绵薄之力。"采访结束罗正红律师深有感触地道。

我们相信，在未来的岁月里，在中国经济逐步实现全球化布局的今天，罗正红律师一定能为中国企业做好保驾护航的工作，为中国企业海外知识产权保护工作书写更加绚丽辉煌的篇章。

# Advocating and Advancing IP Protection

——An Interview with James Luo, Doctor of Laws, a "Top 10 IP Lawyer in Beijing", and Director of Beijing Lawjay Firm

Today, with the deepening of global economic integration, intellectual property has become a prized weapon for competing in the global market. The prediction that "the future competition of the world is the competition of intellectual property rights" has now indeed become a reality.

The thought leader we are going to interview today is a person who has been deeply involved in the field of IP protection for 27 years, especially the protection of the IPs of foreign or multinational companies. He is the director of Beijing Lawjay firm and holds a PhD in law, James Luo.

James Luo is an esteemed legal scholar and a skilled litigator. James Luo earned his LLB in IP in 1991 at the Renmin University of China Law School. In 1999, he stood out from among his peers in the national selection process for the "Young PRC Lawyers Training Program" organized by the Ministry of Justice and sponsored by the British government, and was sent to the University of London where he studied European IP law, and honed his legal practice at a prestigious UK law firm. Through a scholarship granted by the China Scholarship Council, James Luo conducted studies and research in IP as a visiting scholar at the University of London. In 2000, he earned his LLM in IP at King's College London, University of London, and in 2008, obtained his PhD in IP at Renmin University of China Law School. A product of his many years of criminal law practice, his PhD dissertation, a research on the "Criminal Protection of Trademark Rights" is a comparative study of the underlying theories and practices on the criminal protection of IP rights in China, UK and USA, which, even today, remains to be a highly important and practical guide and reference to scholars and practitioners alike.

With nearly 30 years of extensive legal experience, James Luo is an established legal authority in IP litigation and enforcement. He is a former equity partner of top international law firm Bird & Bird LLP, which in itself is an outstanding professional achievement, given that, of over 300 000 lawyers in China, only a handful have served as equity partners in foreign law firms. James Luo have likewise served as IP director for North Asia of Motorola China, sat as arbitrator at the Beijing Arbitration Commission, and have worked for Baker & McKenzie Hong Kong and Beijing and other prestigious law firms.

In addition, James Luo presently sits as a legal expert of the Supreme People's Court's Beijing IP Case Law Center, and have served as trademark committee chair of the Beijing Bar Association, China sub-committee chair of INTA's anti-counterfeiting committee, and vice chair of the Quality Brands Protection Committee (QBPC) of the China Association of Enterprises with Foreign Investment (CAEFI).

Nearly all of James Luo's clients are from Fortune 500 companies. If you search his name on the internet, you will find that he is often associated with Louis Vuitton, Chanel, Gucci, Prada, Burberry, Michael Kors, MCM, Zegna, Armani, Playboy, Microsoft and many other high-profile international companies and world-famous brands. For many years, James Luo has been making profound contributions to protecting the rights and interests of many of the world's most renowned brands.

## Comments made about James and his firm by his peers and major legal publications

•James Luo is counsel of choice amongst overseas clients. His clients comment: "I have always thought very highly of James. He is efficient and we have confidence in him. Noted for his strong track record handling significant IP lawsuits, he is a trusted adviser to prominent luxury brands."—— Chambers and Partners

•Managing partner James Luo has significant experience in trademark and copyright litigation. —— The Legal 500

•Highly effective and a leader in the fight against fakes', James Luo has an in-depth understanding of the courts and is a frequent fixture in important trademark infringement cases. Considered a thought leader, he sits on the Supreme Court's IP Case Law Centre experts committee. "He is at the apex of the profession, widely admired by clients and competitors alike." —— World Trademark Review

In 2012 and 2013, Lawjay Partners was shortlisted by Chambers and Partners for Boutique PRC Law Firm of the

In 2012 and 2013, Lawjay Partners was shortlisted by Chambers and Partners for Boutique PRC Law Firm of the Year, the only IP firm nominated in the category. Recently, the firm was also ranked as among the 2017 Asian Legal Business Top 10 Firms to Watch by Thomson Reuters and the 2016 Top 10 IP litigation law firms by IP House.

**Contributions to IP Protection**

Just as a writer best expresses himself through his books, the greatness of a lawyer is best seen through his cases. Since becoming the director of Beijing Lawjay firm in 2009, James Luo, leading a strong team of top-caliber IP lawyers, represents various top luxury brands and world famous marks in over a hundred of civil and criminal lawsuits trademark and copyright infringement and unfair competition yearly, and many of such cases have become landmark cases setting "precedents" on the subject matter. Among the recent victories he had won for top brands include the "Playboy ICON" trademark infringement retrial case at the Supreme People's Court; the "Too Faced & Envy Device" trademark opposition retrial case at the Supreme People's Court, where the Trademark Review and Adjudication Board was ordered to make a new decision; obtaining an award of RMB 4.3 million in damages in a trademark infringement action against an online counterfeiter and its online service provider, winning a lawsuit against an OEM that exported counterfeit goods, and a triumphant lawsuit against a popular Chinese e-commerce platform that sold fake luxury goods. Likewise, the Supreme Court and the China National Bar Association respectively ranked the "Zhujiazhuang Typhoon Shelter & Device" trademark dispute case he handled as among the top 10 IP litigation cases in China. The joint civil actions of Burberry, Chanel, LVM and Prada against Guangzhou Baiyun Leather Market, Guangzhou Yi Ma Fashion Market for trademark infringement ranked as among the QBPC's top ten best practice cases for 2015-2016. The Supreme Court also ranked LVM's landlord liability case against Hefei Baima Market as among the 2014 top 50 best practices IP litigation cases in China, while other cases were selected as top 10 IP litigation cases in other provinces.

**A Persistent Advocate of IP Protection**

For many years, James Luo has been consistently invited to participate in, deliver presentations at various international IP summits and seminars, and interviewed by the media to promote and advocate IP protection. Among his recent presentations, talks and interviews are:

(1)Presentations on "IP Enforcement Strategy in China" delivered to QBPC, IACC, AmCham, EU Chamber of Commerce, JETRO, etc.;

(2)Presentations on "Anti-Counterfeiting in China" delivered to law students of the Franklin Pierce Law Center and top Chinese law schools;

(3)TV interview: "Creating an Innovative Nation Requires IP Protection" (in Chinese), China Talk, CNTV, 25 November 2013;

(4)TV interview: "A Talk with James Luo: Defender of Intellectual Property Rights" (in English), Huaren Huiketing, HRTV, July 2015;

(5)Lecture on "The Recent Developments on IP Protection in China", 2016 Sino-US IP Seminar, Shenzhen, China, November 2016;

(6)Presentation on "Shaping Your Environment: Building and Managing the Brand Protection Function", World Trademark Review: Brand Protection in China, Shanghai, China, December 2016;

(7)Presentation on "Several Issues on Trademark Prosecution and Trademark Infringement in China", UK IP Office Trademark Workshop, London, December 2016.

Such background, experiences and achievements are enough to show James Luo's passion for his IP law career. He is deeply passionate with his work in advancing and protecting intellectual property rights, has been pouring tremendous efforts in IP protection for decades, and is committed to continuing his distinguished career in IP protection long into the future.

**Contributions to the "Going Global Strategy" of Chinese Enterprises**

In recent years, in light of the Going Global Strategy of Chinese enterprises and China's pursuance of the massive "Belt and Road" initiative, various industry experts have made proposals for and have given their best efforts to realize the globalization of the Chinese economy. In view of James Luo's experience and contributions in the field of international IP protection, he was selected by the intellectual property committee of All China Lawyers Association as the leader of their "Belt and Road" and international business group in 2007. James Luo was very proud about it since it is such an important job. "I have been practicing IP law for 27 years, and it is safe to say that I am a witness to, and a promoter of, the development of IP protection in China. Capitalizing on my experience working overseas and in protecting the IPs of multinational companies, I hope that, in the future, I can contribute to helping more Chinese enterprises venture and expand overseas and vigorously compete in the global market," said James Luo at the end of the interview.

We believe that, in the future, along with further globalization of China's economy, James Luo will be helping more Chinese enterprises, and blaze the trails in providing overseas IP protection to Chinese companies.

# 为"一带一路"建设保驾护航

## ——访中国中小企业协会"一带一路"工作委员会
## 法律服务部部长姚惠娟律师

2013 年 9 月和 10 月，国家主席习近平在出访中亚和东南亚国家期间，先后提出共建"丝绸之路经济带"和"21 世纪海上丝绸之路"的重大倡议，得到国际社会高度关注和响应。2015 年 3 月 28 日，国家发展改革委员会、外交部、商务部联合发布《推动共建丝绸之路经济带和 21 世纪海上丝绸之路的愿景与行动》（简称"一带一路"）。该文件指出："一带一路"将充分依靠中国与有关国家既有的双多边机制，借助既有的、行之有效的区域合作平台，高举和平发展的旗帜，积极发展与沿线国家的经济合作伙伴关系，共同打造政治互信、经济融合、文化包容的利益共同体、命运共同体和责任共同体。这是国家级的顶层设计，对于世界经济的发展意义重大而深远。

2017 年 5 月 4 日，中国国家安全部与 20 多个国家安全部门"一带一路"安全合作对话会在北京举行，会上，中共中央政治局委员、中央政法委书记孟建柱指出：只有安全稳定的环境，才能推动"一带一路"建设更快向前迈进。笔者以为，这里的环境当然包括"一带一路"沿线国家的法治环境。

2018 年 7 月 25 日，在"一带一路"倡议提出 5 周年之际，由中国中小企业协会"一带一路"工作委员成立的"法律服务部"任命了一位在涉外法律领域坚守 30 多个春秋，且仍服务于一线的涉外律师担任该法律服务部的负责人，她就是本文的主人公——北京市东元律师事务所创始合伙人、西安分所主任姚惠娟律师。中国中小企业协会"一带一路"工作委员会法律服务部为何会任命一位专职律师担任该部的负责人？笔者以为，这应该是姚惠娟律师在涉外法律领域丰富的经验，骄人的业绩和丰硕的成果，以及已步入天命之年仍坚持在一线办案的精神得到了委员会的一致青睐和高度认可。今天就让笔者带领大家一起来进一步认识这位被媒体誉为"国际舞台上连接中西方文化交流的铿锵玫瑰"的中国女律师吧。

### 与国际法律事务结缘

姚惠娟律师与国际法律事务的肇始和渊源，还要追朔到 20 世纪 80 年代。姚惠娟律师于 1984 年开始从事律师工作，参加工作不久即被司法部选定（西安市仅一个名额）到上海参加国际律师培训，成为了中国第一批涉外经济律师；她于 1986 年参加首届全国律师资格统一考试，成绩位居西安榜首；1988 年参与组建西安市涉外经济律师事务所，全面负责外贸公司业务，并参与了在陕的 9 大进出口公司中 6 家公司的法律事务；她曾被聘任为联合国艺术家理事会法律顾问，获得"联合国国际友好使者"称号，接受联合国前秘书长潘基文、美国前总统克林顿等的亲切接见；美国历史上著名的第一位华人女议员赵美心、著名的社会活动家华侨陈香梅也与她进行了亲切的交流。所以，媒体评价她为"国际舞台上连接中西方文化交流的铿锵玫瑰"。除此，姚惠娟律师现还担任着中华全国律师协会企业法律顾问专业委员会委员、中国侨联法律顾问委员会委员、中国音乐学院名誉院长金铁霖法律顾问、南京仲裁委员会仲裁员、西安仲裁委员会仲裁员、榆林仲裁委员会仲裁员等。《中国当代优秀律师》这样评价姚惠娟律师："她是一位在中国律师发展史上、在世界的舞台上书写着不凡与传奇的中国女律师"。

作为中国第一批涉外律师，姚惠娟律师在 20 世纪八九十年代就参与了各类国际诉讼和仲裁案件，代表中国企业迈向世界舞台，维护企业权益，帮助中国企业在国际市场上平等参与竞争。我们从近年姚惠娟律师参与的部分国际项目或诉讼仲裁案件中即可见一斑。

2009 年 12 月至 2014 年 3 月，姚惠娟律师与郭阳等律师作为酒钢钢铁（集团）有限责任公司的代理人，办理某公司与酒钢集团国际钢材买卖合同国际仲裁案，在面对某公司聘请的法国、德国律师团队时，她与郭阳律师在事实的细致分析、证据的合理运用、法律的正确使用下，全面维护了酒钢钢铁的合法利益。除此之外，姚惠娟律师代理的海事货物纠纷、国际贸易货物品质纠纷等均维护了委托方的最大合法利益。

2017 年，租赁界"航母"——工银金融租赁有限公司（工银金融租赁有限公司成立于 2007 年 11 月 28 日，是国务院确定试点并首家获中国银监会批准开业的银行系金融租赁公司，是中国工商银行的全资子公司，注册资本 110 亿元人民币）发布法律顾问服务招标公告，数十家律所前往，有着 30 多年企业法律顾问实务经验并始终坚守在一线办案的姚惠娟律师获得公司高层高度重视，最终成功入驻企业律师库。之后作为代理人办理有关案件，取得满意成果。

2018 年 7 月 25 日，被中国中小企业协会"一带一路"工作委员任命为法律服务部部长实属众望所归、人心所向。当然，姚惠娟律师感到肩上的担子更重，责任也更大了，她不能辜负这份信赖和重托。

据美国《财富》杂志报道，美国中小企业平均寿命不到

中国侨联法顾委海外律师团与中国中小企业协会"一带一路"工作委员会共同举办国际法律服务交流座谈会

第一排（从左至右）：日本 TMI 律师事务所律师何连明；西班牙德源房产律师事务所律师陈静；加拿大陈维鹃律师事务所律师陈维鹃；德国温氏律师事务所律师温天敏；新西兰律师奥克兰市政府 WHAU 地区议会议员、议会副主席朱旭东；墨西哥阚凤芹律师与翻译事务所律师阚凤芹；中国中小企业协会"一带一路"工作委员会法律服务部部长姚惠娟；美国赵联律师事务所律师赵联；葡萄牙 PLMJ 律师事务所律师林蔓；泰国尼采律师事务所方文川夫人章红媛；美国黄笑生国际律师行律师黄笑生

第二排（从左至右）：中国中小企业协会"一带一路"工作委员会秘书长吴宏宇；中国中小企业协会"一带一路"工作委员会主任商世伟；德国豪埃森律师事务所律师张志远；巴西天宇会计师、律师事务所律师诸诗琦；美国王志东律师事务所律师王志东；法国德恒律师事务所律师石仁林；南非孙氏律师事务所律师、南非约翰堡市议员、市公共安全局局长孙耀亨；澳大利亚蔡庆伟律师事务所蔡庆伟；马来西亚蔡文洲律师楼律师蔡文洲；香港施若龙律师行律师施若龙；澳大利亚郑玉桂律师事务所律师郑玉桂；美国合众律师事务所律师梁仲平；澳大利亚王柏沂律师事务所律师王柏沂；英国邓汉声律师事务所律师邓汉声；意大利吴恩斌律师事务所律师吴恩斌；泰国尼采律师事务所律师方文川；印尼立诚律师事务所律师张永渊；新加坡正气律师事务所律师萧锦耀；马来西亚罗章武律师事务所律师罗章武；国浩（巴黎）律师事务所孙涛；中国侨联联法律顾文委员会委员、权益保障部副部长黄晖。

7 年，大企业平均寿命不足 40 年。而在中国，中小企业的平均寿命仅 2.5 年，集团企业的平均寿命仅 7～8 年。美国每年倒闭的企业约 10 万家，而中国有 100 万家，是美国的 10 倍。不仅企业的生命周期短，能做大做强的企业更是廖廖无几。据笔者观察，中国企业，尤其是民营企业，其现实情况是因企业经营不善或涉重大诉讼破产，因行政处罚致股价下跌，企业及企业负责人因涉刑事风险而身陷囹圄等不一而足，而这些归根结底皆是法律问题，皆是没有重视规则的问题。而"一带一路"沿线的国家迄今已增至 65 个，每个国家的政治、经济、文化、法律环境又有不同，中国中小企业又普遍缺乏参与国际经营和竞争的人才和经验，这就为中国中小企业"走出去"提出了严峻的考验。中国中小企业协会"一带一路"工作委员法律服务部的成立可谓正当其时，亦是顺应时代发展的大势所趋。当然，无论是"引进来"，还是"走出去"，在这场全球经济治理的深度变革与发展中，中国涉外律师都将任重而道远。

### 对话中国中小企业协会"一带一路"工作委员会 法律服务部部长姚惠娟律师

**赵伟主编：** 姚律师您好，2018 年是中国改革开放的第 40 个年头，而作为在涉外法律领域服务已 30 多个春秋的老一代法律人，您应是最有发言权的涉外律师之一，可否谈谈您对"一带一路"建设中，中国企业参与国际竞争以及国际法律事务的一些看法和想法？

**姚惠娟律师：** 好的，我想先就国际贸易中我们企业所面临的困境在此作下总结。要发展就要先将可能面临的困难和风险做下系统性的评估，这样才能做到胸有成竹稳步发展，而不是"一拍脑门"就做决定，最终造成重大经济损失而无法收场，中国企业在"走出去"的多年中已经交了不少的"学费"，所以我们不能再重蹈覆辙。在"一带一路"发展中，各企业也会不同程度地遇到各种各样的问题。首先是人才匮乏。中小企业普遍缺乏国际化经营人才和经验，在国际市场竞争中往往处于弱势地位，难以有效识别海外各国的法律、政治、经济、社会、环境、安全等方面存在的潜在风险，对沿线国家的行业政策、法律环境、风俗习惯等方面缺乏了解。二是我国大部分中小企业在全球产业链中，处于价值链的低端，缺乏品牌和国际销售渠道，国际竞争能力弱。中国企业与西方跨国公司相比有明显的"后发劣势"，大部分只能到投资环境差、风险高的国家和行业去寻找机会，有的市场看似空间巨大，实则有效需求不足，盲目进入将带来高风险。三是，我国海外投资起步较晚，企业不熟悉国际市场、缺乏

海外投资经验，以及会计、律师、咨询等中介机构发展程度低、风险评估能力弱等问题比较突出。海外国家的政治、经济、社会环境复杂多变，语言文化、商业规则、法律体系、行业标准等与国内截然不同，这就对中国企业的适应能力和管理水平提出了更高的要求。走出去的中国企业还面临着信息不对称、资源碎片化、恶性竞争等问题，既不利于力量整合统筹，也容易造成资源重复浪费。四是"一带一路"沿线国家和地区的金融环境并不完善，对中国企业的金融支持有限。

**赵伟主编：** 既然中国企业"走出去"有这么多困难和风险，那么我们又该如何应对呢？中国律师或海外律师又该如何为中国企业尤其是中小企业提供法律保障呢？

**姚惠娟律师：** 这就是中国中小企业协会"一带一路"工作委员会成立法律服务部的初衷，我们建立的是一个中外律师合作交流的平台。我们通过建立中外律师交流合作的这个平台，已经达成为中小企业国际法律事务健康发展提供优良服务的共识。同时，我们还积极建立宣传联络平台，通过法律、政治、经济、文化的互相沟通和交流，增加了解和加强国际事务处理的民情基础，形成联动；促进国内、国外律师事务所的密切合作；帮助中国中小企业"走出去"，并帮助海外企业"引进来"；积极发挥法律防范风险的作用，做到预防在前，长期提供所在国的法律服务。争取为国际法律事务的建设及各国海外贸易企业，提供更加优质的法律服务。由于"一带一路"沿线国家和地区法律制度参差多态，法治环境复杂多变，所以"一带一路"建设法律服务不可或缺，或者可以说是"刚需"。

**赵伟主编：** 近来您参与了哪些与国际法律事务相关的活动，在此可否与我们做下分享？

**姚惠娟律师：** 好的。参加活动很多，我仅就在2018年8月17日至18日，"一带一路"倡议提出五周年，中国侨联法顾委海外律师团成立十周年纪念及中国侨联法顾委海外律师团与中国中小企业协会"一带一路"工作委员会共同举办的国际法律服务交流座谈会作下简要汇总。

会议开幕式上，中国侨联法顾委主任张耕同志回顾了海外律师团成立的历程，张耕主任表示：经过10年的壮大发展，中国侨联法顾委海外律师团已成为一道亮丽的海外维权风景线。他希望委员们扬法律之利剑、持正义之天平，积极参与推进中外法律机构交流与合作，切实维护海外侨胞权益，为"一带一路"的顺利实施和帮助更多中国企业"走出去"提供优质的法律支持和服务。

我既是中国中小企业协会"一带一路"工作委员会法律服务部的负责人，同时也是中国侨联法顾委海外律师团成员，是中国侨联法顾委的一位老委员。

8月18日，中国侨联法顾委海外律师团与中国中小企业协会"一带一路"工作委员会共同举办了国际法律服务交流座谈会。此次座谈会参会律师包含澳大利亚、德国、法国、英国、俄罗斯、葡萄牙、西班牙、意大利、美国、加拿大、马来西亚、日本、新加坡、印尼、墨西哥、南非、巴西等18个国家以及中国香港地区共28位境外律师代表。

现在也在准备2018年12月15日举办的"一带一路"优秀法律服务项目颁奖礼暨"一带一路"法律服务高端论坛。该活动由法制日报社主办，法制网和中国中小企业协会"一带一路"工作委员承办。

开展中小企业"一带一路"沿线国家法律风险防范指引系列手册工作，整合多项数据，以市场需求、国际需求、专家建议、国家政策导向为标准，结合法律及我国扶持中小企业发展的专门制度，制作该手册。先期纳入出版计划的国家如下：新加坡、马来西亚、印度尼西亚、缅甸、泰国、老挝、柬埔寨、越南、文莱和菲律宾，伊朗、阿联酋、卡塔尔、印度、斯里兰卡、哈萨克斯坦、乌兹别克斯坦、塔吉克斯坦、俄罗斯、乌克兰。

就目前的律师队伍而言，缺乏能够为国际法律市场提供服务的律师，为了能够给"一带一路"沿线企业提供更加专业和精准的法律服务。同时也在考虑，未来要不断地壮大该领域律师团队，与培训机构合作，培养一批能够涉猎国际事物的专业律师。

总之，海外贸易的增加和发展为企业带来了非常广阔的市场空间和发展前景，但机遇总是与风险是并存的，企业在此发展过程中，难免会遇到挫折，遇到风险，而利用法律武器保护自己，防范、控制和杜绝各种法律风险，将成为企业参与其中的必然选择。

中国中小企业协会"一带一路"工作委员会法律服务部现主要承接对外法律事务，与各国律所开展友好合作，共同为中小企业的健康发展保驾护航。

**赵伟主编：** 您对中国中小企业参与"一带一路"建设和参与国际竞争有哪些期待和愿景？

**姚惠娟律师：** 当今世界正发生复杂深刻的变化，国际金融危机深层次影响继续显现，世界经济缓慢复苏、发展分化。在金融危机的严峻情况下，企业资金链断裂等都严重影响着企业的正常运转。作为中国最具创新精神的群体，中小企业不仅是中国经济社会发展的重要力量，也是"一带一路"沿线建设项目不可或缺的参与者。当前，经济全球化不断深入发展，中小企业日益成为对外合作的一支主力军，是世界各国对外经贸关系中最重要的合作领域之一，也是现在和将来面临全球经济发展一体化最大的受益者和风险承担者，所以法律服务对中小企业参与国际合作的意义就更加突出。

随着"一带一路"建设的不断推进和创新驱动发展的深入实施，鼓励和支持我国中小企业参与"一带一路"建设，将为我国中小企业带来新的发展机遇，中国中小企业将迎来一个大发展的时代。只要我们抓住机遇，并有效把握风险，中国企业将在世界的舞台上开创更广阔的发展空间，我们也将在世界的经济大潮中乘风破浪，直挂云帆，创造更加辉煌灿烂的明天。

# Escort for the Building of the "Belt and Road"

—— An Interview with Lawyer Yao Huijuan, Head of the Legal Service Department of the "Belt and Road" Working Committee, China Association of Small and Medium Enterprises

President Xi Jinping proposed a major initiative to jointly build the Silk Road Economic Belt and the 21st Century Maritime Silk Road during his visits to central Asian and southeast Asian countries in September and October 2013, which received high attention and response from the international community. The National Development and Reform Commission, the Ministry of Foreign Affairs, and the Ministry of Commerce jointly issued the Vision and Actions on Jointly Building Silk Road Economic Belt and 21st Century Maritime Silk Road (referred to as the "Belt and Road") on March 28, 2015. The document pointed out that the Belt and Road Initiative, which fully relies on the existing bilateral and multilateral mechanisms of China and relevant countries, and employs existing and effective regional cooperation platforms, is designed to hold high the banner of peaceful development and actively develop economic partnerships with countries along the route, thereby creating a community of interests, a community of destiny and a community of responsibility for political mutual trust, economic integration, and cultural inclusion. I believe that this is a national top-level design, which is of great and far-reaching significance to the development of the world economy. The OBOR Security Cooperation Dialogue between China's Ministry of State Security and more than 20 national security authorities was held in Beijing on May 4, 2017. At the meeting, Meng Jianzhu, member of the Political Bureau of the CPC Central Committee and secretary of the Political and Judiciary Commission under the CPC Central Committee, pointed out that only a safe and stable environment can promote the building of the "Belt and Road" to move forward faster. I believe that the environment here certainly includes the rule of law environment in the countries along the "Belt and Road".

On July 25, 2018, on the occasion of the 5th Anniversary of the Belt and Road Initiative, the Legal Service Department established by the "Belt and Road" Working Committee of the China Association of Small and Medium Enterprises (CASME) appointed a lawyer specially to handle foreign-related matters as the head of the department, who has been dedicated to foreign-related law for more than 30 years and now still serves in the front line. She is Yao Huijuan, the founding partner of Beijing Dongyuan Law Firm and the director of Xi'an Branch. Why did the Legal Service Department of the CASME "Belt and Road" Working Committee appoint a full-time lawyer as the head of the department? I believe it is Ms. Yao's rich experience, impressive performance and fruitful results in the field of foreign-related law and her spirit of handling cases in the front line in her fifties that has been unanimously favored and highly recognized by the committee. Today, let's have a further understanding of this Chinese female lawyer who has been hailed by the media as "the Iron Rose on the international stage who bridges Chinese and Western cultural exchanges".

**Engaged in international legal affairs**

The beginning of Ms. Yao's engagement with international legal affairs may be traced back to the 1980s. Ms. Yao began to work as a lawyer in 1984. Soon after that, she was selected by the Ministry of Justice (only one candidate in Xi'an) to receive international lawyer training in Shanghai, and then she became one of the first foreign-related economic lawyers in China. She participated in the first national bar qualification examination in 1986, ranking first in Xi'an. She participated in the establishment of Xi'an Foreign Economic Law Firm in 1988, where she was fully responsible for the business of foreign trade companies and participated in the legal affairs of six companies among the nine major import and export companies in Shanxi. She was appointed as the legal advisor to the United Nations Artists Council, was awarded the title of "United Nations International Friendship Ambassador" and was warmly received by former UN Secretary-General Ban Ki-moon and former US President Bill Clinton. Zhao Meixin, the first famous female Chinese congresswoman in American history, and Chen Xiangmei, a famous social activist, also had cordial exchanges with her. Thus, Ms. Yao was hailed by the media as "the Iron Rose on the international stage who bridges Chinese and Western cultural exchanges". Ms. Yao is currently a member of the Corporate Legal Advisory Committee

of the All China Lawyers Association, a member of the Legal Advisory Committee of the All-China Federation of Returned Overseas Chinese, a legal adviser to Jin Tielin, the Honorary Dean of the China Conservatory of Music, an arbitrator of the Nanjing Arbitration Commission, an arbitrator of the Xi'an Arbitration Commission, and an arbitrator of the Yulin Arbitration Commission. The Outstanding Lawyer of Contemporary China commented on Yao Huijuan: "She is a Chinese female lawyer who has wrote extraordinary and legendary chapters in the development history of Chinese lawyers and on the world stage." As one of the first lawyers specially handling foreign-related matters in China, Ms. Yao participated in various international litigation and arbitration cases in the 1980s and 1990s, where she represented Chinese companies on the world stage, safeguarded their rights and interests, and helped them compete equally in the international market. Ms. Yao's expertise is evidenced by some international projects or litigation and arbitration cases involving her in recent years.

From December 2009 to March 2014, Ms. Yao Huijuan and Guo Yang, as agents of Jiuquan Iron and Steel (Group) Co., Ltd. (JISCO), handled an international arbitration case for a company's international steel sales contract with JISCO. Facing the team of French and German lawyers hired by the company, Ms. Yao and Mr. Guo fully safeguarded the legitimate interests of JISCO through detailed analysis of facts, rational use of evidences and correct use of the law. Ms. Yao also maintained the greatest legitimate interests of her clients when handling maritime cargo disputes and quality disputes of international trade goods.

In 2017, ICBC Leasing Co., Ltd. (which was established on November 28, 2007, and is one of the first pilot bank-based financial leasing companies designated by the State Council and approved by the China Banking Regulatory Commission. It is a wholly-owned subsidiary of the Industrial and Commercial Bank of China, with a registered capital of RMB11 billion), hailed as the "aircraft carrier" of the leasing industry, issued a tender notice for legal advisory services, which attracted dozens of law firms. Ms. Yao Huijuan, who has more than 30 years of experience in corporate legal counseling and has always handled cases in the front line, was highly recognized by ICBC Leasing's senior management and eventually joined the company's lawyer team. She then handled relevant cases as an agent, achieved satisfactory results.

On July 25, 2018, her appointment as of the head of the Legal Service Department of the CASME "Belt and Road" Working Committee stood high in popular favor. Ms. Yao felt that the responsibility on his shoulders was greater and she could not live up to this trust.

According to the US Fortune magazine, the average life of US SMEs is less than 7 years, and less than 40 years for large enterprises. In China, however, the average life of SMEs is only 2.5 years, and only 7-8 years for group companies. There are about 100 000 companies in the United States that fail every year, compared with 1 million in China, which is 10 times that of the United States. The life of companies is short, and few can grow bigger and stronger. According to my observation, the reality is that Chinese enterprises, especially private enterprises, go bankrupt due to poor management or major lawsuits, the stock price falls due to administrative penalties, and the heads of enterprises are caught in criminal risks, among others. In the final analysis, these are legal issues because companies do not pay attention to rules. The number of countries along the "Belt and Road" has increased to 65 so far. The political, economic, cultural and legal environments of these countries are different. Chinese SMEs generally lack the talents and experience in participating in international operations and competition, which has put a severe challenge on the "going global" of Chinese SMEs. The Legal Service Department of the CASME "Belt and Road" Working Committee has been established in the right time, which keeps up with the trend of the times. No matter for the purpose of "bringing in" or "going global", Chinese lawyers specially who are handling foreign-related matters will have a long way to go in this profound change and development of global economic governance.

**Interview with Lawyer Yao Huijuan, Head of the Legal Service Department of the "Belt and Road" Working Committee, China Association of Small and Medium Enterprises**

**Editor-in-chief Zhao Wei:** Hello, Ms. Yao. 2018 marks the 40th year of China's reform and opening up. As a senior lawyer who has served more than 30 years in the foreign-related legal field, you are best qualified to speak on this issue. Could you tell me your opinions and ideas about Chinese enterprises' participation in international competition and international legal affairs in the building of the "Belt and Road"?

**Ms. Yao Huijuan:** Well, I'd like to start with a summary of the difficulties our companies faced in international trade. For developing purposes, we must first systematically evaluate the difficulties and risks that may be faced, so that we can achieve steady progress with a well-thought-out plan, rather than make a decision recklessly that may result in major economic losses. Chinese companies have cost a lot to "go global" over the past years, so we cannot repeat the same mistakes. In the development of the "Belt and Road", companies may encounter various problems to varying degrees. The first is shortage of talents. Due to lack of talents and experience in international management, SMEs are often in a weak position in the international market competition as they feel difficult to effectively identify the potential risks in law, politics, economy, society, environment and security of overseas countries are lack of understanding of industry policies, legal environments and customs of the countries along the "Belt and Road". Second, most of China's SMEs are at the low end of the value chain in the global industrial chain, as they lack brand and international sales channels and are weak in international competition. Compared with Western multinational corporations, Chinese enterprises have obvious "late mover disadvantages". Most of them could only find opportunities in countries and industries with poor investment environments and high risks. Some markets seem to have huge space, but in reality, effective demand is insufficient, and blind entry would bring high risks. Third, China's overseas investment started late. Companies are not familiar with the international market and lack of overseas investment experience, and accounting, lawyer, consulting and other intermediaries have a low degree of development as well as weak risk assessment capabilities. The political, economic, and social environments of overseas countries are complex and changeable. Language cultures, business rules, legal systems, and industry standards are entirely different from those in China. This puts higher demands on the adaptability and management level of Chinese enterprises. Chinese enterprises that go global are also faced with problems such as information asymmetry, fragmentation of resources, and vicious competition. They are not conducive to the integration and coordination of strengths, and are also likely to cause repeated waste of resources. Fourth, the financial environments of countries and regions along the "Belt and Road" are not perfect, providing limited financial support for Chinese companies.

**Editor-in-chief Zhao Wei:** Since Chinese companies have so many difficulties and risks in "going global" what should we do about it? How can Chinese lawyers or overseas lawyers provide legal protection for Chinese enterprises, especially SMEs?

**Ms. Yao Huijuan:** This is the original intention for establishing the Legal Service Department of the CASME "Belt and Road" Working Committee. What we have built is a platform for cooperation and exchange between Chinese and foreign lawyers. Through the establishment of such a platform, we have reached a consensus on providing excellent services for the sound development of international legal affairs of SMEs. We have also established a publicity and liaison platform to increase mutual understanding and strengthen the basis of popular sentiment in international affairs through legal, political, economic and cultural exchanges; to promote the close cooperation of domestic and foreign law firms; to help Chinese SMEs "go global" and "bring in" overseas companies; and to give full play to the role of law in preventing risks and provide long-term legal services in the host country. We will strive to provide better legal services for the development of international legal affairs and overseas trading enterprises in various countries. As the legal systems are diverse and the legal environments are complex and volatile in countries and regions along the "Belt and Road", the building of "Belt and Road" legal services is indispensable or rigidly demanded.

**Editor-in-chief Zhao Wei:** What activities related to international legal affairs have you participated in recently? Could you please share with us?

**Ms. Yao Huijuan:** All right. I have participated in many activities. Here I will only give a brief summary of the celebration of the 5th anniversary of the proposal of the "Belt and Road" Initiative and the 10th anniversary of the establishment of the Overseas Lawyers Group of the Legal Advisory Committee of the All-China Federation of Returned Overseas Chinese, as well as the international legal service exchange symposium co-organized by the Overseas Lawyers Group and the CASME "Belt and Road" Working Committee on August 17-18, 2018.

At the opening ceremony, Zhang Geng, Director of the Legal Advisory Committee of the All-China Federation of Returned Overseas Chinese, reviewed the history of the establishment of the Overseas Lawyers Group of the Legal Advisory Committee. Mr. Zhang said: After ten years of development, the Overseas Lawyers Group has become a powerful team for overseas rights protection. He hoped that the members will hold the sword of law and the balance of justice to actively promote exchange and cooperation between Chinese and foreign legal institutions, earnestly safeguard the rights and interests of overseas Chinese, and provide quality legal support and services for the smooth implementation of the "Belt and Road" Initiative and the "going global" of more Chinese enterprises.

I am not only the head of the Legal Service Department of

the CASME "Belt and Road" Working Committee, but also a member of the Overseas Lawyers Group and a senior member of the Legal Advisory Committee of the All-China Federation of Returned Overseas Chinese.

On August 18, I participated in the international legal service exchange symposium co-organized by the Overseas Lawyers Group and the CASME the "Belt and Road" Working Committee. The symposium included 28 overseas lawyer representatives from 18 countries such as Australia, Germany, France, Britain, Russia, Portugal, Spain, Italy, the United States, Canada, Malaysia, Japan, Singapore, Indonesia, South Africa, Brazilas well as Hong Kong China and Mexico China regions.

The "Belt and Road" Outstanding Legal Service Awarding Ceremony and the "Belt and Road" Legal Service High-End Forum are to be held on December 15, 2018. The event is hosted by the Legal Daily and organized by the CASME the "Belt and Road" Working Committee.

A series of guidelines for prevention of legal risks for SMEs doing business in countries and regions along the "Belt and Road" will be formulated by integrating data and considering market demand, international demand, expert advice, and national policies, combined with the law and special systems for supporting the development of SMEs in China. The countries that are temporarily included in the publication are as follows: Singapore, Malaysia, Indonesia, Myanmar, Thailand, Laos, Cambodia, Vietnam, Brunei and the Philippines, Iran, United Arab Emirates, Qatar, India, Sri Lanka, Kazakhstan, Uzbekistan, Tajikistan, Russia and Ukraine.

As far as the current team of lawyers is concerned, there is a lack of lawyers who can serve the international legal market. To provide more professional and accurate legal services for companies along the "Belt and Road", it is also considered that in the future, we will continue to develop the team of lawyers in this field, and cooperate with training institutions to train a group of professional lawyers who can handle international affairs.

In short, the increase and development of overseas trade has brought a very broad market space and development prospects for enterprises, but the opportunities always coexist with risks. In this development process, enterprises will inevitably encounter setbacks and risks. Using legal weapons to protect themselves and to prevent, control and eliminate various legal risks will become an inevitable choice for enterprises to participate in international competition.

The Legal Service Department of CASME "Belt and Road" Working Committee now handles the foreign-related legal affairs of the Working Committee and conducts friendly cooperation with law firms around the world, so as to jointly protect the sound development of SMEs.

**Editor-in-chief Zhao Wei:** What are your expectations and visions for Chinese SMEs to participate in the "Belt and Road" building and international competition?

**Ms. Yao Huijuan:** The world today is undergoing complex and profound changes. The deep-seated impact of the international financial crisis continues to emerge, and the world economy is slowly recovering and developing in a differentiated manner. In the wake of the financial crisis, capital chain breaks and other severe situations would seriously affect the normal operation of enterprises. As the most innovative group in China, SMEs are not only an important contributor to China's economic and social development, but also an indispensable player in the construction projects along the "Belt and Road". At present, as economic globalization continues to advance, SMEs are increasingly becoming a major player in foreign cooperation and one of the most important areas of cooperation in foreign economic and trade relations among countries. They are also the biggest beneficiary and risk-bearer of global economic development integration now and in the future, so the significance of legal services for SMEs to participate in international cooperation gets even more prominent.

With the continuous advancement of the "Belt and Road" building and the in-depth implementation of innovation-driven development, encouraging and supporting Chinese SMEs to participate in the "Belt and Road" building will bring new development opportunities for SMEs in China which will usher in an era of great development. As long as we seize the opportunities and effectively control the risks, Chinese enterprises will create a broader space for development on the world stage. We will also brave the wind and the waves in the world economic tide and create a more brilliant future.

# 立足中国、面向世界，做一个善良的法律人
## ——访北京市康达律师事务所高级合伙人、法学博士杨荣宽律师

进入 21 世纪以来，随着科学技术水平的不断进步和产业升级，经济全球化已成为世界经济发展的重要趋势。可以说，任何一个国家、一个企业要想发展壮大，就必须站在全球的高度，用世界的眼光来看世界、定战略，主动顺应经济全球化的潮流，唯如此才能适应新时代发展的需要，成为经济全球化大潮的"弄潮儿"，成为未来时代的引领者。当前，"市场经济即法治经济"已是业界共识，律师在社会经济健康有序发展中所起的作用也越来越大，这一群体已成为推动经济社会向前发展、维护社会稳定的不可或缺的重要组成部分。而随着我国"走出去"战略、"一带一路"建设的逐步深入推进，中国律师的身影不断出现在国际的舞台上，中国律师的声音在各种国际会议中亦越来越响亮……

2018 年 4 月，由《中国商网法治频道》《中国商报法治周刊》评选的"2017 年度中国商事解决十大律师"揭晓，本文主人公——北京市康达律师事务所高级合伙人杨荣宽律师荣列其中。藉此，我们再次采访了这位专啃"硬骨头"案件的法学博士。

### 中国律师要坚守法治精神，依法维护外国企业在华合法权益

改革开放 40 年来，随着我国与世界各国合作、交流的日益扩大，大批外国企业进入我国开展经营活动，它们为我们带来了新技术、新理念、新经验，成为社会经济发展中不可忽视的一支重要力量。俗话说，公正是法治的生命线，没有公正也就没有法治。杨荣宽律师强调："作为一个法律人、一名中国律师，要依法维护外国企业在华合法权益，要大力弘扬法治精神，彰显我国依法治国的决心和信心。"

据笔者调研，在杨荣宽律师的执业生涯中，就有诸多依法维护在华外国企业合法权益的经典之作，当事人合法权益得到了维护，一个大国的法治精神更得到了弘扬和彰显。

2000 年，意大利 EMC 公司遭遇山西某市环保局行政处罚，处罚金额高达 3000 万元人民币，杨荣宽律师应 EMC 公司委托，在行政诉讼一审、二审中坚持原则、据理力争，最终法院判决撤销该行政处罚决定，外方当事人合法权益最终得到维护，其对中国的司法环境更有了信心。

毕马威（KPMG）是一家网络遍布全球的专门提供审计、税务和咨询专业服务的机构，而作为其中国公司多年的首席法律顾问，多年来，康达律师事务所杨荣宽律师团队无论在非诉讼法律服务领域，还是在客户遇有诉讼案件发生时皆得到外方当事人的高度认可和信赖。

2017 年 12 月 20 日，由杨荣宽律师团队代理的毕马威国际（KPMG International）、毕马威中国的相关成员所及国家行政管理总局商标评审委员会（简称"商评委"）商标异议、复审、诉讼等重大商标争议案，历时 9 年，最终委托人（毕马威国际）诉求获得全部支持，商评委复审决定被撤销。

杨荣宽律师非常自豪地道："毕马威是经 KPMG 国际在财会、审计领域广泛使用的字号，具有较高知名度，且毕马威商号已经与 KPMG 国际建立了稳定的指向关系，具有在先商号权。被异议商标的注册侵害了 KPMG 国际在先商号权益，具有实事和法律依据。所以，最终毕马威在本次诉讼中获得支持，也是我国司法公正的应有之义。"在毕马威与锦州港虚假陈述、达能娃哈哈"世纪大战"中皆有杨荣宽律师团队的辛勤深耕。

鉴于康达律师事务所杨荣宽律师团队在维护外资企业合法权益方面突出的业绩，德勤华永会计师事务所、法国国家人寿保险公司、吉野家、泰国红牛、法国卡思黛乐兄弟简化股份有限公司（Castel Freres Sas）、阿斯利康投资（中国）有限公司等外资企业皆先后聘请杨荣宽律师团队担任其法律顾问，提供诉讼、非诉讼法律服务。

在此，我们还需要重点一提的是，在卡思黛乐兄弟简化股份公司与李道之、上海班提酒业有限公司的"卡斯特之战"中，赔偿金额由 3373 万元到 50 万元的大逆转，杨荣宽律师带领团队付出了多少心血，旁人是不能完全感同身受的。据当时媒体报道，2016 年 1 月，经最高人民法院判决，法国 Castel（法国卡思黛乐兄弟简化股份有限公司）最终赔偿李道之、上海班提酒业有限公司 50 万元人民币，本次判决为终审判决。最高人民法院的终审判决终于为这起历时 10 年的"卡斯特之战"画上了圆满的句号。

媒体这样评价道：该案为葡萄酒行业迄今为止最大商标侵权案，法国卡思黛乐兄弟简化股份有限公司（原卡斯特兄弟简化股份有限公司）最终赔偿李道之、上海班提酒业有限公司 50 万元人民币。这一结果不得不说是一个"大逆转"！因为之前在温州中院、浙江高院的两次判决结果都是判定法国卡思黛乐兄弟简化股份有限公司赔偿李道之、上海班提酒业有限公司 3373 万元人民币，而本次最高人民法院的最终判决结果仅 50 万元的赔偿，与之前的判决金额相差甚远。从 3373 万元到现在的 50 万元的赔偿结果，法国卡思黛乐兄弟简化股份有限公司虽负犹胜，甚至从某种程度上来说可以算是取得了一场"大胜利"。而这一案件对整个知识产权界

也是一个年度大事件，影响相当深远。而在这起备受关注的"卡斯特之战"中，代理该案在最高人民法院提起再审的主办律师杨荣宽更是功不可没。我们进一步了解到，当事人（法国卡思黛乐兄弟简化股份有限公司）在温州中院作出一审判决、浙江高院维持原判的情况下，并未抱很大信心，当事人也认为这个案件几无翻案可能，但不自信反而激励了杨荣宽律师。"一定要啃啃这块硬骨头"，杨荣宽律师暗下决心。后经认真查进出口单据、主体文件，终于发现案件突破口。当最高人民法院法官宣读终审判决，赔偿金额为 50 万元人民币，法国卡思黛乐兄弟简化股份有限公司代表听到这个数字时，其喜悦之情可谓溢于言表。

### 无讼与和解才是法律人追求的理想境界

江苏某市引进了国际知名饮品品牌，外方投资数亿元，决定在消费大国大干一场，但中方股东依托地方势力，将外方资金脱壳至其控制的第三方公司，而双方的合资公司却走向了破产的边缘。外方起诉至法院，因标的额巨大、案件重大、证据复杂、地方保护盘根错节等因素，外方一审败诉，二审再败诉，维权之路步履维艰。杨荣宽律师团队接受外方委托后，通过缜密分析，杨荣宽律师说："这个案件不用再诉讼了"。外方一听，惊愕之余不知如何是好。杨荣宽律师继续说："这个案件我来负责与对方谈判。"然而，对方根本不把律师放在眼里，进过几轮交涉，双方才终于坐在了谈判桌上。谈判期间，杨荣宽律师就案件的经过以及对方涉嫌抽逃资金可能面临的法律风险、利弊关系合盘托出，律师的真诚和大度令对方非常钦佩。外方本计划能拿回投资本金的一半就已经很满足，而最终经过杨荣宽律师力争，为外方拿回全部投资。杨荣宽律师将诉讼案件非诉化，终使双方冰释前嫌，握手言和，外方利益得以维护。

再如某知名房地产企业因股东新老交替出现僵局，杨荣宽律师以引进战略投资者、管理层收购、股权内部转让、股权奖励四大法宝为筹码，给予了当事人信心，推进了公司改革，加速了问题的解决。在台湾实联、吉野家等重大争议解决中，杨荣宽律师不畏艰难，克服困难，历获佳绩。"每一涉外案件，均具独特性、复杂性，每一次争议解决，均是成长。"

杨荣宽律师的办法很多很独特，却往往产生奇效，很多方法很简单，却往往常人想不到。他的方法多样、灵活，如同太极，变幻莫测，却也万变不离其宗。"办法总比困难多"是杨荣宽律师的口头禅，话虽简单，却充满自信和力量，让每一位当事人安心，也让每一位团队成员安心。

"法律不仅仅是工具，而应该成为我们内心的信仰。其实诉讼是很残酷的，我们最大的希望不是胜诉，而是没有诉讼，这才是我们法律人所追求的目标和理想！"杨荣宽律师感叹道。

### 为中国企业"走出去"保驾护航，是中国律师义不容辞的责任

中国企业"走出去"战略始于 2001 年《国民经济与社会发展第十个五年计划纲要》的颁布。多年来，为了更好地实施"走出去"战略，上至中央领导下至地方政府皆献智献策共谋发展之道，取得了显著的成就，也付出了沉重的代价，但要发展就不能停滞不前，就要不断融入全球市场经济体系。2013 年，国家提出"一带一路"的倡议，为中国企业参与国际合作与竞争，为中国经济融入全球市场注入了新的活力。

2017 年 11 月 8 日至 10 日，"2017 年亚太经合组织（简称'APEC'）工商领导人峰会"在越南岘港隆重召开。中国、美国、澳大利亚、智利、马来西亚、新西兰、巴布亚新几内亚、秘鲁、菲律宾等 APEC 各成员经济体领导人及 2000 余跨境企业和越南 800 家企业代表出席会议（注：APEC 是亚太区域国家与地区加强多边经济联系、交流与合作的重要组织，成立于 1989 年，同时也是亚洲 - 太平洋地区级别最高、影响最大的区域性经济组织）。

越南国家主席陈大光在此次峰会开幕式上致辞，他表示亚太地区工商界在新技术、能源、商务合作、新一代贸易与投资方式等方面都扮演着先锋者的角色。

秘鲁总统 Pedro Pablo Kuczynski，香港特首林郑月娥（Carrie Lam Cheng Yuet-ngor），墨西哥总统培尼亚、新西兰总理 Jacinda，澳大利亚总理 Malcolm，巴布亚新几内亚总理 Peter，马来西亚总理纳吉布，分别参加商务领袖峰会对话。

美国总统特朗普发表了《建立在公正与对等基础上健康的贸易关系》主题演讲。我国国家主席习近平发表题为《抓住世界经济转型机遇，谋求亚太更大发展》的主旨演讲，他强调："世界正处在快速变化的历史进程之中，世界经济正在发生更深层次的变化。我们必须顺应大势，勇于担当，共同开辟亚太发展繁荣的光明未来。深入推进'一带一路'建设，实行高水平的贸易和投资自由化便利化政策，推动构建面向全球的自由贸易区网络。这是以人民为中心、迈向美好生活的新征程。亚太的和平、稳定、繁荣属于全体亚太人民，亚太的未来要靠亚太人民携手创造。互信、包容、合作、共赢的伙伴关系，是亚太大家庭的精神纽带，是确保亚太合作处在正确轨道上的重要保障。让我们脚踏实地的推进合作，扎扎实实采取行动，共同建设亚太更加美好的明天！"

作为与会嘉宾，康达律师事务所高级合伙人杨荣宽律师

应邀出席了该高峰会议，并与相关方面建立了高层次、高广度、大范围的联系和沟通。据了解，杨荣宽律师团队已持续多年为诸多 APEC 跨境企业提供高效法律服务，其专业、严谨、让人信赖的法律服务深受业界赞誉。

2018 年 5 月，杨荣宽律师随同李克强总理出访印度尼西亚，并受邀参加"中国—印尼工商峰会"，其他受邀参加的高级别国际会议及高峰会包括 2017 年中国—萨尔瓦多贸易和投资论坛、第八届国际资本峰会及国际商事争端解决论坛、中葡企业商机论坛、第八届"一带一路"生态农业与食品安全论坛、第 20 届中国北京国际科技产业博览会主题报告会、第六届世界工商领袖（昆山）大会、中越经贸合作论坛、中蒙两国商务理事会成立大会、中菲经贸合作论坛等。

此外，杨荣宽律师还笔耕不辍，先后发表了《印尼跨境投资土地规制若干问题》《国际商事仲裁透明度走向及保密性弱化——分析及应对》《国际商事仲裁中第三方资助之法经济分析》《国际商事仲裁保密性法律考量》《环境产品协定的价值考虑与跨境投资》《保证责任之免除在疑难商事诉讼中的异化》《对赌协议商事争议评述及司法实践研究》《民法总则诉讼时效修订对商事诉讼影响分析》《商事外观主义原则在疑难商事诉讼中的辩证与适用——股权的显名和隐名之司法实践》《新加坡国际仲裁中心仲裁规则之考虑与借鉴》等多篇专业文章，在商事领域"拓展了崭新的影响力"，在国际商事争议解决中"颇具工匠精神的思维呈现"。

杨荣宽律师说："为中国企业'走出去'保驾护航，是中国律师义不容辞的责任，是新时代中国律师的使命与担当"。

**后记**

英国法学家麦克莱说："善良的心就是最好的法律"，善良的心可以打动人、感化人、温暖人、教育人，诚然，因为善良的法律人总会用心传递法律与司法的温度。杨荣宽律师的善良可以说是无处不在，他的团队成员说："无论是待人接物，还是接陌生电话，乃至接到广告推销的电话，杨律师也始终面带微笑，从不呵斥他人。代理各类诉讼案件时，杨律师首先主张的是息诉止争，对于没有必要提起诉讼的案件，他会坦诚告知当事人该案不宜提起诉讼，因为那样得不偿失，既浪费金钱，又浪费时间，还会浪费司法资源。当然，他还会提出更佳的解决方案，尽最大努力在最短的时间内解决问题，因为没有提起诉讼，杨律师失去了一大笔律师费，但他却赢得了众多当事人的尊重和信赖。"6 月份，夏日开始，在繁忙工作的间隙，杨荣宽律师还将负责康达律师事务所香港办公室的筹建工作，"任重道远，上下求索"。

是啊！善良的心就是最好的法律，作为新时代的中国律师，无论是立足中国，还是面向世界，善良的心就是那张最有效的通行证。

## Based in China and oriented to the world——being a kind lawyer
### ——An Interview with Lawyer Yang Rongkuan, Senior Partner of Beijing Kangda Law Firm, Doctor of Laws

Since the beginning of the 21st century, with the progress of science and technology, and the upgrading of industries, economic globalization has become a major trend of global economic development. It can be said that for any country or enterprise to develop in the new era, and become a future leader of economic development, it must see the world and formulate its strategy, and adapt to the trend of economic globalization with a global vision. Currently, "the market economy is the rule of law economy" is already a common understanding of the industry, and lawyers are playing an increasingly crucial role in healthy and orderly economic and social development. This group is essential to economic and social progress, and social stability. With the further implementation of China's "going global" strategy, and "Belt and Road" initiative, Chinese lawyers are appearing on the global stage more frequently, and their voice at international conferences is increasingly loud……

In August 2018, the "2017 Top 10 Chinese Lawyers in Business Dispute Settlement" selected by *China Business Network Legal Channel* and *China Business Herald News Weekly* were revealed, and the leading character of this article – Lawyer Yang Rongkuan, Senior Partner of Beijing Kangda Law Firm, was one of them. We have interviewed this doctor of laws who specializes in tackling tough cases again.

**Chinese lawyers should stick to the rule of law spirit, and protect lawful rights and interests of foreign enterprises in China according to law**

In the past 40 years of reform and opening, as China expands cooperation and exchanges with foreign countries, a large number of foreign enterprises have entered China for business

operations, bringing new technologies, concepts and experience, and becoming a non-negligible force in economic and social development. As the saying goes, justness is the lifeline of the rule of law. Lawyer Yang stresses, "As a Chinese lawyer, I should protect lawful rights and interests of foreign enterprises in China according to law, and carry forward the rule of law spirit to show China's resolution and confidence of ruling by law."

According to the author's investigation, there have been many classical cases of protecting lawful rights and interests of foreign enterprises in China according to law in Lawyer Yang's career, in which lawful rights and interests of clients were protected, and the rule of law spirit of a great power was carried forward.

In 2000, EMC Corporation in Italy was imposed an administrative penalty of RMB 30 million by the environmental protection bureau of a city in Shanxi Province. Lawyer Yang was appointed by EMC Corporation to argue strongly on just grounds in the first and second trials of the administrative proceedings. The court finally revoked the administrative penalty decision, and the client became more confident in China's judicial environment as its lawful rights and interests were finally protected.

KPMG is an agency specializing in auditing, taxation and consulting services with a global network. As the legal advisor to its Chinese branch, Lawyer Yang's team from Beijing Kangda Law Firm has been highly recognized and trusted by the foreign client over these years whether in non-litigious or litigious legal services.

On December 20, 2017, in the major dispute over trademark opposition, review and litigation of the relevant members of KPMG International and KPMG China versus the Trademark Review and Adjudication Board, State Administration for Industry and Commerce handled by Lawyer Yang's team that had been lasting for nine years, all claims of the client (KPMG) were finally supported, and the review decision of the Trademark Review and Adjudication Board was revoked.

Lawyer Yang said proudly: "KPMG is the famous name used extensively by KPMG International in the finance and accounting area, and the KPMG trademark has a stable targeted connection with KPMG International and has a prior trademark right. The registration of the opposed trademark infringes on the prior trademark right of KPMG International with a factual and legal basis. Therefore, the support for KPMG in this lawsuit reflects China's judicial justice." Lawyer Yang's team worked hard in the KPMG case, the misrepresentation case of Jinzhou Port, and the Danon versus Wahaha acquisition conflict.

In view of the outstanding performance of Lawyer Yang's team in protecting lawful rights and interests of foreign enterprises, foreign enterprises like Deloitte Touche Tohmatsu Certified Public Accountants LLP, CNP Assurances, Yoshinoya, RedBull Thailand, Castel Freres SAS in France, and AstraZeneca Investment (China) Co., Ltd. appoint Lawyer Yang's team as their legal adviser to offer litigious and non-litigious legal services.

It is noteworthy that in the "Castel War" of Castel Freres SAS versus Li Daozhi and Panati Wine (Shanghai) Co., Ltd., the amount of compensation dropped dramatically from RMB 33.73 million to RMB 500 000. Others cannot feel personally how much effort Lawyer Yang and his team paid.

According to a media report, the Supreme People's Court judged in January 2016 that Castel (France) should finally pay RMB 500000 in compensation to Li Daozhi and Panati Wine (Shanghai) Co., Ltd. This final judgment put a perfect end to the decade-long "Castel War".

The press commented like this, "In this ever-largest trademark infringement case in the wine industry, Castel Freres SAS finally paid RMB 500 000 in compensation to Li Daozhi and Panati Wine (Shanghai) Co., Ltd. This result is absolutely surprising!" The two prior judgments made by the Wenzhou Municipal Intermediate People's Court and the Zhejiang Provincial Higher People's Court were that Castel Freres SAS should pay RMB 33.73 million in compensation to Li Daozhi and Panati Wine (Shanghai) Co., Ltd., while the final judgment of RMB 500 000 only entered by the Supreme People's Court differed significantly. Castel Freres SAS seemingly lost but actually won, and this in a sense could be considered as a great victory. This case was an annual event with far-reaching influence for the whole intellectual property community. In this remarkable "Castel War", Lawyer Yang who brought this case to the Supreme People's Court for retrial made an indelible contribution. We further learned that the client (Castel Freres SAS) had little confidence in this case when the first-instance judgment made by the Wenzhou Municipal Intermediate People's Court was affirmed by the Zhejiang Provincial Higher People's Court, and thought that it was almost impossible to reverse the verdict. Instead, its lack of confidence motivated Lawyer Yang to solve this hard nut. He finally found a breakthrough point in this case after checking the import and export documents carefully. When the Supreme People's Court announced the final judgment with an amount of compensation of RMB 500 000, Castel's representative showed great joy when hearing that.

**Non-litigation and reconciliation is the ideal state pursued by lawyers**

A world-famous drink brand was introduced into a city in Jiangsu Province. The foreign side invested hundreds of millions of RMB to do something great in this consuming country, while the Chinese shareholder transferred the foreign capital to a third party company controlled by it, and their joint venture was on the verge of bankruptcy. The foreign side brought a suit, but lost in the first and second trials because the subject amount was tremendous, the evidence was complex, and the Chinese side had strong local forces.

After Lawyer Yang's team was appointed by the foreign side, Lawyer Yang said after a rigorous analysis, "Litigation is no longer necessary for this case." The foreign side was shocked at this. Lawyer Yang went on, "I will negotiate on your behalf." However, the other side was unwilling to negotiate with him until several rounds of bargaining. During the negotiations, Lawyer Yang stated the course of the case, and the potential legal risks, pros and cons of the other side's suspected capital withdrawal. His sincerity and generosity impressed the other side. The foreign side planned to settle for taking back half of the investment, but it finally took back the full investment through Lawyer Yang's struggle. Lawyer Yang made this case non-litigious to reach a compromise between both sides, and the foreign side's interests were protected.

For another example, a well-known real estate enterprise went into a deadlock in shareholder replacement, Lawyer Yang made the client confident, drove corporate reform and accelerated problem solving with the four measures of strategic investor introduction, acquisition by the management, internal equity transfer and equity reward. Lawyer Yang overcame difficulties and got good results in settling major disputes of Taiwan Shihlien, Yoshinoya, etc. "Every foreign-related case is unique and complex, and the settlement of each dispute is growth for me."

Lawyer Yang has many unexpected, unique, flexible yet simple ways that often proved surprisingly effective. He always acts changefully but on the same principle. His catch phrase is "There are always more solutions than difficulties." This simple sentence shows his strong confidence and power, and reassures every client and team member.

"The law is not only a tool, but also our inner faith. In fact, litigation is very cruel. As lawyers, our greatest hope and ultimate goal is not winning lawsuits but eliminating litigation," exclaimed Lawyer Yang.

**Protecting outgoing Chinese enterprises is an imperative obligation of Chinese lawyers**

The "going global" strategy of Chinese enterprises began with the promulgation of the *Outline of the Tenth Five-year National Economic and Social Development Plan* in 2001. Over these years, the central leadership and local governments have been seeking paths of development in order to implement this strategy more effectively. In this process, remarkable achievements have been made at heavy costs. However, we must be integrated into the global market economy system to go further. In 2013, the state proposed the "Belt and Road" initiative, inspiring Chinese enterprises to participate in international cooperation and competition, and the Chinese economy to be integrated into the global market.

During November 8-10, 2017, the 2017 APEC Economic Leaders' Meeting was held in Danang, Vietnam. Economic leaders from APEC member economies, including China, the U.S., Australia, Chile, Malaysia, New Zealand, Papua New Guinea, Peru and the Philippines, and delegates of over 2 000 transnational corporations and 800 Vietnamese enterprises were present (Note: Founded in 1989, the APEC is an important organization through which Asian-Pacific countries and regions seek to strengthen multilateral economic connections, exchanges and cooperation, and also the highest-level and most influential regional economic organization in the Asia-Pacific region).

Vietnamese President Tran Dai Quang delivered a speech at the opening ceremony of this summit, saying that the Asian-Pacific business community played a pioneering role in new technologies, energy, business cooperation, and new-generation trade and investment modes.

Peruvian President Pedro Pablo Kuczynski, Chief Executive of Hong Kong Carrie Lam Cheng Yuet-ngor, Mexican President Pena, Prime Minister of New Zealand Jacinda, Prime Minister of Australia Malcolm, Prime Minister of Papua New Guinea Peter, and Malaysian Prime Minister Najib attended the business leaders' summit dialogue.

U.S. President Trump gave the keynote speech "Healthy Trade Relations Based on Fairness and Equity". Chinese President Xi Jinping made the keynote speech "Seizing the Opportunity of a Global Economy in Transition and Accelerating Development of the Asia-Pacific", stressing that, "We live in a fast changing world, and the global economy is undergoing more profound changes. We must advance with the trend of times, live up to our responsibility and work together to deliver a bright future of development and prosperity for the Asia-Pacific. We will promote the implementation of the "Belt and Road" Initiative, adopt policies to promote high-standard liberalization and facilitation of trade and investment, and establish a global network of free trade areas. This is a new journey toward a better life for the people. All of our people in the Asia-Pacific deserve peace, stability and prosperity, and all of us in the region should jointly deliver a bright future for the Asia-Pacific. Partnerships based on mutual trust, inclusiveness, cooperation and mutual benefit. This is what keeps our big Asia-Pacific family together and ensures the success of Asia-Pacific cooperation. Let us take solid steps to promote cooperation and usher in an even brighter future for the Asia-Pacific!"

Lawyer Yang was invited to attend the summit as a guest, and established high-level and extensive connections with the parties concerned. It is learned that Lawyer Yang's team has provided efficient, professional, rigorous and trustworthy legal services to numerous APEC transnational corporations for many years, and won extensive praises in the industry.

In May 2018, Lawyer Yang visited Indonesia, and was invited to attend the China-Indonesia Business Summit. Other high-level international conferences and summits that he was invited to attend include without limitation the 2017 China-Salvador Trade and Investment Forum, 8th International Capital Conference and International Business Dispute Resolution Forum, China-Portugal Business Opportunity Forum for Enterprises, 8th "Belt and Road" Eco-Agriculture and Food Safety Forum, Keynote Session of the 20th China Beijing International High-tech Expo, 6th World Business Leaders (Kunshan) Conference, China-Vietnam Economic and Trade Cooperation Forum, inaugural meeting of the China-Mongolia Business Council, and China-Philippines Economic and Trade Cooperation Forum.

In addition, Lawyer Yang has kept writing and published a number of professional articles, such as "Some Land Regulation Issues in Cross-Border Investment in Indonesia" "Transparency Trend and Confidentiality Weakening in International Commercial Arbitration——Analysis and Response" "Economic Analysis of Third Party Funding in International Commercial Arbitration" " Legal Considerations of Confidentiality in International Commercial Arbitration" "Value Consideration and Cross-border Investment of Environmental Product Protocols" "Dissimilation of the Exemption of the Guarantee Liability in Difficult Commercial Litigation" "Review of Commercial Disputes in and Study on the Judicial Practice of Valuation Adjustment Mechanisms" "Analysis of the Impact of the Amendment of Limitation of Action on Commercial Litigation in the General Principles of the Civil Law" "Dialectics and Application of Exterior Right Theory in Difficult Commercial Litigation——Judicial Practice of Equity Dominance and Recessiveness" "Consideration and Reference of the Arbitration Rules of the Singapore International Arbitration Centre", generating new influence in the commercial field, and presenting thoughts ingeniously in the settlement of international commercial disputes.

Lawyer Yang said: "Protecting outgoing Chinese enterprises is an imperative obligation of Chinese lawyers."

**Postscript**

British jurist McLean said: "The good heart is the best law." A good heart can touch, warm and educate others, because a good lawyer would always deliver the warmth of laws and justice with his or her heart. Lawyer Yang's goodness is everywhere. His team members said, "When dealing with people or matters, or even answering strange calls, lawyer Yang always smiles, and never reproaches others. When handling lawsuits, lawyer Yang wants to settle disputes first. For any cause that is not necessarily brought to court, he would tell the client frankly that a lawsuit not only consumes money and time, but also wastes judicial resources. Of course, he would offer a better solution to solve the problem as soon as possible at his best. When no suit is brought, Lawyer Yang loses a considerable attorney fee, but wins the respect and trust of the client." In this June, lawyer Yang will also be responsible for the establishment of the Hong Kong office of Beijing Kangda Law Firm. He never stops working.

Right! The good heart is the best law. For Chinese lawyers of the new era, the good heart is the most effective pass whether in China or the world.

# 肩负律师使命、维护司法公正

## ——访全国优秀律师、上海市联合律师事务所管委会主任、

## 党支部书记曹志龙律师

司法环境是衡量一个国家、地区竞争力的重要指标之一。俗话说，筑好"巢"方能引来"金凤凰"，良好的司法环境是吸引投资的重要手段，是保持市场经济活力的必要条件，同时也是一个国家、区域经济发展和腾飞的有力保障。而打造一个良好的司法环境，更是所有法律人应尽的职责、应有的使命和担当。

进入 21 世纪以来，随着我国正式加入 WTO 以及中国企业"引进来""走出去"战略及"一带一路"建设的逐步深入推进，中国经济正在完成市场化、国际化进程，并早已融入世界经济体系和经济全球化的浪潮中。

作为一名执业 16 个春秋，又曾荣获全国律师行业最高殊荣"全国优秀律师"的本文主人公——上海市联合律师事务所（简称"联合所"）管委会主任、党支部书记曹志龙律师，无论是谈"引进来"还是聊"走出去"，他首先研究和关注的就是企业法律风险以及法律风险防范之道。正是因为他每年皆代理上百起案件，练就了他的一双"火眼金睛"。他崇尚"大道至简""知行合一"，只要他接手的案件或项目，他总能在纷繁复杂、千头万绪的案件中梳理出明晰的法律关系和头绪，化繁为简并最终维护当事人的合法权益。他常说："法律面前人人平等，不论是外方还是中方当事人，其权益都要受到法律的保护，因为公正是司法的灵魂和生命线，也是一个国家法治水平、司法环境、投资环境优劣的最好体现。"

**案例解析**

1. 公正是法治的灵魂和生命线

中国改革开放 40 年来在各个领域皆取得了巨大的成就，尤其是广大华侨华人对我国经济文化建设领域的贡献可谓有目共睹。华侨华人发挥其在资金、技术、管理经验、商业资源等方面的优势，在祖国大地投资兴业，用智慧和汗水，有力地促进了中国经济社会的发展，推动了中国同世界的交流与合作。而当华侨华人投资利益受损时，作为守护公平正义的法律人理应保护他们的合法权益，展现中国的法

治精神，为社会经济的可持续发展竭尽全力，优化投资环境，树立公正的形象。下面介绍一下曹志龙律师竭力维护华侨华人投资权益的经典案例。

（1）事起：2003 年 7 月 22 日，山东某市经济技术开发区管理委员会（简称"管委会"）与香港某发展有限公司（简称"香港公司"）签署《建设成立股份制医院协议书》，初步约定由管委会、香港公司及某市医院（简称"合作医院"）三方在某市经济技术开发区内共同设立一家股份制医院。一年零三个月后，开发区国有资产经营管理公司、香港公司委托的投资主体——某投资公司、某市耳神经外科研究所详细约定了各方各项权利义务。2005 年 1 月 17 日，开发区国有资产经营管理公司向投资公司、耳神经研究所发出《通知》，告知管委会建议将医院项目分为两期，第一期先成立某市经济技术开发区亚健康科研中心（简称"科研中心"）。接到通知后，投资公司会同地方股东迅速展开了科研中心的筹设工作。2005 年 9 月前夕，经济技术开发区社会事业局、科技与工业发展局亦分别作出批复，准予筹建。

科研中心拿到政府部门的"准行令"后，又于 2005 年 11 月、2006 年 4 月将某市国土资源局经济技术开发区分局的两张国有土地使用权证办理完毕，确认科研中心取得了开发区内位于渤海南路的两块国有土地的使用权。然而，就在科研中心的场所建设进行之际，原先大开绿灯的社会事业局却突然"倒戈"，于 2007 年 4 月 21 日发出《关于停止某市经济技术开发区亚健康科研中心筹建活动的通知》，决定立即停止科研中心的"筹建活动"。

2007 年 8 月 27 日，山东某市公安局经济技术开发区分局在没有解释原因及执法依据的前提下，突然对投资公司的公司章、财务专用章采取了扣押措施；3 日后，又再发通知收缴了科研中心的行政、财务章、合同章。同日，某市国土资源局也向科研中心发出"某注销（2007）字第 01 号""某注销（2007）字第 02 号"《注销土地登记通知书》，注销科研中心此前取得的国有土地使用权。

香港公司的董事长、华侨蒋某在收到上述 4 项行政决定后，与该市政府主管部门多次沟通无果。鉴于自身力量薄弱，遂将公司遭遇反映到国务院侨办，后此案转至在当时有着 20 多年发展历史的联合所，联合所接到案件后，立即由曹志龙律师等 3 名律师组成了维权律师团前往山东办理此案。

（2）办案：接受香港公司委托后，3 位律师发现 4 个具体行政行为均存在程序违法、事实认定有误的情况，遂确定了先复议再谈判的代理方案，提出撤销 4 个具体行政

行为的复议。几经努力，最终使复议机关山东省人民政府撤销了以上 4 个具体行政行为，为后续的成功和解与权利维护打下了有力的基础。

（3）曹志龙律师解析：该案属于涉侨案件，受到国务院侨办的高度重视。承办律师妥善处理该案件，有效地化解了外商与当地政府的矛盾；纠正了当地政府的错误行政行为，促进了地方政府依法行政，同时树立了外商对于大陆投资环境及投资法律、政策的信心。该案还属于为当事人挽回重大经济利益的案件，切实维护了当事人的合法权益，获得国务院侨办、某市当地政府及香港公司的高度评价，对当地的外商投资环境产生了积极的影响。

2. 国际贸易货款受损，律师历尽艰辛维权

上海某实业发展有限公司（简称"上海公司"）是一家从事太阳能硅材料贸易的公司，在对外采购时因汇款不慎导致货财两空，带来近 3000 万元人民币的重大经济损失。本案件中，他作为主办律师，为了证明采购汇款与交易的一致性，虽然没有书面合同但买卖合同关系客观存在，历尽艰辛，最终为上海公司挽回了重大经济损失。当然，维权之路何等艰险，或只有经历者才能深刻感受。

（1）事起：英属维尔京群岛某硅片公司（简称"硅片公司"）是注册在英属维尔京群岛的公司，德国某股份公司（简称"德国公司"）注册地在德国，硅片公司属德国公司的全资子公司。硅片公司在上海设立了代表处，首席代表为黄某，担任硅片公司中国片区的销售总监。

2006 年 9 月起，硅片公司通过其上海代表处与上海公司进行业务合作，从硅片公司处购买抛光片等货物，并通过花旗银行（中国）有限公司上海分行等各种付款途径向硅片公司支付预付款。起初硅片公司尚能正常发货，但随着订单数量的增大，硅片公司在收取上海公司的预付款后却无法交付货物，而作为控股股东的德国公司在将硅片公司及上海代表处高管悉数更换后又拒绝承认上海公司所付款项。没有正式买卖合同，汇款单据的收款方大多是黄某指定的第三人，累积预付款项已达 4 235 760.30 美元，这样的境况该如何主张自身权益？上海公司遭遇困境，极有可能物财两空，只得求助律师。

（2）维权：接受上海公司委托后，两律师深觉此案虽只是采购预付款，但双方没有正式买卖合同，又没有将款项汇入供货方主体公司，且该案还涉及中国法律与外国法律等问题，诸多因素皆增加了本案的复杂性。经过认真研究，代理律师提出代理方案：要证明上海公司与硅片公司具有实际买卖交易行为，还要证明 2006 年 9 月以来上海公司所付款项实际确为购买硅片公司的产品。经调取上海公司与硅片公司多年来进行交易的部分报关单、提单、来往邮件及发票等材料终于获得有效证据；后又取得上海代表处原首席代表黄某签字出具的 10 份情况说明，其在情况说明中确认尚欠上海公司货款 4 235 760.30 美元，此证据经上海市卢湾区公证处公证，黄某的证言对上海公司与硅片公司之间的货物买卖关系再次进行了确认；硅片公司财务于 2008 年 8 月 8 日发给上海公司的电子邮件，邮件的附件中详细记载了该公司自 2006 年以来收到上海公司通过其他公司和个人支付货款的时间和金额（共计收到 13 073 819.14 美元），硅片公司总裁 Paul 亦在该附件中签字。以上证据均表明上海公司与硅片公司间存在买卖关系已无争议，确实存在因买卖关系而形成的债权债务。而且德国公司在硅片公司存在欠款的情况下还通过分红的方式从硅片公司"分得" 600 万美元的利润，这侵害了债权人的利益。

所有证据材料收集和固定后代理律师提出：1. 上海公司与硅片公司之间存在因长期买卖关系而形成的债权债务；2. 作为控股股东的德国公司所谓分红行为侵害了上海公司利益，应对硅片公司的债务承担连带责任的代理意见。

（3）判决：法院经审理判决被告硅片公司向原告上海公司支付 4 235 760.30 美元，并偿付自 2009 年 7 月 27 日起至该判决生效之日止的利息（按中国人民银行同期美元存款利率计算），但法院因硅片公司所在英属维尔京群岛及德国公司法的规定与中国公司法不同，而驳回了要求被告德国公司对被告硅片公司的债务承担连带责任的诉讼请求。

（4）曹志龙律师解析：本案中原告上海公司与被告硅片公司之间没有签订买卖合同，也没有原告直接向被告支付货款的凭证，但货物买卖通常会有对账单、发票，双方的往来函件等，上述证据若综合考虑，即能够让法院采信双方确实存在买卖关系，在被告硅片公司以及其控股股东德国公司未能举证已履行发货义务的情况下，被告硅片公司理应将原告上海公司预付的货款及相应利息予以退还。

此外，由于该案属涉外案件，首先应确定法律适用问题，同时还需要律师对法律关系涉及的外国法律进行研究，律师作为原告当事人的代理人往往会对法律条款做有利于当事人的理解和解释，在思维上也可能会受到惯有的中国法律的影响。如我国《公司法》中规定了"公司股东滥用公司法人独立地位和股东有限责任，逃避债务，严重损害公司债权人利益的，应当对公司债务承担连带责任"。这就是涉及公司人格混同问题，人格混同主要表现为人员混同、业务混同、财务混同。但本案中对此问题应适用的法律是被告硅片公司登记地，即英属维尔京群岛的相关法律。法院认为，英属维尔京群岛《商业公司法》中并未明确人格混同的法律构成要件，也没有规定因人格混同及股东利用法人独立地位损害公司债权人利益后的法律责任，且主张利润分配不当的主体是公司而非债权人，所以并未支持由被告德国公司对被告硅片公司的债务承担责任的诉讼请求。该案例也说明了英属维尔京群岛《商业公司法》对于公司人格混同规则的特殊性，这需要在从事国际投资与贸易时特别关注。

（5）曹志龙律师建议：从整个判决结果来看，法院支

持了被告硅片公司向原告上海公司支付全部诉讼请求的货款金额及利息，维护了原告的合法权益，使原告上海公司避免了重大经济损失。

在此，作为长期研究世界各国法律环境、投资环境的律师，我们建议：买卖或交易时应认识到签订书面合同以及商谈与确定具体合同条款的重要性；若买卖或交易一方或双方是公司的，希望能够同时规范公司相关规章制度，避免在交易过程中产生争议，造成损失。

曹志龙律师的解析和建议由点及面，条例清晰，直击要处，足见其背后的良苦用心及深厚的法学功底，希望我国企业在国际贸易中、在"走出去"战略、"一带一路"建设中，亦如曹志龙律师所愿，将法律和风险防范意识常记心间，如此方能无往而不利。

**为中国企业"走出去"和"一带一路"建设建言献策**

笔者了解到，曹志龙律师参与发起建立了"八方联盟"和"国际律师事务所联盟"（ADVOC）并担任上海区代表；坚持与港、澳、台及多个国家之间的双边业务合作和交流；多次参与"企业兼并重组与海外投资高层论坛"；参加莫斯科交易所与上海清算所联合主办的"'一带一路'建设的投融资暨中俄金融基础设施建设国际研讨会"；担任国际商品和原料交易业务合作之专家顾问等。

2017年10月26日，曹志龙律师受邀出席了莫斯科交易所与上海清算所联合举办的"'一带一路'建设的投融资暨中俄金融基础设施建设国际研讨会"，并以"企业跨境投融资面临的法律风险与防范"为题进行交流发言。曹志龙律师围绕企业跨境投融资现状、投融资的监管和主要法律规定、企业投融资所面临的主要问题及法律风险，提出企业在"一带一路"的投融资中应当加强尽职调查、熟悉投融资目的国法律法规、掌握金融工具和熟悉金融产品、完善项目运作与公司治理、加强与专业机构和国际组织合作，并建议企业建立和完善ACE法律风险管理体系建设。曹志龙律师同时提出企业在"一带一路"投融资过程中应当充分发挥律师的作用：律师在法律查明、尽职调查及法律风险防范方面具有独特的优势，在"一带一路"新形势下能够为企业跨境投融资提供优质高效的法律服务。与会嘉宾对曹志龙律师的发言积极响应，提出今后将加强与律师事务所的合作与交流，进一步了解金融工具与金融产品，

防范"一带一路"投融资带来的法律风险。

笔者还了解到，早在2009年第七届华东律师论坛上，曹志龙律师就已将自己的研究和实务经验撰写成文章《谈谈中国律师如何更好地为跨境投资提供法律服务》与同仁无私分享。文章中，曹志龙律师根据自己的实务经验，提出了律师在跨境投资中可提供的法律服务的独到见解。文章结尾，曹志龙律师提出：中国律师事务所和律师们应当从不断完善内部管理、加强对律师专业分工、开展国际经验交流等方面，不断提高中国律师的专业化水平，不断提高中国事务所的核心竞争力，不断开拓新的法律服务市场，使中国律师业在经济全球化的浪潮中，真正走向专业化、规模化和国际化。

**后记**

曹志龙律师说："律师不仅是一种职业，一种专业，更是一项事业。是法治梦想的力量，指引我们不断前行；是律师事业的召唤，让我们为之终身奋斗。"

正是秉持这样一份对律师事业的热爱，对法治梦想的执着，让曹志龙律师获得了行业内外的高度认可。曹志龙律师现担任联合所管委会主任、党支部书记，兼任中华全国律师协会战略发展委委员、中华全国律师协会民事专业研究委员会委员、中华全国律师协会公司法专业研究委员会委员、上海市律师协会公司与商事业务研究委员会主任、上海市律师协会社会责任促进委员会主任、上海市律师协会规划与规则委员会副主任、上海市律师协会第十届理事、上海法学会商法研究会常务理事、华东政法大学律师学院特聘教授、中国国际经济贸易仲裁委员会仲裁员、上海国际经济贸易仲裁委员会仲裁员、上海仲裁委员会仲裁员、上海经贸商事调解中心调解员、黄浦区人大代表等社会职务。近年来，他的努力获得了多项荣誉：荣获2009年度"第十届上海市青年岗位能手""第四届上海市优秀青年律师"称号；被评为2011～2015年度上海市优秀律师，2011～2014年度全国优秀律师。

据悉，曹志龙律师还是本届中华全国律师协会修订和完善"律师法"课题的主持人，从律师定位、执业权力保障和救济、律协定位、维护法律服务市场秩序等12个方面提出了建设性的法律修改意见。

笔者了解到，在从事律师工作前，曹志龙律师曾有过4年人民教师的职业生涯。20年来，从教师到律师，从"万金油"律师到专业律师，从专业律师到"优秀青年律师"，从"优秀青年律师"到"全国优秀律师"、律师行业建设工作的参与者，曹志龙律师一直坚守着一个信念，那就是要肩负时代使命，大力弘扬法治精神，竭力维护法律尊严，做一名司法公正的维护者。

眼界决定人生格局，格局决定人生高度。作为上海滩老牌律所联合所的管委会主任、党支部书记，曹志龙律师正身处世界潮流的前沿，与律所同仁一起书写着他们的法律人生和法治梦想，书写着法律的公平与正义。

中国涉外律师

# Shouldering a lawyer's mission and protecting judicial justice

## ——Lawyer Cao Zhilong, National Excellent Lawyer and Chairman of the Management Committee and Secretary of the CPC Branch of Shanghai United Law Firm

The judicial environment is an important indicator of the competitiveness of a country or region. As the saying goes, a good nest attracts the golden phoenix. A good judicial environment is an important means of attracting investment, a prerequisite to an active market economy, and a strong guarantee of the economic development and take-off of a country or region. Creating a good judicial environment is a duty and mission of all lawyers.

Since the beginning of the 21st century, with China's accession to the WTO, and the further implementation of China's going global strategy, and "Belt and Road" Initiative, the Chinese economy is being liberalized and globalized, and has been integrated into the global economic system and the wave of economic globalization. Lawyer Cao, Chairman of the Management Committee and Secretary of the CPC Branch of Shanghai United Law Firm is a lawyer who has practiced for 16 years, and a winner of "National Excellent Lawyer" —— the highest honor of the Chinese lawyer community. When talking about "bringing in" and "going global", he always focuses on legal risks of enterprises and how to prevent such risks. It is because he handles over 100 cases per annum that he has got penetrating insights. He advocates that "Great truths are always simple" and "Knowledge and action should go hand in hand". For whatever case he handles, he can always find out clear legal relationships and clues from complicated facts, turn complexity into simplicity, and finally protect the clients' lawful rights and interests. He often says: "All people are equal before the law. For any client, Chinese or foreign, its rights and interests must be protected by law, because justice is the soul and lifeline of judicature, and also the best embodiment of a country's rule by law, judicial environment and investment environment."

## Case analysis

### 1. Justice is the soul and lifeline of rule by law

China has made tremendous achievements in all sectors in the past 40 years of reform and opening up. In particular, the contributions of overseas Chinese to China's economy and culture are obvious to all. Overseas Chinese investors have promoted China's economic and social development, exchanges and cooperation with other countries using their advantages in capital, technology, management experience and business resources. When they suffer losses in investment interests, lawyers ought to protect their lawful rights and interests, show China's rule by law spirit, and endeavor to create a better investment environment that promotes sustainable economic and social development as guardians of fairness and justice. Typical cases in which lawyer Cao strived to protect investment interests of overseas Chinese are presented below.

(1)Origin: On July 22, 2003, the management committee of an economic and technological development zone in a city in Shandong Province entered into an agreement on the establishment of a joint-stock hospital with a Hong Kong development limited liability company (hereinafter referred to as the "Hong Kong Company"), specifying that the management committee, the Hong Kong Company and a municipal hospital (hereinafter referred to as the "Cooperative Hospital") would establish a joint-stock hospital jointly in the economic and technological development zone. After one year and three months, the state-owned asset management company of the development zone, an investment company —— the investor appointed by the Hong Kong Company, and a neurotology institute agreed on their respective rights and obligations in detail. On January 17, 2005, the state-owned asset management company of the development zone gave a notice to the investment company and the neurotology institute, stating that the management committee suggested developing the hospital project in two phases, where the sub-health research center of the economic and technological development zone (hereinafter referred to as the "Research Center") would be established in the first phase. After receiving the notice, the investment company started the preparation of the Research Center quickly together with local shareholders. Immediately before September 2005, the social affairs bureau, and science, technology and industry development bureau of the economic and technological development zone approved preparation respectively.

After the Research Center got the government approvals, it received two certificates of the right to use state-owned land from the economic and technological development zone branch of the municipal land and resources bureau in November 2005

and April 2006, certifying that the Research Center obtained the right to use two pieces of state-owned land located on Bohai South Road. However, when the Research Center was about to be built, the social affairs bureau that formerly granting an approval changed its decision by issuing the notice on stopping the preparation of the Research Center in the economic and technological development zone on April 21, 2007.

On August 27, 2007, the economic and technological development zone branch of the municipal public security bureau detained the corporate and financial seals of the investment company suddenly without explaining the reason and the basis of law enforcement, and issued a notice three days later to seize the administrative, financial and contract seals of the Research Center. On the same day, the municipal land and resources bureau issued notices of cancellation of land registration ("X Zhu Xiao (2007) No.01" and "X Zhu Xiao (2007) No.02") to the Research Center, cancelling the right to use state-owned land obtained by the Research Center earlier.

Jiang X, Board Chairman of the Hong Kong Company and overseas Chinese, communicated with the competent municipal authorities many times after receiving the above four administrative decisions, but his efforts proved futile. Due to his own limited power, he reported the matter to the Overseas Chinese Affairs Office of the State Council, and this case was later transferred to Shanghai United Law Firm with a history of over 20 years. After accepting this case, the law firm dispatched a legal team composed of Lawyer Cao and two other lawyers to Shandong to handle this case.

(2)Case handling:After appointment by the Hong Kong Company, the three lawyers found that all the four administrative decisions involved illegal procedures or erroneous determination of facts, determined a handling program of reconsideration before negotiation, and filed a reconsideration application of revoking the four administrative decisions. Through their efforts, the Shandong Provincial People's Government revoked the four administrative decisions, laying a solid foundation for subsequent

successful reconciliation and rights protection.

(3)Lawyer Cao's analysis: This case involved overseas Chinese, and was highly valued by the Overseas Chinese Affairs Office of the State Council. The handling lawyers handled this case properly, resolved the conflict between the foreign investor and the local government, corrected the wrong administrative act of the local government, caused the local government to carry out administrative work according to law, and built up the foreign investor's confidence in the investment environment, laws and policies of Mainland China. In this case, major financial losses were retrieved for the client, and its lawful rights and interests protected practically. This case was thought highly of by the Overseas Chinese Affairs Office of the State Council, the municipal government and the Hong Kong Company, and had a positive impact on the local foreign investment environment.

2.Payments in international trade impaired, and rights protected by lawyers through hard work

A Shanghai industrial development limited liability company (hereinafter referred to as the "Shanghai Company") is a company dealing with solar silicon material trading. It suffered major financial losses of nearly RMB 30 million due to inadvertent remittance in foreign purchase. In this case, lawyer Cao managed to prove that the purchasing remittance was consistent with the transaction, and a sales contract relationship existed though there was no contract, and eventually retrieved major financial losses for the Shanghai Company. Of course, perhaps only those who experienced this case in person know how difficult it was.

(1)Origin: A silicon wafer company of the British Virgin Islands (hereinafter referred to as "the Silicon Wafer Company") is a company registered in the British Virgin Islands, and a wholly-owned subsidiary of a German joint-stock company (hereinafter referred to as the "German Company"). The Silicon Wafer Company has set up a representative office in Shanghai, and its chief representative is Huang X, who is also the China region chief sales officer of the Silicon Wafer Company.

Since September 2006, the Silicon Wafer Company has been in business cooperation with the Shanghai Company through its Shanghai representative office, purchasing polished wafers and other goods from the Silicon Wafer Company, and making down payments to the Silicon Wafer Company via the Shanghai branch of Citibank (China) Co., Ltd. and by other means of payment. At the beginning, the Silicon Wafer Company delivered goods normally. However, with the increase of order quantity, the Silicon Wafer Company was unable to deliver goods after receiving down payments from the Shanghai Company. As the controlling shareholder, the German Company denied down payments of the Shanghai Company after replacing all executives of the Silicon Wafer Company and the Shanghai representative office. There was no formal sales contract, and the remittance documents were mostly to the order of a third party designated by Huang X, with down payments amounting to $4 235 760.30. How should the Shanghai Company protect its own rights and interests in this case? In this difficult situation, the Shanghai Company had to resort to lawyers.

(2)Protection of rights: After appointment by the Shanghai Company, the two lawyers thought that though this case involved down payments only, there was no formal sales contract, and the sums were not remitted to the supplier directly. Besides, this case involved Chinese and foreign laws, and was extremely complicated. After a careful study, the lawyers proposed a handling program——first proving that there were practical transactions between the Shanghai Company and the Silicon Wafer Company, and then proving the sums paid by the Shanghai Company since September 2006 were actually used to purchase products of the Silicon Wafer Company. After referring to some customs declaration forms, bills of lading, e-mails, invoices and other materials of transactions between the two companies, valid evidence was finally available, and 10 statements issued by Huang X, former chief representative of the Shanghai representative office were obtained later, confirming that the Silicon Wafer Company still owed the Shanghai Company $4 235 760.30. This evidence was notarized by the Luwan District Notary Office of Shanghai Municipality, and Huang X's testimony further confirmed the trading relationship between the two companies; the attachment to an e-mail sent by the finance department of the Silicon Wafer Company to the Shanghai Company on August 8, 2008 specified the times and amounts of the sums for goods received by the Silicon Wafer Company from the Shanghai Company via other companies and individuals since 2006 (totaling $13 073 819.14), and Paul, President of the Silicon Wafer Company, also signed in this attachment. The above evidence showed that there was an undisputed trading relationship between the two companies, together with the resulting credits and debts. Moreover, the German Company received $6 million in profits from the Silicon Wafer Company in the mode of profit sharing while the latter had debts, thereby infringing on the interests of the creditors.

After all evidentiary materials were collected and confirmed, the lawyers gave the following opinions: There were credits and debts arising from the trading relationship between the Shanghai Company and the Silicon Wafer Company; The so-called profit sharing act of the German Company as the controlling shareholder infringed on the interests of the Shanghai Company, and should assume a joint and several liability for the debts of the Silicon Wafer Company.

(3)Judgment: Through trial, the court judged that the defendant (the Silicon Wafer Company) should pay $4 235 760.30 to the plaintiff (the Shanghai Company), and compensate for the interests thereon from July 27, 2009 to the effective date of the judgment (at the prevailing US dollar deposit rate of the People's Bank of China). However, the court rejected the claim that the defendant (the German Company) should assume a joint and several liability for the debts of the defendant (the Silicon Wafer Company) because the company laws of the British Virgin Islands and Germany were different from the Chinese company law.

(4)Lawyer Cao's analysis: In this case, there was no sales contract between the plaintiff (the Shanghai Company) and the defendant (the Silicon Wafer Company), nor there was any voucher of direct payment by the plaintiff to the defendant. However, the sale of goods was often accompanied by account statements, invoices, letters, etc., and such evidence could make the court believe that there was a trading relationship between both parties. Since the defendant (the Silicon Wafer Company) and its controlling shareholder (the German Company) failed to prove that they had performed the delivery obligation, the defendant (the Silicon Wafer Company) ought to refund the down payments of the plaintiff (the Shanghai Company) and the interests thereon.

In addition, since this was a foreign-related case, the applicable

laws should be first determined, and the lawyers should study the foreign laws involved in the legal relationship. As the agent of the plaintiff, the lawyers would often understand and interpret legal provisions in favor of the plaintiff, and their thinking might also be habitually affected by Chinese laws. For example, the Chinese company law stipulates, "If a shareholder of a company abuses the independent status of the legal entity and the limited liability of shareholders to evade debts, thereby infringing on the interests of the company's creditors seriously, it shall assume a joint and several liability for the company's debts." This involves the confusion of corporate personality, which takes the form of staff, business and financial confusion mainly. However, the laws applicable in this regard in this case are the relevant laws of the British Virgin Islands——the place of incorporation of the defendant (the Silicon Wafer Company). The court thought that the Business Company Act of the British Virgin Islands did not define the legal constituents of personality confusion, nor did it stipulate the legal liability arising from personality confusion, and a shareholder's infringement on any creditor's interests using the independent status of the legal entity, and that the subject claiming improper profit distribution was the company other than any creditor, so it did not support the claim that the defendant (the German Company) should be liable for the debts of the defendant (the Silicon Wafer Company). This case also shows the special nature of the rules on the confusion of corporate personality in the Business Company Act of the British Virgin Islands, so special attention should be paid to this in international investment and trade.

(5)Lawyer Cao's advice: Based on the judgment, the court supported that the defendant (the Silicon Wafer Company) should pay all the claimed sums and the interests thereon to the plaintiff (the Shanghai Company), protecting the lawful rights and interests of the plaintiff, and helping the plaintiff avoid major financial losses.

As lawyers studying legal and investment environments of all countries around the world, we suggest that the importance of entering into a written contract, and negotiating and defining contract terms should be realized in trading, and if one party or both parties is or are a company or companies, relevant corporate rules and regulations should also be regulated to avoid disputes and losses.

Lawyer Cao's analysis and advice are well organized and direct to the point, from which his well-meant intention and profound legal knowledge can be seen. As expected by lawyer Cao, Chinese enterprises should always keep law and risk prevention in mind in international trade, and the implementation of China's going global strategy, and the "Belt and Road" Initiative in order to remain successful.

**Giving advice on the implementation of the going global strategy, and the "Belt and Road" initiative for Chinese enterprises**

The author has learned that Lawyer Cao participated in the establishment of the "Grand Compass Alliance" and the international network of independent law firms (ADVOC), and serves as the representative of the Shanghai region; he has been engaged in bilateral cooperation and exchanges with Hong Kong China, Macao China, Taiwan China regions as well as many countries, attended the High-level Forum on Business M&A and Overseas Investment many times, and the International Seminar on "Belt and Road" Investment and Financing & China-Russia Financial Infrastructure Construction jointly organized

by Moscow Exchange and Shanghai Clearing House, and served as an expert adviser on international cooperative commodity and raw material trading.

On October 26, 2017, lawyer Cao was invited to attend the International Seminar on "Belt and Road" Investment and Financing & China-Russia Financial Infrastructure Construction jointly organized by Moscow Exchange and Shanghai Clearing House, and gave a speech titled "legal risks in cross-border corporate investment and financing, and prevention". Based on the current situation of cross-border corporate investment and financing, regulation, key legal provisions, key issues and legal risks, he proposed that enterprises should strengthen due diligence, get familiar with laws and regulations of destination countries, understand financial tools and products, improve project operations and corporate governance, and strengthen cooperation with professional and international organizations in investment and financing activities under the "Belt and Road" Initiative, and advised enterprises to establish a sound ACE legal risk management system. He also proposed that enterprises should give full play to the role of lawyers in this process, because lawyers had unique advantages in due diligence and legal risk prevention, and were able to provide high-quality and efficient legal services for cross-border corporate investment and financing in the new situation. The guests present responded actively to lawyer Cao's speech, and said that they would strengthen cooperation and exchanges with law firms, further understand financial tools and products, and prevent legal risks arising from investment and financing activities under the "Belt and Road" Initiative.

The author has also learned that at the Seventh Eastern China Lawyer Forum in 2009, lawyer Cao shared his article "A talk on how Chinese lawyers should provide better legal services for cross-border investment" written based on his research and practical experience selflessly with peers. In this article, lawyer Cao expressed an insightful view on legal services that could be offered by lawyers in cross-border investment based on his practical experience. At the end of the article, lawyer Cao wrote, "Chinese law firms and lawyers should improve their professionalism and core competences, and keep developing new legal service markets by improving internal management, strengthening specialization, and conducting international experience sharing, thereby enabling the Chinese legal service industry to be truly specialized, expanded and globalized in the wave of economic globalization."

**Postscript**

Lawyer Cao said, "The lawyer is not only an occupation or profession, but also a career. It is the dream of rule by law that guides us forward, and the mission of the lawyer career that inspires to devote our lifetime to it."

It is his commitment to the lawyer career and the dream of rule by law that makes lawyer Cao highly recognized in and out of the industry. Currently, lawyer Cao is Chairman of the Management Committee and Secretary of the CPC Branch of Shanghai United Law Firm, and also holds many social positions, such as member of the Strategic Development Committee of All China Lawyers Association, the Civil Research Committee of All China Lawyers Association, and the Company Law Research Committee of All China Lawyers Association, Director of the Corporate and Business Affairs Research Committee of Shanghai Lawyers Association, Director of the Social Responsibility Promotion Committee of Shanghai Lawyers Association, Deputy Director of the Planning and Rules Committee of Shanghai Lawyers Association, member of the Tenth Council of Shanghai Lawyers Association, executive council member of the Commercial Law Research Branch of Shanghai Law Society, Distinguished Professor of the Lawyers Institute of East China University of Political Science and Law, arbitrator of the China International Economic and Trade Arbitration Commission, arbitrator of the Shanghai International Economic and Trade Arbitration Commission, arbitrator of the Shanghai Arbitration Commission, mediator of the Shanghai Commercial Mediation Center, and deputy to the Huangpu District People's Congress. In recent years, he has won a number of honors, including the "Tenth Shanghai Excellent Young Job Performer Award" in 2009, the "Fourth Shanghai Excellent Young Lawyer Award", Shanghai Excellent Lawyer during 20112015, and National Excellent Lawyer during 2011 ~ 2014.

It is learned that lawyer Cao is also the leader of the Lawyer Law amendment project of All China Lawyers Association, and has given constructive amendment advice in 12 aspects, including lawyer positioning, practicing power protection and relief, lawyers association positioning, and the order of the legal service market.

The author has learned that lawyer Cao served as a teacher for four years before becoming a lawyer. From a teacher to a lawyer, a "utility" lawyer, a specialized lawyer, an excellent young lawyer, a national excellent lawyer, and a participant of legal service industry development, lawyer Cao always believes that he should shoulder a lawyer's mission to carry forward the rule by law spirit, and protect the dignity of law and judicial justice.

The vision determines how successful one can be in his or her career. As chairman of the Management Committee and Secretary of the CPC Branch of Shanghai United Law Firm —— a well-established law firm in Shanghai, lawyer Cao is endeavoring to realize the common dream of pursuing the fairness and justice of law together with his colleagues.

# 发展才是硬道理

## ——访上海市协力律师事务所创始合伙人、中日经贸律师姚重华

"发展才是硬道理"这句广为流传的至理名言深深地影响着国人以及改革开放40年来我国经济的变迁与发展。进入21世纪以来，世界各国为了谋求更好的发展，皆在穷尽一切办法开拓全球市场，为未来谋篇、布局。当前，世界经济全球化已是必然，对于我国而言，中国企业"走出去"，外国企业"引进来"早已成为一种经济常态。

我国与日本自1972年正式建交至今，因历史原因，两国的经贸往来可谓崎岖不断、饱经风雨，而无论在"政冷经热"还是"政冷经凉"的状态下，两国的经济一直有着极强的互补性，这种实际现状是毋庸置疑的，两国之间也唯有合作和向前发展才是"硬道理"。我们今天要采访的主人公就是一位为中日间经贸往来提供30年专业法律服务，且是一位具有中国律师、日本国外国法事务律师（日本律师联合会注册号:G373）双重执业资格的法律人，他就是上海市协力律师事务所创始合伙人姚重华律师。

30年弹指一挥间，40载沧海已桑田。今天就让我们走近姚重华律师，在他的人生之路、执业之旅中看中国改革开放40年的变迁与发展，观一代中国法律人的情怀与坚守。

**业务领域**
国际投资、国际贸易

**学历**
日本京都大学 法学博士课程履修
日本京都大学 法学硕士
上海大学（原复旦大学分校）法学学士

**办公地点**
上海、大阪

**执业经验**
姚重华律师为中国律师、日本国外国法事务律师，执业于上海市协力律师事务所和日本的日中协力律师事务所，并担任大阪商工会议所和大阪国际经济振兴中心的中国法律咨询律师。

姚重华律师1987年在上海市第二律师事务所初涉以刑事辨护为主的律师业务；1988年春到日本京都大学留学，主攻民商法学；1994年春，在京都大学完成了法学硕士和博士课程后回国，就职于上海市第五律师事务所；1998年创设了以专业团队运作为主的协力律师事务所。

姚重华律师从1988年开始涉足中日两国间的投资贸易等法律事务，代理过诸多涉外仲裁和诉讼案件，解决了近百起纠纷案件。20年来，以优良业绩而获得当事人的信赖。2003年作为第一位中国籍的日本国外国法事务律师，在日本商事仲裁协会成功代理了中日两国企业间的国际商事仲裁案件。2004年，成功代理了在中国法院相当罕见的、以日本国法律为准据法的商事诉讼案件。目前，担任着50多家企业的常年法律顾问或独立董事、监事的工作。

**工作语言**
中文，日语

**勤勉尽责，不负所托**
俗话说，"科学技术是第一生产力"，若想在世界未来经济的发展中拥有更多的话语权，必需掌握先进的科学技术。

当前，集成电路应用技术领域（因涉及商业秘密，下文只能简述）的高端设计制造技术一直为美日韩台等企业所掌握，且拥有极强的国际定价话语权，中国内地虽为全球最大的制造和消费市场之一，但因未掌握核心技术，一被"禁售"软肋就露出。若想在世界经济一体化的浪潮中屹立潮头，获得国际定价话语权，实现全球化布局和发展，海外收购不啻为一种最佳方案。2018年4月，一个尽职调查委托电话打到了姚重华律师的日本手机上，要求15日内完成对日本一家某高新技术企业的尽职调查，姚重华律师听了情况介绍后感到15日内根本无法办好。这是一份标的金额达数十亿日元的收购项目——系中国企业收购日本企业，此收购项目若成功，将为中国填补IT关联的高端制造产业链中的一个空白，同时也能为中国企业在该领域增强定价话语权，其积极意义不可估量。但目标企业的具体情况以及收购金额是否合理均不清楚。收购目标企业持有的相关技术是否需要日本政府的审批或备案？这些正是他所考虑的问题。15日内完成尽职调查程序几无可能，至少需要20个工作日甚至更长的时间。"一般这类业务，我们的尽职调查程序至少是40天，因为整个工作需要经过组织团队、收集相关资料、列出尽调提纲、实施、汇编报告初稿至定稿的过程，但双方已经签订意向协议书，我方企业求购心切。"

时不我待，唯有立刻行动并做好前期所有的尽职调查工作，越详细、完备越好。首先，姚重华律师组织尽调团队对该日企的财务状况及资产负债表、损益表、内外合同以及所持有的知识产权等做了细致的调查，初步判断国际产业链的

环境适宜该项技术在中国大规模运用，但目标企业因与整个产业链对接不畅，一直处于亏损状态。姚重华律师在同尽调会计师对企业产品的成品率进行对比发现，企业的成品率为81%多一点，而毛利率只有2%，再加上销售和管理成本肯定是亏损的，如果能将成品率提高到85%，那么企业的毛利率即可达到5%，这样才能持平。同时，姚重华律师还对近年来该领域的国际收购价格进行了深入的调研，发现意向协议价格明显偏高，遂建议降低收购价格。本来只是委托姚重华律师负责前期的尽职调查工作，但随着工作的深入推进，中方企业对姚重华律师财税业务的专业程度也极为认可，由委托尽职调查业务扩大到了委托姚重华律师负责收购价格的商务谈判。在接下此任务后，姚重华律师向对方出示了目标公司详细的财务资料和近期国际IT行业收购价格的数据，在客观资料和国际市场发展现状与实际行情面前，仅两个回合就将该收购案标的金额定下，最终收购价较原意向协议价格降低了约45%，为中方企业节省了大笔收购成本。2018年7月中旬，该收购案完美收官，中方企业又委托姚重华律师担任收购后的目标公司的监事，并负责后续的目标公司整合与协调工作。当然，后续工作虽与法律工作无太大关系，但姚重华律师更乐意看到一个中日企业成功合作的新范例。

"能为中国企业实现全球化布局和发展尽自己的绵薄之力是一件很自豪也很荣幸的事，当然，我们做国际业务的律师，本身就需要拥有国际化的视野和思维。合作共赢无关国别。"姚重华律师欣慰而自豪地说。

### 东渡求学，专注中日经贸

上文提到，姚重华律师自1988年赴日本京都大学留学后开始涉足中日两国间的投资贸易等领域的法律事务，30年来参与了诸多涉外仲裁和诉讼案件，解决了上百起民商事纠纷案件。有一起案件处理和一项技术的引进更值得我们记录。一是，在20世纪90年代东南亚经济危机导致日本商业集团八佰伴破产倒闭的案件中，姚重华律师带领刚设立的协力律师事务所同仁担任了与八佰伴公司相关企业的清算业务，其严谨的工作态度和专业的敬业精神获得各方的高度评价，并为后续接盘企业顺利重启项目奠定了基础。二是，业内众所周知的，世界上第一条高速铁路是建于1964年的日本"东海道新干线"，这意味着日本拥有先进的高铁技术和丰富的高铁运营经验。进入21世纪以来，我国经济取得突飞猛进的发展，但与之不匹配的是我国连200公里准高速的动车组技术还有许多难关没有攻克，国家遂考虑引进日本、德国、法国等发达国家的高铁技术。作为长期致力于中日经贸往来的姚重华律师自此受聘于日本高铁技术的团队成员之一，并为"动车组制动系统"的谈判和引进提供了专业的法律服务。纵观我国由铁路大国到高铁强国的崛起过程，姚重华律师也成为我国高铁发展的一位历史见证者和参与者。

专注于中日经贸往来的30年间，姚重华律师几乎每月都要在中日间往返数趟，里程有数百万公里之多，今天他还在日本谈判，明天可能就到了上海、北京，还要不时地回到老人身边报个平安。忙碌、奔波，为中日间经贸往来牵线

搭桥，他用专业和敬业赢得了委托人的信赖，更获得中日双方当事人的高度肯定和赞赏。

近年来，IT行业、锂电池、人工智能等科技前沿成为姚重华律师关注和服务的重点，他也成了青年人学习的榜样，成为律师界开拓进取、与时俱进的楷模和典范。

### 牢记使命，支持青年发展

姚重华律师在创设了协力律师事务所后，先后送团队7位年轻律师去日本的大学留学。2017年6月，已经成长为协力律师事务所高级合伙人的叶晨律师获日本法务大臣认可，取得日本国外国法事务律师资格，注册于日本律师联合会（注册号G1013号），隶属福冈律师协会，同时叶晨律师也成为首位在日本福冈登记注册为日本国外国法事务律师的中国律师。至今为止，协力律师事务所投资贸易团队已有姚重华、叶晨两位律师于日本律师联合会在册，目前在国内律所中尚无出其右者。

近年来，协力律师事务所团队律师以"迅速""正确""有效"为行动指南，采取专业分工合作、重大或疑难案件集体讨论以及业务流程动态管理的运作模式，保证了办案质量，维护委托人的最大合法权益。

2018年，随着日本《住宅住宿事业法》（简称《民宿新法》）的正式实施，各大民宿销售平台下架所有不合法民宿。2018年6月底，笔者从中国网报道获悉途家取得了国内首个在日本合法经营民宿资质。在日本观光厅公布的一批"住宅宿泊仲介业者"名单中，途家也成为中国境内最早、也是唯一取得日本民宿经营合法资质的中介平台。这意味着日本民宿的监管进一步细化加强，而途家的运营资质和房源已得到日本政府的双重认可，从此消费者在平台预定民宿将更有保障。而此次为途家取得国内首个在日本合法经营民宿资质提供法律服务的就是叶晨律师带领团队成员经过数月艰辛努力完成的项目。

### 考察列国，思索人类社会发展之路

1954年出生的姚重华律师按说早已到了耳顺之年，应该可以过上含饴弄孙的闲适生活了，但他却选择了如孔子一样"周游列国"，砍掉了九成业务后，专注看世界、观社会、思民生。关注"一带一路"的实施以及遇到或可能遇到的问题。诸如东南亚各国、欧洲各国、美国、澳新、墨西哥以及南美一些国家均留下了他的足迹，更留下了他对整个社会发展方向的深深思索。

姚重华律师为中日间经贸的合作与发展服务了30年，贡献了30年，见证和体味了合作、共赢、发展才是硬道理的千古箴言，合作共赢不仅适合我们，更适合整个世界。我们相信，在未来人生之路和执业之旅中，姚重华律师仍将执着于为中日间合作共赢抓住时机和构建平台，为整个人类的发展贡献自己的才智和力量，力量虽微薄，但那是正能量。

# 社会発展は人類共通の目標である

## ——上海協力法律事務所の創立者、日中間投資貿易法務専門の弁護士、
## 姚重華氏とのインタビュー

「社会発展は人類共通の目標である」という名言は、中国経済の発展と40年にわたる改革開放に深く影響している。21世紀の初めから、より良い発展を追求し、未来を切り開くために、世界のすべての国々は、グローバル市場を開拓し、あらゆる知恵を使って取り組んでいる。現在、世界経済のグローバル化は決まっているトレンドである。中国にとっては、中国企業の「海外進出」と外国企業の「中国進出」はすでに経済的な常態化となっている。

中国と日本は、1972年に正式な外交関係を回復してから、歴史的な要因によって両国間の経済と貿易交流は度重なる困難に遭遇し、紆余曲折を経てきた。経済交流が順調に進んでも、進まなくても両国の経済は切っても切れない状態にあることは疑いのないことであり、両国の協力は唯一の道である。　今回、インタビューした方は、中日間の経済貿易取引のため、30年間専門的な法律サービスをしてきた中国弁護士と日本国外国法事務弁護士（日本弁護士連合会登録番号：G373）の両方の資格を持つ法律専門家であり、上海協力法律事務所の創業パートナー弁護士の姚重華氏である。

30年瞬く間に過ぎ去った。インタビューを通じて姚重華弁護士の人生の旅から、中国改革後の変化と発展を一緒に顧みましょう。

### 姚重華弁護士

法律業務専門分野；国際投資、国際取引及びその紛争解決

### 学歴

京都大学大学院法学研究科　法学博士；京都大学大学院法学研究科　法学修士；上海大学（元復旦大学分校）法学学士。

### 法律事務所

上海、大阪

### 執務経歴

姚重華弁護士は、中国弁護士と日本国外国法事務弁護士として上海市協力律師事務所と日本の日中協力法律事務所にて執務して、大阪商工会議所及び大阪国際経済振興センターの中国法律相談員も担当する。

1987年、姚重華弁護士は、上海市第二律師事務所に入り、刑事弁護からその弁護士人生を始められた。1988年の春、京都大学へ留学して民商法などを専攻にして、京都大学大学院にて法学修士と法学博士課程を修了しました。その間数多くの日本の弁護士先生に協力し、中国法務関係の業務に携った。1994年の春、帰国して上海市第五律師事務所の弁護士になった。1998年、専門チームを組んで上海協力律師事務所を創設し、現在は約15拠点を開設し、弁護士が二百人以上ある総合的な法律事務所に成長させた。

姚重華弁護士は、1998年から日中間の投資貿易取引の法律業務に携わってきて数多くの渉外仲裁、訴訟事件を処理したことがあり、百件近く紛争事件を解決した。この20年間、優良な実績で当事者から厚く信頼を得られた。2003年、日本商事仲裁協会にて初めて中国籍の外国法事務弁護士として日中間企業の国際仲裁事件を代理し、かつ中国の裁判所においてその仲裁判断も承認された。2004年、中国の裁判所にて、稀に見る日本法を準拠法とする日本当事者間の商事訴訟事件を担当しました。現在、五十数社の法律顧問弁護士、社外取締役、監査役を担当する。

### 謹厳実直

「科学技術が第一生産力である」と言われているが、世界経済のグローバル化に従って、中国は日本の技術をいかに活用するか考えなければならない。この二三十年間で中国は、世界の工場になり、貿易摩擦問題があっても、その製造拠点及び人口約14億による巨大市場であり、また日本が先端技術をもって、その高いレベルの研究開発力がうまく中国に取り入れされるのが日中両国は期待されていることである。

姚重華弁護士は、日中両国のハイテック産業関連企業の技術取引もサポートしています。半導体産業、液晶製造関係、スマートホン等の精密部品製造、イオン電池製造関係等の技術取引に関わる業務も多くなり、2018年4月から7月にかけて、ある中国民間企業の代理人として、日本の技術を発明して産業化してそして中国などの海外市場に移されたことにより、経営が苦しくなった技術企業の買収を担当された。デューデリジェンスチームの構成、数年間の貸借対照表と損益計算書及びキャッシュフロー計算書などの資料チェック、歩留まりを含む製造原価の分析、基本意見の提出等は、担当のチームメンバーと協力し合って依頼者の要望により最短期間で完成した。事件処理の正確さと速さが依頼者に評価され、その後のビジネス交渉まで依頼された。姚重華弁護士は、世界のIT関連のM&A市場資料も用意され、価格交渉の場で目的会社の関係資料を説明しながら、国際的なIT企業M&A市場の状況も説明して、

中国涉外律师

且つ目的会社の進路見通しについても積極的に意見を提出した。最終的に、交渉相手も姚重華弁護士の意見に納得し、価格交渉は五時間で完了した。また、この M&A 対象である日本企業を製造だけではなく、この企業グループの研究開発センターとして発展させていく案に力を入れています。姚重華弁護士の法的な専門知識、国際取引の経験、交渉力及び企画力は、依頼者からの信頼を得て、現在当該日本会社の監査役に就任する。もちろん、本件 M&A においては、多くの業務が、弁護士業務とは言えませんが、姚重華弁護士は、新たな日中間の企業協力成功例として楽しむのではないかと推測する。

### 日本留学、日中間の法律業務一筋

　　上に書いてあるように、姚重華弁護士は、1988年の春、京都大学へ留学してから日中間の投資貿易取引に関わる法律業務に携わってきた。それから30年間、数多くの渉外仲裁、訴訟事件を担当して、百件近くの紛争事件を解決した。その中の二件を見てみましょう。まず、90年代、東南アジア金融危機が起こり、いち早く中国に進出したヤオハングループが倒産し、これは当時、「おしん」というドラマによって、中国の人々に周知されていた会社で、中国社会にもショックを与えた。当時、姚重華弁護士は、設立したばかりの協力律師事務所の弁護士チームを率いてヤオハン倒産に影響を受けた日系合弁企業の撤退を担当した。合弁相手の中国パートナーとの折衝、撤退計画の立案、従業員の解雇、債権回収と債務整理、債権者との交渉、訴訟の対応などを、姚重華弁護士は会社清算チームの皆と一緒にほぼ計画通りに完了した。当時は業務担当者である弁護士の冷静さも必要とされ、小売り関係の会社で、仕入先、即ち債権者も多く、興奮した債権者たちに囲まれ、110番を三回かけたこともあった。また、ご存知の通り、世界で初めて高速鉄道が実現したのが1964年の東海道新幹線であり、日本は、高速鉄道の技術を有し、豊富な運営経験をもっている。二十一世紀に入り、中国経済は目覚ましく発展してきたが、鉄道技術は、未だ遅れている。中国政府はまず既存の在来線を利用して日本、フランス、カナダ等の時速200キロEMU技術を導入しようと決めた。長い間、日中間の法律業務をやってきた姚重華弁護士は、日本の時速200キロEMU制御システムのチームの一員としてその技術契約の成立に尽力された。その後、中国鉄道の在来線において、EMU車両は時速250キロでも走りだし、世界中に注目されたが、姚重華弁護士は、安全第一を忘れないように警笛を鳴らした［笛は流れない］。現在、中国では、高速鉄道網が整備されつつあり、姚重華弁護士も仕事の合間を利用して中国各地を巡られ、高速鉄道の開通による各地方の経済発展の成果を確認する。最近、中国奥地にある恩施、利川へ向かわれ現地の人達から高速鉄道の開通による経済効果を確認した。中国鉄道発展の一参加者としてその今後

を見守っている。

### 使命を忘れず若い世代の成長を支えていく

　　姚重華弁護士は、協力律師事務所を創設してから、日本語だけではなく日本社会の理解も大事なことだと思って、チームの若手弁護士7名を日本に留学させた。2017年6月、すでに協力律師事務所のシニアパートナーになった叶晨弁護士は、日本国法務大臣の許可を受け、日本国外国法事務弁護士の資格を取得し、日本弁護士連合会に登録（登録番号 G1013 号）し、福岡弁護士会に属されている。これにより、協力律師事務所の投資貿易法務チームでは、姚重華弁護士、叶晨弁護士の二名が、日本の外国法事務弁護士として日弁連に登録したことになり、中国の律師事務所では初めてのことである。

　　協力律師事務所は、設立されてから、「迅速、正確、有効」という行動指針が確立され、専門チームを結成し、重大な案件または複雑な案件の内部討論及び業務のフローチャートのプロセス化による運営制度で、業務品質を確保し、依頼者の利益が最大限になるよう努力してきた。

　　2018年日本の「住宅宿泊事業法」の実施によって、各民泊予約サイトでは、違法な民泊を削除しました。2018年6月末、中国網の報道から途家が日本の民泊経営資格を取得した初めての中国企業であり、日本観光庁が公布した「住宅宿泊仲介業者」名簿には、途家も載ってあった。これにより、途家は、日本政府の認可で日本においての民泊の運営資格を得て、その営業ができるようになった。この途家の日本民泊資格取得は、叶晨弁護士がチームのメンバーと共に数か月の努力の末になした事案である。

### 諸国を考察し、人類社会発展の道を思考している

　　孔子は、「吾十有五にして学に志す。三十にして立つ。四十にして惑はず。五十にして天命を知る。六十にして耳順（したが）ふ。七十にして心の欲する所に従へども、矩（のり）を踰（こ）えず」と言ったが、1954年に生まれた姚重華弁護士はすでに耳順ふという年を過ぎたが、悠々自適な生活を選ばず、業務を減らして、孔子のように諸国周遊を選んだ。視野を世界に向け、人類の共通課題や、中国が法治社会になるようにと考えて、アジア・アセアン諸国、欧米諸国、ANZ、中南米の一部の国々に足跡を残した。勿論、中国政府が提唱してきた「一帯一路」についても、時間かけて関係国を巡り、関係の問題点を真剣にリストアップする。

　　姚重華弁護士は、30年間、日中間の法律業務を中心にしてその両国の経済発展に尽力した。その経験と力を活かして、今後、弁護士の現場仕事だけではなく、日中両国間の橋渡し役としての一層のご活躍を我々は期待している。

# 顺势而为，方能行稳致远

## ——访广东环宇京茂律师事务所首席合伙人、主任何培华律师

40年弹指一挥间。2018年，中国迎来改革开放40周年。改革开放40年来，我国的经济建设取得重大成就，人民生活水平获得极大提高，为经济发展保驾护航的中国律师业自恢复重建至今也获得了长足的发展。

2018年，有一位法律人迎来了他律师执业的第30个年头。在中国律师的发展尤其在涉外法律服务业从无到有再到蓬勃发展的历程中，广东环宇京茂律师事务所首席合伙人、主任何培华律师的名字以及他所代理的美国公民诉中国"马牌烟花爆炸索赔案"、美国对中国"对虾反倾销案""广东生益科技公司遭美国337调查案"等重大涉外案件早已成为各大法学院校、涉外研究机构的典型范例并载入了史册。

值此中国改革开放40周年，何培华律师执业30周年之际，我们再次采访了这位仍奋斗在涉外法律服务第一线的中国涉外律师。

注释：1. 美国公民诉中国"马牌烟花爆炸索赔案"（时间：1993年；结果：为中国挽回经济损失4亿元人民币）；2. 美国对中国"对虾反倾销案"（时间：2004年；结果：成功地获得0关税的有利裁决）；3. "广东生益科技公司遭美国337调查案"（时间：2008年；结果：最终使美国原告方撤诉，取得了中国企业应对美国337调查史上前所未有的胜利）。

## 走近何培华律师

### 砥砺奋进，夯实基底

"不是我成就了这些重大涉外案件，而是这些重大涉外案件成就了我。"何培华律师总是非常谦逊地对待自己过往的成就和荣誉。在笔者看来，若没有扎实的功底、丰厚的学养、高瞻远瞩的眼光以及充足的准备，即使机遇迎面而来，也会失之交臂。正是何培华律师具备了这些素质，所以在遇到重大涉外案件时，他才能挺身而出力挽狂澜，并能最大限度地维护国家利益，维护当事人的合法权益。我们从他的经历和履历中可见一斑。

何培华律师1957年生于中国的最南端，汉代"海上丝绸之路"始发港之一——广东徐闻，20世纪70年代他曾下乡插队3年经受磨砺。1978年9月恢复高考后考上了湛江师范学院英语系，毕业后当了4年中学老师。这些经历为他以后从事涉外法律工作打下了坚实的语言基础；1985年，他考取中国政法大学第二学士班，毕业后考入该校研究生院，师从中国著名法学家江平教授；1988年，他通过全国

律师资格考试；1989年毕业并获民商法硕士学位。同年开始，他在中国国际贸易促进委员会广东分会和广东对外经济贸易委员会从事多年涉外法律工作，历任副科长、科长、副处长等职。1993年创办广东环宇商务律师事务所，并出任主任一职至今；2000年8月至2001年9月在美国哥伦比亚大学作访问学者；2001年7月至2002年8月在美国加州大学法学院攻读国际商法硕士学位；2002年9月起在中国政法大学研究生院攻读民商法博士学位，仍师从江平教授，并于2005年取得博士学位。可以说，这些丰富的工作和学习经历为何培华律师办理重大涉外案件奠定了坚实的基础。

此外，何培华律师还先后担任《民商法律评论》执行主编；广东省律师协会第七、第八届WTO法律专业委员会主任；广东省人大常委会立法顾问；中国政法大学兼职教授；中山大学法学院硕士研究生兼职导师；暨南大学兼职法律硕士研究生导师，厦门大学陈安国际法发展基金讲座教授、国际经济法研究所兼职研究员；中国国际经济法学会常务理事等众多社会职务，在不同的场合和国际舞台上为中国律师发声。

## 对话何培华律师

### 名誉侵权，必须担责

**赵伟主编：**何律师您好！非常感谢您能在百忙中接受我们的这次专访，作为较早从事涉外法律工作的中国律师，可以说在您的执业生涯中，代理的诸多重大涉外案件皆受到多方关注和报道，有的案件已经成为涉外领域的标杆，在此我们已毋庸赘言。我们注意到，2015年，在"甄子丹诉檀冰案"中，您作为中国香港影星甄子丹的诉讼代理人，帮助其维权并取得了非常圆满的结果。可否在此以一个法律人的角度，与我们分享一下该案。

**何培华律师：**好的。依照最高人民法院关于适用《中华人民共和国涉外民事关系法律适用法》若干问题的解释：涉及香港特别行政区、澳门特别行政区的民事关系的适用该法律，所以该案亦属涉外案件。

2012年，内地青年导演耿卫国（檀冰）在与甄子丹方既无合同关系、也无雇用关系的情况下召开新闻发布会，发表了一系列不实言论，将甄子丹塑造成一个黑恶人物形象，严重侵害了其名誉权，故我们将耿卫国（檀冰）起诉至法院，诉请：（1）耿卫国停止侵权行为；（2）在媒体上作出书面赔礼道歉；（3）赔偿经济损失和精神损害赔偿500万元；（4）承担本案诉讼费、律师费和公证费。

该案经过两次开庭，历经两年多时间，2015年11月17日，北京市海淀区人民法院作出一审判决：檀冰构成名誉侵权，支付甄子丹精神赔偿5万元并书面在媒体致歉。法院经审理认为，耿卫国（檀冰）在不同场合和时间发表的针对甄子丹的言论构成对甄子丹名誉权的侵犯。耿卫国（檀冰）在

传播其所称他人提供的与甄子丹相关的信息时，亦未经核实即在公共场合进行传播，其行为构成诽谤。

虽然在赔偿金额上与诉求有很大差距，但法律总算还原了事实和真相，还了被侵害人甄子丹先生一个公道。

### 与其坐以待毙，不如主动出击

**赵伟主编**：多年来，您作为诸多涉外案件的代理人为中国企业在海外维权，为中国企业"走出去"保驾护航，在此，我们不能要求您一一讲述。我们了解到，在前几年，您代表广东某企业成功为其挽回经济损失数千万元人民币，可否与我们分享一下此案的办案历程？

**何培华律师**：好的。前几年，广东某公司与新加坡某公司发生纠纷，涉及纠纷金额数千万元人民币，但新加坡公司却要求该案在伦敦国际仲裁院仲裁，且伦敦国际仲裁院已作出初步裁决。我自1989年在中国国际贸易促进委员会广东分会和广东对外经济贸易委员会工作就一直从事涉外仲裁工作，遂立即判断出该案在伦敦国际仲裁院仲裁肯定对我方不利。经过认真审阅双方签署的协议后发现，在双方签订协议约定的仲裁条款中，只有对方的签字，并没有我方的签字，遂提出管辖权异议，该案必须接受中国法律的管辖，这是毋庸置疑的。我们在国内法院对新加坡公司提起诉讼后，新加坡公司聘请的律师也认定该案应适用中国法律，这些我们都做了笔录，并将在法庭上达成适用中国法律的协议及笔录发给了新加坡公司。

伦敦国际仲裁院虽作出初步裁决，却迟迟未将仲裁结果发给广东某公司，后我国法院作出裁决，认定协议中的仲裁条款无效，现我们已报请最高人民法院审核，此役初战告捷。

在此，我想提醒中国企业，在涉外投资和经营活动中，签署协议一定要谨慎。对于已在境外提起诉讼或仲裁的案件，一定要聘请有充分涉外法律实务经验、经历的律师给予专业的指导，切不可匆忙应诉或置之不理，谨慎应诉是最好的应对办法。

### 商务未动，规则先行

**赵伟主编**：作为老一代涉外律师，您还经常在众多国际研讨会上发声，为中国企业"走出去"鼓与呼，为"一带一路"建设建言献策，请问您对中国企业"走出去"有哪方面的思考和建议？

**何培华律师**：近年来，随着全球经济一体化进程的逐步推进和中国"一带一路"建设的步伐加快，中国企业在"走出去"过程中遭遇不公平待遇的案件屡有发生。

我们环宇京茂律师事务所对于"一带一路"建设非常重视，并对"一带一路"沿线国家尤其东南亚一带法律环境进行了深入研究。作为中国国际经济法学会的常务理事，每年度的年会我都会参加，在2017年年会中，我重点提出："一带一路"建设应建立一个公平、公开、公正的游戏规则，并严格按规则执行，意旨就是，无论遇到任何阻碍，也要优先执行该规则。当前，"一带一路"建设虽如火如荼，但却还未形成一个整体的法律框架或公约，而目前学界大部分讨论的是国与国之间的协议，当前应重点关注并解决共建"一带一路"法律服务框架问题，希望各级有关领导能对此问题引起足够重视。

### 寄语青年涉外律师

**赵伟主编**：您对致力于涉外法律服务的青年律师有哪些寄语和忠告？要想成为一名优秀的涉外律师，您认为应该具备哪些素质和需要做好哪些工作？

**何培华律师**：提供优质的涉外法律服务，语言是第一关。外语是与外商当事人沟通交流的工具，外语水平不过关，即使你有再大的能力，人家也很难相信你。第二，最好能在国外读个学位。我也是在江平老师的鼓励下，于2000年申请到哥伦比亚大学做的访问学者，后又到美国加州大学法学院攻读国际商法硕士学位。第三，要多参加国际研讨会和国际组织。美国律师协会、亚太律师协会、国际仲裁协会等国际组织中国律师都可以申请加入。要多认识国际法学专家，向他们学习的同时，也让他们认识我们中国律师，这样发展起来就如鱼得水了。第四，就是要有社会责任感。我们的青年人若有责任和担当，国家必将走向繁荣和富强。

正如习总书记所说的，我们要不忘初心，砥砺前行。中国经过40年改革开放已经成为世界第二大经济体，人民生活水平获得极大提高，我们要珍惜这来之不易的成果，做一个有责任、有担当的中国法律人。

### 后记

是啊！我们要不忘初心，砥砺前行，做一个有责任、有担当的中国法律人。希望在老一代法律人的带领和传承下，在全面依法治国新时代的大背景下，中国的企业、公民在世界的每一个角落，其权益都能得到中国律师的保护，因为法律就是最好的保障。

回顾往昔，可以说，何培华律师的脚步总是与时代的发展同步而行，在每一个时间节点都做好了充足的准备并抓住了机遇，顺势而为、成就自我。20世纪70年代下乡插队，当他人劳累了一天进入梦乡时，他却拿起了课本，遨游在书的海洋，国家恢复高考的第二年考入湛江师范学院英语系，毕业后又担任英语教师4年。1988年通过律师资格考试；1989年进入中国国际贸易贸促会委员会广东分会和广东对外经济贸易委员会从事多年涉外法律工作；后又赴美留学、回到中国政法大学深造；1993年创办广东环宇商务律师事务所；2000年，他响应律师制度改革要求，辞去公职创办广东环宇京茂律师事务所至今；2013年，国家提出"一带一路"倡议，他又带领团队进入对"一带一路"建设法律的研究中……

俗话说，顺势而为，方能行稳致远。数十年来，何培华律师带领团队在每一个重要的时间节点，挺身而出力挽狂澜，承接一个又一个涉外大案，为国家、为当事人维护权益、挽回损失。我们相信，在未来的律师生涯中，何培华律师仍将带领同仁继续维护当事人最大合法权益，继续为中国的法治建设做出更多更大的贡献。

# Following the trend to go steadily and far
## ——An Interview with Lawyer He Peihua, Principal Partner and Director of Guangdong International Business Law Firm

40 years is a short span. In 2018, the 40th anniversary of reform and opening up, China sees significant achievements in economic development, and has dramatically improved people's living standard, the Chinese legal service industry which protects economic development growing rapidly since its restoration.

In 2018, a lawyer celebrates the 30th anniversary of his law practice. In the course of development of the Chinese legal service industry, especially foreign affairs legal services that have started from scratch and are now flourishing, the lawyer He Peihua, principal partner and director of Guangdong International Business Law Firm, has been widely known as an example among law schools and foreign-related research institutes for the major foreign-related cases handled by him, such as "American citizens' claim for the explosion of Chinese Horse™ fireworks" "U.S. shrimp anti-dumping case vs. China"; "U.S. Section 337 investigation on Guangdong Shengyi Technology Co., Ltd.".

On the 40th anniversary of reform and opening up of China, and the 30th anniversary of Mr. He's practice, we interviewed this Chinese foreign affairs lawyer who was still working on the forefront of foreign-related legal services.

Notes 1.American citizens' claim for the explosion of Chinese Horse™ fireworks (time: 1993; result: recouping financial losses of RMB 400 million for China); 2. U.S. shrimp anti-dumping case vs. China (time: 2004; result: receiving a favorable judgment of zero duty successfully); 3. U.S. Section 337 investigation on Guangdong Shengyi Technology Co., Ltd. (time: 2008; result: eventually making the American plaintiff withdraw its accusation, and winning an unprecedented victory in the history of Chinese enterprises coping with U.S. Section 337 investigations).

## A closer look at Mr. He

### Working hard to lay a solid foundation

"It is not I who make these major foreign-related cases well-known, but these cases that define my career." Mr. He is always modest when facing his past achievements and honors. In the author's opinion, one cannot seize a good opportunity without a solid foundation, extensive knowledge, an elevated vision and adequate preparations. It is because Mr. He has these qualities that he can make a difference in major foreign-related cases to protect the interests of both the country and his clients to the greatest extent, as can be seen from his past experiences.

Mr. He was born in Xuwen, Guangdong——one of the ports of departure of the Maritime Silk Road of the Han Dynasty, located at the southernmost tip of Mainland China——in 1957. He lived and worked in the countryside in the 1970s, was admitted to the English Department of the Zhanjiang Normal College after the college entrance examination was restored in September 1978, and served as a high school English teacher for four years after graduation. These experiences laid a solid lingual foundation for his future career. He was enrolled by the Second Bachelor Class, China University of Political Science and Law in 1985, and then by the Graduate School of this university after graduation as a student of famous Chinese jurist Prof. Jiang Ping. He passed the national lawyer qualification examination in 1988, and graduated with a master's degree in civil and commercial laws in 1989. Since then, he has been doing foreign-related legal work at the Guangdong Branch of the China Council for the Promotion of International Trade, and the Guangdong Foreign Trade and Economic Cooperation Commission, serving as deputy section chief, section chief, deputy division chief, etc. He founded Guangdong International Business Law Firm in 1993, and has been director to date; he was a visiting scholar at Columbia University from August 2000 to September 2001, studied for a master's degree in international commercial law at the School of Law, University of California from July 2001 to August 2002, studied for a doctor's degree in civil and commercial laws from September 2002, still as a student of Prof. Jiang Ping, and received a doctor's degree in 2005. It can be said that these rich working and learning experiences have laid a solid foundation for Mr. He's future practice.

In addition, Mr. He has also served as executive editor of *Civil and Commercial Law Review*; director of the Seventh and Eighth WTO Law Committees of Guangdong Lawyers' Association; legislative consultant to the Standing Committee of the Guangdong Provincial People's Congress, part-time professor of the China University of Political Science and Law; part-time graduate student tutor of the School of Law, Sun Yat-sen University; part-time tutor of master's degree candidates in law of Jinan University; chair professor of Chen An international Law Development Foundation and part-time research fellow

of International Economic Law Institute, Xiamen University; executive director of the Chinese Society of International Economic Law and other social positions, speaking for Chinese lawyers on different occasions and on the global stage.

## A dialog with Mr. He

### Reputation infringers must be held liable

**Chief Editor Zhao Wei:** Hello, Mr. He! Thank you very much for accepting our interview in spite of your busyness. As a Chinese pioneer in foreign-related legal work, you have handled many major cases that have been much reported in your career, some of which have become benchmarks in this field. We have noticed that in the "Donnie Yen versus Tan Bing case" in 2015, you protected the rights of Hong Kong China movie star Donnie Yen successfully as his agent ad litem. Can you share this case with us as a lawyer?

**Mr. He:** Okay. According to the interpretation of the Supreme People's Court on some issues concerning the application of the Law of the Application of Law for Foreign-related Civil Relations of the People's Republic of China, this law applies to cases involving civil relations in the Hong Kong and Macao Special Administrative Regions. Therefore, this case is also a foreign-related one.

In 2012, young movie director Geng Weiguo (Tan Bing) of Mainland China held a press conference and made a series of untruthful remarks with neither contractual nor employment relationship with Donnie Yen, describing Donnie Yen as an evil guy, and infringing on his reputation right severely. Therefore, we prosecuted Geng Weiguo (Tan Bing) with the following claims: (1) Geng Weiguo should stop his infringing act; (2) He should make a written apology on media; (3) He should pay economic and mental damages of RMB 5 million; (4) He should bear the legal, attorney and notary fees of this case.

This case experienced two court sessions and lasted over two years. On November 17, 2015, the Haidian District People's Court made a first-instance judgment: Tan Bing's act was a reputation infringing act, and should pay mental damages of RMB 50 000 to Donnie Yen and make a written apology on media. Through trial, the court thought that the remarks about Donnie Yen made by Geng Weiguo (Tan Bing) on different occasions and at different times constituted an infringement on Donnie Yen's reputation right. Geng Weiguo (Tan Bing) disseminated information on Donnie Yen allegedly provided by others in the public without verification, constituting a slander.

Although the actual amount of damages differed greatly from

the claim, the facts were finally unveiled, bringing justice to Mr. Donnie Yen.

### We would rather do something than do nothing!

**Chief Editor Zhao Wei:** Over these years, you have been protecting Chinese enterprises' rights overseas as the agent of many foreign-related cases to serve the "going global" strategy. Of course, we cannot ask you to explain these cases one by one. We know that you retrieved financial losses of tens of millions of RMB for a Guangdong company. Would you tell us how it was handled?

**Mr. He:** Well. Several years ago, a dispute arose between a Guangdong company and a Singapore company, involving tens of millions of RMB. The Singapore company required that this case be arbitrated by the London Court of International Arbitration (ICIA), and the LCIA had made a preliminary ruling. Since I joined the Guangdong Branch of the China Council for the Promotion of International Trade, and the Guangdong Foreign Trade and Economic Cooperation Commission in 1989, I have been working on foreign-related arbitration. I judged at once that the arbitration of this case by the LCIA was certainly adverse to our side. After reviewing the agreement between both sides carefully, I found that the arbitration clause in this agreement was signed by the opposite side only, and not signed by our side, so I raised an objection to jurisdiction, and claimed that this case must be governed by Chinese laws. This was no doubt. After we brought a suit against to the Singapore company at a Chinese court, the lawyer engaged by the Singapore company also affirmed that this case was governed by Chinese laws. We kept relevant records, and sent the agreement on the application of Chinese laws entered into at the court and the records to the Singapore company.

Although the LCIA made a preliminary ruling, it had not sent the arbitration award to the Guangdong company. The Chinese court later made a ruling, affirming that the arbitration clause in the agreement was invalid. We have now referred the case to the Supreme People's Court, and got a preliminary victory.

I'd like to remind Chinese enterprises to enter into agreement prudently in foreign-related investment and business activities. For cases for which a suit or arbitration has been initiated overseas, a lawyer with rich foreign-related legal practice experience must be engaged to give professional guidance, and should not respond to or ignore the prosecution hastily. The best way is to respond prudently.

## Rules are precedent to business activities

**Chief Editor Zhao Wei:** As a pioneering foreign affairs lawyer, you often speak for the "going global" strategy of Chinese enterprises, and give advice on the development of the Belt and Road at international seminars. What's your advice for this strategy?

**Mr. He:** In recent years, with the further progress of economic globalization, and the accelerated development of the "Belt and Road", Chinese enterprises have been treated unfairly repeatedly in this process.

Our law firm attaches great importance to the development of the "Belt and Road", and made in-depth research on the legal environments of the countries along the "Belt and Road", especially Southeast Asian countries. As an executive director of the Chinese Society of International Economic Law, I would attend every annual convention. At the 2017 annual convention, I suggested that open, fair and just rules should be established for the "Belt and Road" Initiative, and strictly observed whatever obstacle may be encountered. Although the "Belt and Road" is developing vigorously, there is no overall legal framework or convention, and the academic community is discussing agreements among countries most of the time. Leaders concerned at different levels should pay their attention to how to establish a legal framework for the "Belt and Road" jointly.

## Messages for young foreign affairs lawyers

**Chief Editor Zhao Wei:** What are your messages and suggestions for young lawyers devoted to foreign-related legal services? What qualities are needed and what should be done to become an outstanding foreign affairs lawyer?

**Mr. He:** In order to provide high-quality foreign-related legal services, language is the primary condition, and a tool to communicate with foreign parties. However capable one may be, if one is not proficient in foreign languages, one can hardly be trusted. Second, we should preferably receive an academic degree overseas. Encouraged by Prof. Jiang Ping, I became a visiting scholar at Columbia University in 2000, and later studied for a master's degree in international commercial law at the School of Law, University of California. Third, we should attend international seminars often and join more international organizations, such as the American Bar Association, National Asian Pacific American Bar Association, and Association for International Arbitration. We should get to know more international law experts to learn from them and also let them know us, so we can develop more effectively. Fourth, we should have a sense of social responsibility, because only if young people are responsible can our country prosper.

As President Xi Jinping has said, we should always stick to our original aspiration and forge ahead against all odds. China has become the world's second largest economy after 40 years of reform and opening up, and people's living standard has improved dramatically. We should cherish this hard-won outcome, and be responsible in our careers.

## Epilogue

Yes! We should always stick to our original aspiration and forge ahead against all odds, and be responsible Chinese lawyers. In the new era of managing the country by law in all aspects, we expect that Chinese enterprises and citizens can be protected by Chinese lawyers under the leadership of pioneers in every corner of the world, because the law is the best protection.

It can be seen from his past experiences that Mr. He has always kept step with the times, made adequate preparations and seized opportunities to achieve today's success. When he lived and worked in the countryside in the 1970s, he kept studying at night while others were resting. He was later admitted to the English Department of the Zhanjiang Normal College in the second year of restoration of the college entrance examination, and served as an English teacher for four years after graduation. He passed the national lawyer qualification examination in 1988, and has been doing foreign-related legal work at the Guangdong Branch of the China Council for the Promotion of International Trade, and the Guangdong Foreign Trade and Economic Cooperation Commission since 1989; he later studied in the U.S. and pursued advanced studies at China University of Political Science and Law; he founded Guangdong International Business Law Firm in 1993, and resigned from public service and reorganized the law firm in 2000; when the state proposed the "Belt and Road" Initiative in 2013, he led his team to conduct relevant legal research……

There is a saying that only if one follows the trend can one go steadily and far. For decades, Mr. He has led his team to win major foreign-related cases, protecting rights and retrieving losses for the country and clients. We believe that Mr. He will continue to do this together with his colleagues in his future career, thereby making greater contributions to China's legal system building.

# 中国涉外知识产权领军人才张民元律师

张民元律师毕业于武汉大学图书情报学院，获文学学士学位，中国政法大学在职法学博士结业，现担任中国侨联法律顾问、最高人民法院知识产权案例指导（北京）基地专家、中华全国律师协会标准化专家工作组组长等职，系第四批国家级知识产权高层次人才，专业方向为知识产权、法律顾问。在中国律师网开设有"张民元律师专栏"，受邀担任《中国律师》杂志"民元思问"专栏撰稿人。

## 1. 为外国投资者在中国投资与发展提供专业法律顾问服务

从事涉外法律业务，要从张民元律师承接第一家法律顾问单位说起，孚宝仓储是由荷兰皇家在中国与宁波港务局合资的中外合资企业，企业当时的管理者是来自新加坡的李世民总经理。外资股东进入中国投资，迫切需要了解中国的法律环境，并且需要一名中国律师帮助协调与政府及周边企业的关系。在担任孚宝仓储20年法律顾问期间，张民元律师帮助这家外资企业开展员工法律培训、建立健全公司规章制度、协助调解企业与政府和周边企业之间发生的纠纷及企业内部管理的纠纷、为企业内部绩效考核提供专业的法律意见，并为企业的日常诉讼纠纷管理和应急事件处理提供法律帮助。

在为外资企业提供法律顾问服务期间，张民元律师根据自身多年的执业经验，总结了一套为外商投资企业提供法律顾问服务的理论和操作实务，将经验撰写为《企业品牌法律顾问服务指南》作为浙江素豪律师事务所的企业标准在国家标准委"企业标准公共信息服务平台"上自我公开并发布实施，指导专业从事法律顾问的团队"中观法律顾问"付诸实施。

在20年专业从事法律顾问的执业生涯里，张民元律师分别担任了东光五金（宁波）有限公司（台商独资）、海利化工（宁波）有限公司（港资）、龙星物流有限公司（丹麦马士基与中国合资企业）、德贝里克电器有限公司（中美合资）、枫叶科技园有限公司（港资）等数十家外商投资企业的法律顾问，为境外投资者在中国大陆的投资和发展提供专业的法律帮助和法律咨询。

## 2. 为中国创业者提供专业法律顾问服务，引进外资组建合资企业

王伟国先生创业投资的迅达仓储有限公司，在聘请张民元律师担任法律顾问的时候，还只能算是一个小微企业，经过几十年的打拼，王伟国先生将迅达仓储公司从一家只有十几辆车的小微企业发展成为拥有几百辆车、占地40多亩的小型物流企业，在宁波的物流行业中处于龙头地位。在多次与张民元律师聊天的过程中，王伟国先生一直觉得宁波的物流企业之所以做不大，主要原因是缺少自身的知识产权和优秀的管理经验，王伟国总经理萌生了与外国先进的企业合资的意向，但在当时普遍"宁为鸡头，不做凤尾"思潮的控制下，王伟国总经理顾虑重重，一直未能迈开脚步。

2002年，王伟国总经理抱着边谈边看的态度，委托张民元律师与世界500强企业丹麦马士基物流公司的代表开始合资谈判，谈判的过程是艰难的，合资双方的股权如何设置，这首先就是一个难题，外方股权比例过大，王伟国总经理担心会失去企业的控制地位，而外方的投资比例过小，对于一家全球收购的世界500强企业来说，可能根本没有兴趣。外方收购中方企业，中方的资产如何作价，看得见摸得着的固定资产和车辆等有形资产，都可以委托第三方评估机构来评估作价，但对于一家多年打拼的企业在市场上形成的商业信誉和市场渠道这些无形的资产如何作价，这便成为谈判中非常艰难的课题。特别是对于外国收购方来说，他们是很难理解中国的企业经营者在企业经营中需要依赖人脉关系，外商能够认可的无形资产是专利、商标、著作权等有权利证明的知识产权，而对于中国企业经营者所珍惜的商业信誉、市场渠道、人脉关系都不在谈判的考虑之列。所以整个谈判过程是艰难的，从2002年开始谈判一直断断续续谈到2005年龙星物流公司注册成立，可以说是历经艰辛。

龙星物流公司注册成立之后，在宁波北仑港区征地200亩，投资总额1140万美元，成为浙江物流行业的第一名。合资成功之后，王伟国总经理握住张民元律师的手说："我让你成为我企业终身的法律顾问！"

## 3. 引导中国企业走出去，投资海外打进世界商务圈

林允华董事长是个非常有商业头脑和善于经营管理的人，林董从挖煤工人开始打拼，一路从煤炭行业拓展至酒店和房地产，从一贫如洗奋斗至身价十多亿元，足以显现林允华董事长的胆识和过人的商机判决能力。

当林允华董事长在煤炭行业打拼了近20年之后，他深切感受到中国国内的矿产资源紧张所带来的能源危机，毅然决定到国外去找矿。在经过一番轮回地排摸之后，林允华董事长选择了非洲加蓬共和国。

非洲加蓬是个森林大国，矿产资源非常丰富，但作为一名中国商人要远去非洲投资，其艰难程度可想而知。而对于张民元律师来说，非洲加蓬是个非常陌生的国家，该国的法律制度和人文环境都是完全陌生的，但作为林允华董事长的法律顾问，董事长的指挥棒指向哪里，法律顾问的智慧就必须触及到那里。

查找资料，了解非洲加蓬的公司法、矿产资源法、劳动法、合同法以及安全法成为必须的功课，好在林允华先生投资非洲加蓬的计划得到了温州商会和国家商务部的大力支持，通过商会组织和商务部，张民元律师团队获取了非洲加蓬投资

的第一手法律资料，华州矿业工贸有限公司在非洲加蓬正式注册成立，从公司注册到矿藏前期勘探，直到在加蓬总理比约盖·姆巴的主持下，华州矿业工贸有限公司总经理农德连与加蓬矿业部长贝加雷、经贸部长恩冈比亚在总理府共同签署蒙贝利锰矿开采矿权协议，非洲加蓬投资项目才前期宣告成功落定。

华州矿业工贸公司从非洲加蓬政府手中获得 2000 平方公里锰矿详细勘探权，后又获得了 2000 平方公里铅锌矿详细勘探权，其矿石储量约 3000 万吨，平均品位 40%，市场价值达 300 亿人民币。非洲加蓬项目获得预想不到的成功，这期间，林允华董事长经常熬夜，脾气也变得有些火爆，作为公司的法律顾问，张民元律师团队唯一可做的就是耐心解答，细心解释，尽心尽力调查。对于非洲加蓬投资项目来说，张民元律师的总结便是："法律顾问最重要的职责就是在老板遇到重大事件时能够平息老板内心的恐惧、担忧、焦虑与狂躁，运用法律技能帮助老板控制内心的平和与稳重，可能才是法律顾问的真正价值所在。"

**4. 帮助中国企业自主研发知识产权，突破国外贸易知识产权壁垒**

金华美佳科技公司（简称"美佳公司"）是一家从事遮阳篷加工出口的外贸性企业，从产值不过几百万元逐渐做大到出口额突破亿元大关，产品远销到欧美和非洲国家，公司的科技研发团队发挥了重要作用。但就在企业蒸蒸日上的时候，竞争对手却利用国外的专利向美佳的所有客户发出警告函，几乎所有的客户收到警告函之后都不敢下单进货，美佳公司上亿元成品货物滞留工厂，企业面临倒闭危机。

金华美佳公司聘请张民元律师团队担任公司专项法律顾问，破解国外客户收到专利警告函而停止下单进货的难题。

张民元律师带领"中观法律顾问"团队的成员深入工厂，与公司科研人员召开多次产品分析会和技术讨论会，在公司研发团队的共同努力下，美佳公司绕过国外专利的技术特征，研发了新的产品结构并且申请了中国专利。

张民元律师向美佳公司的所有海外客户发出专利不侵权的法律分析意见和律师建议书，并向客户承诺，若侵权将由美佳公司承担全部的赔偿责任。国外客户收到律师意见书后纷纷下单出货，公司危机解除。

与此同时，国内竞争对手在宁波海关查封了美佳公司的出口产品，并且在宁波市中级人民法院提起侵权诉讼。张民元律师团队从容应诉，在对方主张相同侵权时以"禁止反悔"原则相对抗，宁波市中级人民法院依法判决美佳公司不侵犯专利权，对方不服上诉至浙江省高级人民法院，浙江省高级人民法院二审判决维持不侵犯专利权的裁决。对方继续申诉至最高人民法院，最高人民法院仍维持了宁波中级人民法院的判决，并且将"在主张相同侵权时提出禁止反悔原则"作为经典指导案例刊登在《人民法院报》的案例指导栏目中。

美佳公司的专利战争取得完胜，成功突破国外知识产权贸易壁垒，从此产品出口海外畅通无阻，生意越做越大，越做越顺。张民元律师团队将该案作为典型案例，在浙江省知识产权宣传巡回演讲活动中多次宣讲，指导参会企业如何应对国外的知识产权壁垒，在国际商海大战中如何运用自主知识产权保护自身合法权利，如何合理利用知识产权武器打击竞争对手，破解国际贸易领域中的技术壁垒。

**5. 协调解决国际交易中的贸易争端，化解国际贸易中的商业风险**

中化集团是宁波一家综合性的外贸出口和国内生产加工型企业集团，2010 年，中化集团与以色列 B.V 公司因出口产品定牌加工合同发生贸易争端，以色列商人向中化集团提出索赔 500 万美元。

张民元律师团队接受聘请出任该争议解决的中方专项法律顾问，在接受委托之后，张民元律师带领团队深入以色列调查，并借助国际互联网的互通资源调查出以色列所主张的专利权是很早在以色列曾申请过外观设计专利并且专利保护期限已经届满而进入社会公众领域的公知技术。尽管以色列商人就该项技术在美国又重新申请了美国专利，并且取得了美国的专利证书，但根据张民元律师的专业判断，以色列商人的专利是无效专利。

为了保证商业谈判的成功概率，同时确保在商业谈判中居于主动地位，张民元律师团队与美国欧夏梁律师事务所合作，帮助中化集团在美国成功申请了产品设计更新的外观设计专利，并且取得了美国专利局颁发的外观设计专利证书。在与以色列律师多次斡旋之后，当张民元律师团队出具了中化集团已申请成功的美国专利证书并且提供了以色列专利已进入社会公众领域的相关证据之后，以色列律师放弃了 500 万美元的索赔计划，而选择继续跟中化集团在吊床领域开展长期合作。

**6. 调解国际投资与并购合作中股东权益争议，为跨境企业稳定经营提供法律支撑**

远成石化电力机械有限公司是一家中美合资企业，2008 年外资股东去世，其财产继承人依据美国公证的遗嘱向公司主张财产继承，并且主张持有该公司 95% 的股权。该公司的实际控制人是中方股东，且从公司正式合资开始便一直在实际经营管理这家公司，公司从注册资本 60 万美元起步，发展到后来的市值超过两亿元，都是由中方股东一手实际经营，外资股东除了最初在国内工商登记时出面办理企业登记之外，一直未曾露面，公司的实际经营管理和对外投资一直由中方股东负责。

该公司中方股东聘请张民元律师团队担任该项涉外股权争议的专项法律顾问，外资股东在上海提起国际仲裁，仲裁裁决的结果是外资股东拥有该公司 95% 的股权，也就意味着中方股东实际经营了十几年的公司资产几乎全部归外方所有。

张民元律师团队在经过一系列调查之后发现该外资股东最初设立公司出资时与中方股东之间实际有其它的交易发生，其出资的目的和实际出资的事实受到质疑，而且外方股东从公司登记成立之后一直未参与公司的实际经营管理。张民元律师根据调查的事实向宁波市中级人民法院提出执行异议，宁波市中级人民法院裁定上海国际贸易仲裁的裁决书不予执行。外资股东不服，上诉到浙江省高级人民法院，省高

级人民法院维持了宁波市中级人民法院的裁决。中方股东另行向宁波市镇海区人民法院提起股东确认之诉，确认其股东资格，经过一系列的诉讼和协调后，中方股东终于夺回公司控制权。

7. 宣传知识产权，推进标准化，引导企业与国际接轨

宣传知识产权，推进法律顾问标准化，引导企业与国际接轨，一直是张民元律师的心愿。2009年，张民元律师在浙江省司法厅、浙江省科技厅、浙江省知识产权局的联合指导下，组织策划由浙江省律师协会在浙江省范围内开展知识产权宣传巡回演讲，活动得到浙江省委的表彰，并受到国务院知识产权战略实施工作部际联席会议办公室发文表彰，该宣讲活动已开展8年，现仍在知识产权宣传周稳步实施。

2016年，张民元律师协助中华全国律师协会申报了社会管理与公共服务综合标准化试点，获得国家标准委员会的立项，张民元律师担任全国律师协会标准化专家工作组组长，致力于推进法律顾问服务标准化工作。

从业20年，张民元律师以浙江素豪律师事务所专业从事法律顾问的团队"中观法律顾问"为平台，与美国欧夏梁律师事务所（OshaLiang LLP）、法国基德律师事务所、巴西 CésarA.LeãoBarcellos&Cia.Ltd.、秘鲁 Omcabogados & Consultores、马来西亚 Tiger Intellectual Sdn Bhd、德国 Casalonga & Partners 等专利商标事务所在知识产权领域开展广泛合作，为企业申请马德里商标国际注册、PCT专利国际申请以及在各个国家单独申请商标注册和专利申请提供专业的法律帮助。

让中国企业走向世界，让中国律师与国际标准接轨，一直是张民元律师奋斗的目标和心愿，随着互联网的发展和国际经济全球大融合，相信像张民元律师这样，以涉外知识产权为专业通道，广泛提供涉外法律服务的中国涉外律师领军人才将会大有作为。

# Leading Talent of Chinese Foreign–related Intellectual Property Rights —— Lawyer Zhang Minyuan

Lawyer Zhang Minyuan was admitted to the Degree of Bachelor of Arts in the College of Library and Information Science of Wuhan University. Later, he completed an on-the-job Doctor of Laws course of China University of Political Science and Law. Now he is the legal adviser of China Federation of Returned Overseas Chinese, the expert of Intellectual Property Case Guidance (Beijing) Base of The Supreme People's Court, the standardization expert working group leader of All China Lawyers Association, etc. He is also one of the fourth batch of national intellectual property rights high-level talents, whose professional orientation is intellectual property and legal adviser. Furthermore, there is "Zhang Minyuan Column" in the website of All China Lawyers Association, and he has been invited to work as a columnist for the column named "Min Yuan's thoughts and questions" of the magazine called *Chinese Lawyer*.

## 1.To provide professional legal consultancy services for foreign investors to invest and develop in mainland China

Engaged in foreign-related legal services, it should talk about from the first company of legal counsel that lawyer Zhang undertook. Vopak Warehouse is a Sino-foreign joint venture invested by Royal Vopak and Ningbo Port Authority in mainland China. The manager of the enterprise at that time was general manager Li Shimin from Singapore. Foreign shareholders were urgent to know about Chinese legal environment when they made investments in mainland China, and a Chinese lawyer was needed to help coordinate the relationships with governments and businesses around. During the twenty years as the legal counsel of Vopak Warehouse, lawyer Zhang helped this foreign-capital enterprise to conduct legal trainings for its employees, establish and improve its rules and regulations, assist to mediate disputes between companies and governments or businesses around as well as the internal management disputes of the enterprise. Moreover, lawyer Zhang provided professional legal advice for internal performance evaluation and legal help for the daily litigation dispute management and emergency event handling of the enterprise.

During the period of providing legal consultancy services to foreign-capital enterprises, lawyer Zhang has summed up a set of theory and practical operation for providing legal consultancy services to foreign-invested enterprises according to his own perennial practical experiences. Furthermore, these experiences have been written into "Corporate Brand Legal Adviser Service Guide", which is as the enterprise criteria of Zhejiang Su Hao Law Firm, publishing by itself and implementing on the "Corporate Standard Public Information Service Platform" of National Standards Committee, and guiding the professional legal adviser team "Deep Research Legal Adviser" into practice.

In the twenty years of professional legal adviser career, lawyer Zhang has served dozens of foreign-funded enterprises respectively, such as Tong Kwang Valve Industrial Co., Ltd. (Taiwan China funded), Ningbo Haili Chemical Industry Co., Ltd. (Hong Kong funded), Blue Dragon Logistics Co., Ltd.

(Denmark MAERSK Chinese joint venture), Dayrelax Electrical Appliance Co., Ltd. (Sino-American joint venture), Maple Technology Park Co., Ltd. (Hong Kong funded), providing professional legal services and legal advice for the investment and development of foreign investors in mainland China.

## 2.To provide professional legal consultancy services for Chinese entrepreneurs, and introduce foreign capital to form joint ventures.

Xun Da Warehouse Co., Ltd. is invested by Mr. Wang Weiguo for starting a business. When lawyer Zhang was hired as the legal adviser, it was just a small and micro company. After decades of struggling, Xun Da Warehouse has become a small logistics enterprise with hundreds of cars covering an area of more than forty acres, which has placed in a leading position of logistics industry in Ningbo. In the process of multiple chats with Lawyer Zhang, Mr. Wang always held the view that the reason why logistics enterprises in Ningbo develop slowly was they lacked their own intellectual property rights and excellent management experience. Thus, Mr. Wang came up an intention to found a joint venture with foreign advanced enterprises. However, at that time, under the control of the general trend of thought that "better be the head of an ass than the tail of a phoenix", Mr. Wang was full of worries and did not take a step.

In 2002, the general manager Mr. Wang held the attitude of trying over the time, entrusting Lawyer Zhang to negotiate with the representatives of Denmark MAESK, which is one of the world top 500 enterprises about joint venture. The process of negotiation was tough, how to set up parties' equity in the joint venture was the first challenge. If the equity ratio of foreign party was too large, Mr. Wang would fear of losing the control of the enterprise. On the contrary, if the investment proportion of foreign party was too small, for a world-top-500 enterprise that acquires companies around the world, it may have no interests. When a foreign enterprise acquires a Chinese enterprise, how to evaluate Chinese enterprise's assets becomes a very difficult topic during the negotiation. Tangible assets like fixed assets, vehicles and so on can be assessed by entrusting an appraisal institution as the third party. Nevertheless, for an enterprise that has struggled for many years, it is difficult to evaluate those intangible assets such as the business reputation formed in the market and market channels. Especially for foreign acquirers, it is also difficult for them to understand the fact that relationship is indispensable during business operation in China. They regard the intellectual property rights that have certificate of rights like patent, trademark, copyright as intangible assets, regardless of business reputation, market channel and relationship while Chinese business operators cherished. Therefore, the whole negotiation process was difficult. Since 2002, the negotiation had been intermittent until 2005 when Blue Dragon Logistics Co., Ltd. was established, which was full of hardship.

Since the incorporation of Blue Dragon Logistics Co., Ltd. land acquisition has been 200 mu in Beilun Port District, Ningbo, the total investment has been $11.4 million, it has become the No.1 of logistics industry in Zhejiang Province. After the success of the joint venture, the general manager Mr. Wang held the hands of lawyer Zhang, saying that "I will make you become the lifelong legal adviser for my enterprise!"

## 3.To guide Chinese enterprises to go out, and invest overseas into the world business circle

The chairman of the board, Lin Yunhua, is a person who has strong business mind and is good at management. He begins to struggle from a coal worker, and then expands the coal industry to the business of hotel and real estate. Striving from as poor as a church to worth more than ten million of social status, it is enough to show Mr. Lin's boldness and outstanding business judgment ability.

Having engaged in the coal industry for nearly 20 years, Mr. Lin deeply felt the energy crisis brought by the tension of domestic mineral resources, and he decided to go abroad to find mineral resolutely. After investigation, Mr. Lin chose The Gabonese Republic in the end.

The Gabonese Republic is a big forest country, and its mineral resources are abundant. However, as a Chinese business man, it is hard to invest in Africa. As for lawyer Zhang, the Gabonese Republic is a very strange country, the legal system and cultural environment are also totally strange. Nonetheless, as the legal adviser of Mr. Lin, the wisdom should reach the direction where the chairman of the board has pointed.

Finding information and understanding the Gabonese company law, mineral resources law, labor law, contract law and security law were the prerequisite assignments. Fortunately, the plan was supported strongly by the Wenzhou Chamber of Commerce and the Ministry of Commerce. Through these two organizations, the lawyer Zhang's team obtained the first-hand legal information about Gabonese investment, Hua Zhou Mineral Industry and Trade Co., Ltd. was officially registered in Gabon. From the registration to the mineral exploration at the early stage, until the general manager Nong Delian of Hua Zhou Mineral Industry and Trade Co., Ltd. cosigned Mombelli Manganese Mining Agreement with the Gabonese Minister of Mining and Minister of Commerce, presided over by Gabonese Prime Minister, the investment project settled at the early stage to declare success.

Hua Zhou Mineral Industry and Trade Co., Ltd. acquired manganese ore exploration rights in detail of 2000 square

kilometers from Gabon government, and then obtained lead zinc ore exploration rights in detail of 2000 square kilometers, where the ore reserves were about 30 million tons, the average grade was 40%, the market value could reach 30 billion yuan. Gabon project achieved unexpected success. During that time, Mr. Lin often stayed up late, causing hot temper sometimes. As the legal adviser of the company, the only thing that lawyer Zhang's team can do was to answer questions patiently and explain carefully, as well as to do some in-depth investigations. For the Gabon investment projects, the conclusion of lawyer Zhang is that: "the most important duty for a legal counsel is to make the boss calm down when he or she meets a major event and use legal skills to help him or her to maintain peace and steady from the heart, which may be the real value of a legal adviser".

**4.To help Chinese enterprises develop their own intellectual property rights, and break through the barriers of intellectual property rights in foreign trade**

Zhejiang Homey Electrical Technology Co., Ltd. is a foreign trade corporation, which works on the process and export of awning. Its amount of exports has gradually expanded to more than one billion, and its products are exported to Europe, the United States and countries in Africa, in which the technology research and development team of the company plays an important role. However, as the enterprise has been becoming flourishing, its competitor issued a warning letter to all of customers making use of foreign patents, after that, almost all the customers were afraid to make an order stock. As a result, millions of finished goods were stranded in the factory, the enterprises faced a crisis of insolvency.

Zhejiang Homey Electrical Technology Co., Ltd. entrusted lawyer Zhang's team to serve as a special legal counsel for the company, solving the problem that foreign customers receive the patent warning letter and stop the purchase orders.

Lawyer Zhang led members of "Deep Research Legal Adviser" team into the factory, and convoked product analysis and technical seminars with scientific research personnel of the company for many times. Under the joint efforts of the research and development team, the company circumvented the technical features of foreign patent, developed a new product structure and applied for a patent in China.

Lawyer Zhang sent out legal analysis opinion and lawyer proposal of no infringement of the patent to all overseas customers of Homey. Further, he committed to the customers that if tort existed, the company would bear all the compensation liability. Foreign clients made orders one after another since they

received the lawyer's letter, thus, the bankruptcy crisis of the company was relieved.

At the same time, the domestic competitor seized the export products of Homey in Ningbo Customs, and litigated of tort infringement in the Ningbo Intermediate People's Court. The team of lawyer Zhang dealt with it calmly and fought against the claim of "same infringement" with the "no regret" principle. Finally, the Ningbo Intermediate People's Court judged that Homey did not infringe the patent right according to the law. The domestic competitor refused to accept the decision and appealed to the Zhejiang Higher People's Court, however, the court affirmed the original judgment. Later, the competitor continued to appeal to the Supreme People's Court, the court still maintained the decision, and published "presenting 'no regret' principle when the same infringement is proposed" as a guide for classic cases in the case guidance column of People's Court Daily.

The patent war of Homey was completed successfully, and it successfully breached the foreign intellectual property trade barriers. Since then, the export of products overseas has been unimpeded, and the business has become more and more flourishing. Lawyer Zhang's team considers the case as a typical one, and has preached many time in intellectual property publicity speaking tour activities of Zhejiang province, in order to guide the attending enterprises to deal with foreign intellectual property barriers, and use their own intellectual property rights in the international trade war to protect their legal rights and interests, as well as to reasonably use the intellectual property weapons against the competitors to crack technology barriers in the field of international trade.

**5.To coordinate and solve trade disputes in international transactions, and resolve business risks in international trade**

Sinochem (Ningbo) is a comprehensive enterprise group engaged in foreign trade export and domestic production and process. In 2010, Sinochem Group had trade dispute with Israeli B.V company account for nominating brand and processing contract of export products, for which the Israeli party claimed $5 million compensation.

Lawyer Zhang's team accepted the authorization as the special legal adviser of the Chinese party during the process of dispute resolution. After that, lawyer Zhang led the team to do in-depth survey of Israel, and with the help of the Internet communication resources, it figured out that the patent which Israel was proposed had applied for design patent at very early time and it had been into social public area known as the prior art because the patent protection period had expired. Although the Israeli party applied for patent in the United States again and obtained the patent certificate, pursuant to lawyer Zhang's professional judgment, such patent was invalid.

In order to assure the success of commercial negotiation and the initiative position meanwhile, lawyer Zhang's team helped

Sinochem Group successfully apply design patent of updating product design under the cooperation with Osha Ling LLP in the United States, and obtain the design patent certificate issued by the U.S. Patent Office as well. After many times to mediate with Israeli attorneys, when lawyer Zhang presented the aforementioned evidence, they gave up the compensation scheme and chose to continue long-term cooperation with Sinochem Group in the field of hammock.

**6. To mediate the disputes of shareholders' rights and interests in the cooperation of international investment and acquisition, and provide legal support for the stable operation of cross-border enterprises**

Yuan Cheng Petrochemical Power Machinery Co., Ltd. is a Sino-US joint venture. In 2008, the foreign shareholder dead, the successors claimed to inherit the property according to the will which was notarized in the US. Moreover, the successors claimed to own 95% equity of the company.

The actual controllers of the company are Chinese shareholders, who have been in actual operation and management since the joint venture was established officially. At the beginning, the registered capital of the company is $600 000, under the efforts of Chinese shareholders, the market value has been over two billion dollars now. The foreign shareholder only showed up at the first time to handle business registration, consequently, the Chinese shareholders are responsible for the actual operation and management of the company as well as the foreign investment.

The Chinese shareholders of the company employed lawyer Zhang's team as the special legal counsel for the foreign-related equity controversial. The foreign shareholders filed international arbitration in Shanghai, the arbitration award was that the foreign shareholders own 95% equity of the company, which meant almost all the company's assets were belonging to the foreign party, which were actually operated by the Chinese party for more than ten years.

After a series of investigation, lawyer Zhang's team found that the foreign shareholder had other deals with Chinese shareholders when the company was originally established. Therefore, the purpose and fact of the investment should be doubted. Moreover, the foreign shareholder is not involved in the actual operation and management after registration and establishment. Based on these facts, lawyer Zhang claimed an execution objection to Ningbo City Intermediate People's Court execution objection, and the court judged that the arbitration award would not be executed. Foreign shareholders were not satisfied with the result and appealed to the Zhejiang Higher People's Court, however, the court affirmed the judgment. In addition, the Chinese shareholders filed an action of shareholder confirmation to Ningbo Zhenhai District Court, and the court confirmed the qualification of shareholders. After a series of lawsuits and coordination, the Chinese Party finally recaptured the actual control of the company.

**7. To publicize intellectual property rights, promote standardization, and guide enterprises to integrate with the world**

To publicize intellectual property rights, promote the standardization of legal counsel, and guide enterprises to integrate with the world, has always been the wish of lawyer Zhang. In 2009, under the joint guidance of Department of Justice of Zhejiang Province, Department of Science of Zhejiang Province and Intellectual Property Office of Zhejiang Province, lawyer Zhang organized intellectual property publicity speaking tour activities carried by the Lawyers Association in the scope of Zhejiang province, which was praised by Zhejiang Provincial Committee, and also recognized by the Intellectual Property Rights Strategy Implementation department, joint meeting office of the State Council. The activity has been carried out to preach for eight years, and it is still implemented steadily in the intellectual property rights of publicity week every year.

In 2016, lawyer Zhang assisted All China Lawyers Association to declare the comprehensive standardization pilot project of social management and public service, which gained approval from the National Standard Committee. Furthermore, lawyer Zhang became the leader of standardization expert working group, devoting himself to promoting the standardization work of legal consultancy services.

Having taken an occupation for 20 years, lawyer Zhang regards "Deep Research Legal Adviser" in Su Hao Law Firm that specializes in legal adviser as a platform, and carries out extensive cooperation with patent and trademark law firms such as Osha Liang LLP in the US, Gide Loyrette Nouel in France, César A. Leão Barcellos & Cia. Ltd in Brazil, Omcabogados & Consultores in Peru, Tiger Intellectual Sdnbhd in Malaysia, Casalonga & Partners in Germany, etc. Professional legal assistance is provided for enterprises to apply for Madrid international registration of trademarks and PCT international patent, as well as apply for trademark registration and patent applications separately in each country.

To make Chinese enterprises go towards the world and Chinese lawyers be in line with international standards, are always the goal and desire of lawyer Zhang. With the development of the Internet and global economy, there is no doubt that leading talents of Chinese foreign-related lawyers like Zhang Minyuan widely provide foreign-related legal services by considering foreign-related intellectual property rights as professional channel will go a long way.